JEWISH
MARRIAGE

JEWISH MARRIAGE

RABBINIC LAW, LEGEND, AND CUSTOM

Mendell Lewittes

JASON ARONSON INC.
Northvale, New Jersey
London

This book was set in 12 point Bem by TechType of Upper Saddle River, New Jersey, and printed and bound by Haddon Craftsmen in Scranton, Pennsylvania.

Library of Congress Cataloging-in-Publication Data

Lewittes, Mendell.
   Jewish marriage : rabbinic law, legend, and custom /
Mendell Lewittes.
      p.   cm.
   Includes bibliographical references and indexes.
   ISBN 1-56821-201-1
   1. Marriage—Religious aspects—Judaism.   2. Marriage (Jewish law)
3. Marriage customs and rites, Jewish.   I. Title.
BM713.L48   1994
296.4'44—dc20   94-9185

Manufactured in the United States of America. Jason Aronson Inc. offers books and cassettes. For information and catalog write to Jason Aronson Inc., 230 Livingston Street, Northvale, New Jersey 07647.

CONTENTS

PART II
DIVORCE IN JEWISH LAW AND CUSTOM

PREFACE

Let it be understood: This volume was not designed as a manual to advise people how to stay happily married, though reading it may help one develop a more positive view of married life.[1] Nor do the chapters on divorce contain detailed advice on divorce settlements that avoid the problems usually confronting divorcées. It is, rather, a survey of marriage laws and customs that have prevailed in Jewish life from biblical times to the present, with a corresponding survey of divorce proceedings that have also been determined by Jewish law and custom.

JEWISH LAW: For a proper understanding of this material, one should have an appreciation of law and custom in Judaism and the interrelationship between them. Jewish law is denominated *Halakhah*, derived from the basic Hebrew root *halakh*, which means walking or going. Thus *Halakhah* represents "a way of life." Its roots are in biblical law, especially that of the

Pentateuch;[2] its trunk has grown out of the rabbinic interpretation of biblical law and is incorporated in the Mishnah and Talmud;[3] its branches are the commentaries to the Talmud by the rabbis of the Middle Ages and their subsequent codification in the Code of Jewish Law denominated *Shulchan Arukh* (literally "prepared table"); and its leaves are the *Responsa*, the responses by scholars of all ages to inquiries posed to them by persons who wish to conduct themselves in accordance with Jewish law. The *Responsa* are called in Hebrew *She'eilot U-Teshuvot*, Questions and Answers. The Bible is referred to as "The Written Law" (*Torah she-bi-khtav*), and all subsequent discussion of Jewish law comprises "The Oral Law" (*Torah she-bé al peh*).

Talmudic references are to the Babylonian Talmud unless preceded by J.T., designating the Jerusalem (Palestinian) Talmud. "The Sages" refers to the Sages of the Talmud.

CUSTOM: These are practices followed by some Jewish communities without having been previously required by the *Halakhah* and are denominated *Minhag*. *Minhag* originally was a local custom, binding only upon the local inhabitants, but the tendency was for local practice to spread and become adopted by other communities, many in the course of time becoming almost universally practiced. Customs that attained the approval of rabbinic authorities gradually became incorporated in the corpus of the *Halakhah*, so that what originally was a matter of spontaneous local practice became obligatory as a matter of law. However, the *Halakhah* recognizes many differences in practice still prevailing in various communities as being in accordance with Jewish law. Thus there are differences in the scope of its legislation, some rulings binding on all Jews and some binding only on some.

These differences began early on in Jewish life. The division of the Jewish kingdom in the days of King Solomon's son Reheboam led to a division in custom between the Jews in Judea and those in Galilee, a division that became more pronounced in mishnaic times, as we shall see from some marriage customs. Volumes have been written about the differences in practice between the Jews of Palestine and those of Babylonia in talmudic times. In the days of the *Geonim* (sixth to eleventh centuries C.E.) there were differences between the Jews of one city in Babylonia and those of another city, a consequence of the different rulings of the respective heads of the local Academies. As time went on, with the increased dispersal of the Jewish people in Europe and North Africa, the number of peculiar local customs increased, and the leading rabbinic authorities in the Middle Ages attempted, in their halakhic works, to codify many of these customs as law for all Jews. By this time, however, a major division that could not be eliminated existed, each division embracing within itself many minor differences in custom. Generally speaking, this is the division between Sephardim, or Oriental, Jews and Ashkenazim, or European, Jews, leading to the codification of their major differences in the *Shulchan Arukh*. Thus in the course of our discussion, I will distinguish between practices that are obligatory today for all Jews and those that still remain a matter of local practice.

AGGADAH: The Jewish tradition comprises not only the legal injunctions of the *Halakhah* but also that other branch of the literary heritage of the rabbis, the *Aggadah*. The *Aggadah*—as recorded both in the Talmud and in the homiletical discourses of the Sages collected in the various volumes called *Midrash*—is comprised of sermonic exposition of Scripture, moral exhortation, parable and proverb, and folklore and legend. From this compendium of Jewish lore, I cite on

occasion statements that reflect the attitude of the Sages toward marriage and divorce, which have profoundly influenced Jewish family life through the ages.

Finally, it should be understood that this volume is not an
academic treatise. It is neither a product of the examination of
ancient manuscripts nor a survey of the scholarly works that
abound in this field, and therefore I do not engage in any
polemics with the opinions of others who have written on this
intriguing subject.[4] Rather, I express my own views based on
years of study of the rabbinic sources and personal experience
in the rabbinate. I have attempted to present to the intelligent
and curious layman a review of the Jewish people's ideas and
practices in so important an area of human life, arranged in
chronological sequence and, as far as possible, in nontechnical
language. It is intended not only for the Jew interested in the
traditions of his own people but also for the non-Jew, who
shares with his Jewish neighbor the universal phenomenon of
marriage and divorce.

ACKNOWLEDGMENTS

My profound appreciation to my daughter Rhona, her son Eyal, her daughters Avigayil and Nili, and to Mr. Abba Engelberg for their assistance in processing the manuscript on the computer. My sincere thanks to the staff of Jason Aronson for their kind encouragement and guidance.

PART I

A Survey of
Jewish Marriage

CHAPTER 1

THE INSTITUTION OF
JEWISH MARRIAGE

The Lord God said, It is not good for man to be alone, I will make for him a helper appropriate for him. . . . So the Lord God cast a deep sleep upon the man and he slept; and He took one of his ribs and closed up with flesh in its place. And the Lord God fashioned into a woman the rib He had taken from the man, and He brought her to the man. Then the man said, This now is bone of my bones and flesh of my flesh; she shall be called Ishah [Woman], for she was taken out of Ish [Man]. Hence a man leaves his father and mother and clings to his wife, and they shall be one flesh. (Genesis 2:18–24)

The *Midrash* relates: Rabbi Levi began his discourse on the verse "For God is the Judge" (Psalm 75:8) as follows: A Roman matron once asked Rabbi Jose ben Halafta, "In how many days did God create His world?" He replied, "In six days." She then asked, "From then on till now how does God occupy Himself?" He said, "He arranges couples for marriage, saying, 'This person's daughter shall be that person's wife.' " She said, "Is this all? Even I can do this. I have many manservants and many maidservants, and I can pair them in one hour." Rabbi Jose countered, "You may think it easy; God finds it as hard as the splitting of the Red Sea,"[1] and he left her. What did she do? She brought one thousand manservants and one thousand maidservants, lined them up, and said, "This man shall marry this woman," and paired them for the night. In the morning they came to her, one with his skull cracked, another with his eye dislodged, and a third with his elbow broken. They all said, "I don't want this one [as my spouse]." Whereupon she sent for Rabbi Jose and said to him, "Rabbi, your Torah is true; everything you said is right." The rabbi responded, "The happily married couple sings, the unhappy one cries; however, God pairs them notwithstanding their preferences."[2]

Rabbi Levi was giving here vivid expression to the rabbinic conviction that it is God (some might call this "fate") Who impels a person to marry a particular individual. Indeed, they found confirmation in several biblical verses that "a man is paired to a woman by God."[3] They even asserted that "forty days before a child is born a heavenly voice proclaims, 'This person's daughter shall be the wife of that person.' "[4] However, some rabbis had reservations about this premise. Resh Lakish preached that such pairing is not arbitrary; couples are paired according to their deeds.[5] Shmuel of Pumbeditha contended that it is possible to change this prenatal destiny by prayer.[6] No doubt, the rabbis were attempting to explain to King Solomon—and to many an ordinary observer—what was beyond comprehension: "the way of a man with a maid" (Proverbs 30:19).

In any event, the feeling that marriage is arranged by heavenly decree—in Yiddish the expression is *"es iz beshert"* (it is predestined)—served to strengthen marriage ties and encouraged couples to stay married despite hardships and problems of incompatibility. The stability of Jewish marriages, until very recent times, has been attested to by independent observers in all ages. The first and best-known appreciation of the Jewish home is that of Bilaam, who said, "How goodly are your tents, O Jacob; your dwellings, O Israel" (Numbers 24:5).[7]

SEARCHING FOR A WIFE

Notwithstanding preordained destiny, ever since Adam and Eve it behooves both man and woman to go forth and seek a spouse. A classic example of such a search is the familiar story of the patriarch Abraham, who sent his household manager Eliezer to look for a wife for his son Isaac (Genesis, chap. 24). The search focused upon two requirements: a family connection that ensures a somewhat similar upbringing, and thus making for compatibility, and a person of good character. Unless the candidate for marriage is stricken with a strong passion, which makes him or her blind to such qualities, it is strongly advised by both Scripture and Sage to use one's head as well as one's heart in seeking a partner in life. This is the way the Sages understood the verse in Psalm 32:6, "Therefore let every benevolent man pray to you at a time of finding, that the torrent of many waters [i.e., a blind passion] not overtake him."[8]

To underscore the importance of compatibility and character, the Sages pronounced a series of exhortations for one seeking a mate. These pronouncements were addressed primarily to the man, for especially upon the male falls the obligation. They said, "It is the way of a man to go after a woman."[9] They exhorted,

> A man should sell all his possessions, if necessary, in order to marry the daughter of a scholar. If he can't find a scholar's daughter, he should look for the daughter of a person distinguished for his righteous deeds; if unsuccessful, then a synagogue president's daughter; or of a trustee of charitable funds; or of a school teacher. Under no circumstances should he marry the daughter of an ignoramus.[10]

Nor should he marry a woman for the sake of her money.[11] By no means should a man decide to marry a woman before he has seen her and finds her pleasing in his eyes.[12] One sage even suggested that a young scholar—whose contact with females is very circumscribed—going out to meet his intended bride should take with him an ignoramus—much more knowledgeable as far as women are concerned—to make sure they give him the right lady.[13] Additional practical advice given by the Sages for one seeking a mate includes the following: A young man should not marry an old woman, nor should an old man marry a young woman, for such disparity in ages would lead to infidelity.[14] Furthermore, a man should not marry a woman in whose family there is a hereditary disease;[15] and I might add "what goes for the goose goes for the gander."

THE AGE TO MARRY

To marry, we shall soon see, is a *mitzvah*, a religious obligation. However, it differs from other *mitzvot* as to the age of obligation. For all other *mitzvot*, the age of obligation begins at twelve for girls and thirteen for boys; for marriage, the *mitzvah* devolves upon the male when he reaches the age of eighteen.[16] Nevertheless, the Sages gave the matter some latitude, saying that any time between the ages of sixteen and twenty-four is appropriate, though the earlier the better. This is because they advised that one should first build a house and plant a vineyard, and then marry.[17] One sage, Rav Hisda, boasted that he was better than his companions because he married when he was sixteen. His colleague Rav Huna asserted that if a man isn't married by the time he is twenty he will suffer the rest of his life from sexual fantasies.[18] These ages are for the male; for the female the practice was to marry her off even before the age of puberty, though this was discouraged. One sage went so far as to say, "If your daughter has reached the age of maturity [i.e., after the age of twelve and a half] and she is not yet married, then liberate your slave and marry her off to him."[19]

THE DIVINE PURPOSES OF MARRIAGE

Scripture states it unambiguously: "It is not good for man to be alone" (Genesis 2:18). Man, by his very nature, requires companionship. The blessing for bride and groom invoked under the wedding canopy speaks of "love and brotherhood [I don't have the feminist equivalent], peace and companionship." The rabbis of the Talmud were quite emphatic about this; they averred that "a man without a wife is without joy, blessing, goodness, Torah, a protective wall, and peace."[20] A modern philosopher of Judaism, commenting upon the verse cited above, speaks of "the lonely man," suffering from an existential loneliness arising out of a sense of insecurity and alienation in the face of an inscrutable and overwhelming cosmos.[21]

To save man from loneliness, God said, "I will make for
him a helper *k'negdo.*" This last word has baffled the transla-
tors, for it contains several nuances of meaning. One (Hark-
avy) translates "suitable"; another (old JPS,)[22] "meet"; and
yet another (new JPS) "fitting." I have suggested "appropriate for him." Perhaps a closer rendering might be "com-
plementing him." The woman brings to the union certain
female qualities that complement the male qualities of her
husband, thus making for an integrated union. Man's aggres-
siveness is balanced by woman's passiveness, his rationalism
by her emotionalism. Her qualities are the "extra intelligence"
that the rabbis imputed to the woman, an intuitive understanding of a situation.[23] They therefore advised the husband,
"If your wife is short, bend down and consult with her."[24]

The rabbis have also seen in *k'negdo* a hint of opposition, for
the Hebrew *neged* means "opposed to" or against. Thus they
said, "If the man is worthy [by virtue of his good conduct],
then she is a helper; if unworthy, then she opposes him."[25]
There is a recognition on their part of the subtle tension that
lurks in every marriage, a tension, however, that if properly
understood is positive rather than negative. It controls and
stimulates at one and the same time.

Procreation

The biblical story of the first marriage concludes, "Hence a
man leaves his father and mother and clings to his wife, and
they shall be one flesh." The concluding phrase is understood
by Jewish commentators to refer to the offspring resulting
from the marital union, for in the child are united the human
characteristics of the two parents.[26] Thus, the primary purpose of marriage is the producing of children. In general, God

made certain that His creative works would perpetuate themselves and therefore implanted in them the seeds for their
reproduction. God said, "Let the earth sprout vegetation;
seed-bearing plants and fruit trees of every kind that bear fruit
with the seeds in it" (Genesis 1:11). For the animal kingdom—
the fish of the waters, the birds of the skies, the beasts of the
field—God pronounced a blessing saying, "Be fruitful and
multiply, fill the waters in the seas, and let the birds multiply
on the earth" (Genesis 1:22).[27] For man, however, who also
received this blessing, it was more than a blessing; it was a
command, a *mitzvah*, a religious obligation: Go and reproduce. This is the way our Sages viewed it, as the first of the 613
commandments of the Torah.[28] And as a *mitzvah*, it had to be
defined in a series of halakhic rulings. How many children
does one have to produce in order to fulfill the obligation?
Some say one male child and one female, others two male
children.[29] However, this does not imply that once having
produced the required number, one may cease to bring children into the world. On the contrary, the ruling is, "If one had
children in his youth, he should have children in his old age."
A confirmation of this was found in the verse, "Sow your seed
in the morning, and don't let your hand rest in the evening, for
you don't know which is going to prosper" (Ecclesiastes
11:8).[30] Nevertheless, a man who has already fulfilled the·
minimum obligation may marry an infertile woman. Even if
he is no longer capable of producing offspring, he is obliged to
remain married; bachelorhood is no good in any event.[31]

CONTRACEPTION AND ABORTION

The "spilling of seed," the wasting of one's capacity to breed,
is a most serious offense,[32] and sterilization is specifically

prohibited.[33] Contraceptive measures are frowned upon, permitted only when a pregnancy may be detrimental to health.[34] By the same token, and with even greater force, is Judaism's objection to abortion. To the wasting of one's seed is added the grievous sin of terminating a potential life. It is permitted only when allowing the fetus to come to full term endangers the mother's life.

The importance of the *mitzvah* to reproduce was reinforced by another verse, "He did not create it [the world] a waste, but formed it for habitation" (Isaiah 45:18). Thus the Sages ruled that if a man lived with his wife for ten years and they did not produce any offspring, he is not allowed to remain childless but must marry another woman.[35]

In this connection, the Mishnah relates a poignant story. It happened once in the city of Sidon that a man was married ten years and his wife bore him no children. He appeared before Rabbi Simon ben Yohai and requested a divorce. But first he said to his wife, "Any precious item that I have in my house, take it and go with it to your father's house." Rabbi Simon said to the husband, "Just as you celebrated your marriage with a feast, so celebrate your divorce with a feast." What did the wife do? She made a grand feast and caused her husband to be drunk. She then whispered to her servants to take him to her father's house. He woke up in the middle of the night and asked, "Where am I?" She said to him, "Didn't you say to me, 'Any precious item that I have in my house, take it and go with it to your father's house'? Now nothing is more precious to me than you." When Rabbi Simon heard this, he prayed for them and they were blessed with child.[36]

This rabbinic attitude that procreation is a religious duty sanctioned by God is in sharp contrast to the classic Christian attitude, which saw in celibacy a higher value. The early

Church fathers in particular saw marriage as a concession to man's libidinous nature and a preventive of fornication; for those who devote themselves to religious pursuits ("married to the Church") celibacy is preferable.[37] Reflected in Judaism's positive attitude toward marriage is its positive attitude toward the sexual act within the framework of marriage. Though sexual intercourse is common to both beast of the field and the human species, cognitive man, if he sees in it a divine purpose, approaches it with a special sense of intimacy and delicacy, enhancing both the marital bond and the physical pleasure for both partners. Thus there is no restriction against sexual intercourse between married partners, even when there is no possibility of impregnation. (More will be said about this in Chapter 7, in which conjugal relations are discussed.)

A rather strange rabbinic ruling—one sage disagreed—states that the *mitzvah* of procreation is incumbent only upon the man; the woman is exempt thereof.[38] This exemption allowed women who experienced extreme pain during childbirth to drink a potion that rendered them sterile.[39] However, a woman is obliged to be married even though unable to bear children, lest she be suspected of lewd conduct. On the other hand, a woman may sue for divorce on the grounds that she found her husband infertile; even though there is no *mitzvah* for her to have children, she needs them for support in her old age.[40]

The Sages based the woman's exemption from the *mitzvah* of procreation on the words *and conquer it* (the world) added to the command to be fruitful (Genesis 1:28), arguing that it is man's role, not woman's, to be a conqueror. Similarly in marriage, man assumes the initiative, while woman's role is to be passive and respond to the man's fulfillment of the *mitzvah*.[41] It by no means follows from this that woman's role in procreation is less significant; indeed, it is indispensable. For the woman, however, the exemption makes it dispensable in exceptional circumstances.

Some commentators have explained that this exemption of women from the *mitzvah*, even though they are indispensable to its fulfillment, was made because of the Torah's reluctance to impose an imperative upon them whereby obeying involves severe pain. Furthermore, it has been argued that it was necessary to command men to perform this natural act lest they neglect to do so on the grounds that it would deter them from the study of Torah.[42] Women, who are exempt from the *mitzvah* of studying Torah, lack this excuse and thus naturally want to marry and bear children without being called on to do so by divine fiat.

It should be noted that though a Jewish community would pressure a recalcitrant individual to perform a *mitzvah*, when it comes to the *mitzvah* of marrying, the *Shulchan Arukh* (sixteenth century) states that it is no longer customary to pressure an individual who refuses to marry.[43]

MONOGAMY VERSUS POLYGAMY

From the verse "Hence a man leaves his father and his mother and clings to his wife," one assumes that the circumstance of "one wife to one husband" was regularized then and there in a law banning polygamy. That this was not the case becomes apparent two chapters later, where Scripture tells us, without registering any objection, that Lemech took unto himself two wives (Genesis 4:19). The Sages say it was a common practice in the generation of the flood to take two wives, one for bearing children and the other for sexual pleasure. The one for bearing children sat alone like a widow (her husband would pay her little attention), while the other was given a potion to render her sterile, and she sat with him adorned like a prostitute.[44] Generations later we find that the patriarch Jacob took two wives, though only as a result of Laban's deceit. (I shall discuss the concubines later.) Furthermore, the Torah lays down a certain ruling concerning a man who has two wives (Deuteronomy 21:15–17), though that does not necessarily mean that it was a common practice. The Torah also has a special ruling for kings: "He shall not have too many wives, lest his heart goes astray" (Deuteronomy 17:17), which the Sages understood to limit him to eighteen.[45] Kings, however, are exceptional. We should note at the same time King Solomon's advice to cling to the wife of one's youth: "Let your fountain be blessed: find joy in the wife of your youth. A lovely hind, a graceful doe, let her breasts satisfy you at all times; be infatuated with love of her always" (Proverbs 5:18–19). "Enjoy happiness with the woman you love all the fleeting days of your life that have been granted to you under the sun, for that is your portion in life" (Ecclesiastes 9:9). Similarly, the prophet Malachi affirms, "For God is witness between you and the wife of your youth. . . . She is your companion and the wife of your covenant" (Malachi 2:14). One talmudic sage phrased it this way: "For everything there is a replacement, except for the wife of one's youth."[46]

The Sages approached the problem of polygamy from two angles. First, they considered the effect on the first wife. If the first wife objected to her husband's having taken another wife, Rabbi Immi ruled that the husband was ordered to divorce her and pay her the financial rights due her from her *ketubah*.[47] In a polygamous marriage, each wife was called a *tzarah*, a "trouble" for the other, and therefore the testimony of one wife in a matter affecting the other wife was not acceptable; she was suspected of attempting to cause trouble to the other, her rival for the affection of her husband.[48] The second curb on polygamy was the ability of the husband to support more than one wife. Thus, Rava ruled that a man could marry as many wives as he desired only if he could support them.[49]

RABBENU GERSHOM'S BAN

At the beginning of the eleventh century, Rabbi Gershom, head of the *yeshivah* in Mainz, Germany, pronounced, among other new regulations, a ban against polygamy.[50] It was readily accepted by Ashkenazi-European Jewry, then concentrated in Germany and northern France. It was not accepted by Sephardi-Oriental Jewry, a small percentage of which continued to practice polygamy until recent times.[51] Some would see in this division the influence of the environment on Jewish practice. Ashkenazi Jews lived among their Christian neighbors, who banned polygamy; Sephardi Jews lived among their Muslim neighbors, who did practice polygamy (up to four wives). This division affected the performance of the *mitzvah* of *Yibbum*, levirate marriage (Deuteronomy 25:5–10). Where polygamy is permitted, a married man may perform the *mitzvah* and marry the widow of his childless brother;[52] where polygamy is forbidden, only the alternative to *Yibbum* provided by the Torah—namely, *Chalitzah*, the release of the widow to marry outside the family by the ceremony of removing the shoe—is performed. In the State of Israel today, as in Western countries, polygamy is forbidden by law, and consequently *Yibbum* has become obsolete.

THE TORAH'S BAN AGAINST ADULTERY

Though the law of the Torah permits multiple wives to one husband, it does not permit multiple husbands to one wife. Indeed, any sexual intercourse between a married woman and a man other than her husband is adultery, an offense punishable by death. Thus, the Sages expounded the phrase "clings to his wife, but not to his neighbor's wife."[53] The obvious reason for this command is the questionable paternity of the offspring of a woman who has had intercourse with more than one man. And paternity is crucial in Judaism, for it establishes the tribal affiliation of the child. If the father is a *kohen*, a member of the priestly clan, then the child is a *kohen* even if the mother is not of priestly descent. Conversely, if the mother is of priestly descent but the father is not, the child is not a *kohen*.[54] Moreover, if the paternity is unknown, a man may unknowingly marry his sister or some other close relative.[55]

It seems to me that there is a more profound rationale for this distinction between the man and the woman, reflecting the different intensity of emotional involvement in the sexual act. No matter what feminists might say, hormones and emotions interact. For the woman, since a single act of sexual intercourse may lead to pregnancy, it expresses a profound emotional attachment to the male partner. For her, accepting a partner other than her husband indicates a weakening of her attachment to him and portends a breakdown of the family bond. As for the man, the sexual act does not necessarily indicate a serious emotional attachment to his paramour; it may be for him a casual relationship, a fleeting submission to a carnal urge. For this reason, a married woman who voluntarily submits to a man other than her husband, be he married or unmarried, commits adultery; both she and her partner are equally guilty and both are forbidden by the *Halakhah* to continue any relationship.[56] On the other hand, if a married man has an extramarital affair with an unmarried woman, it is not an act of adultery in the halakhic sense and does not compel the philanderer to divorce his wife.[57]

However, let it be clear that Jewish law does not grant any license for male promiscuity. The Torah has laid down penalties for raping or seducing an unmarried woman (Exodus 22:15, Deuteronomy 22:28). Furthermore, the Sages ruled that a man may not charge his wife with a suspicion of adultery if he himself is not clean of sexual misconduct.[58]

CONCUBINAGE

Father Jacob, in addition to the two wives mentioned above, had two other wives, each a handmaiden to one of the first wives. Even before him, his grandfather Abraham married his wife Sarah's handmaiden, Hagar, because Sarah was barren. Actually, these handmaiden wives were not wives in the fullest sense of the term; they were semiwives, or concubines (*pilegesh* in Hebrew).[59] The Talmud explains the difference: A wife becomes one by a ceremony of betrothal (*Kiddushin*, described in a later chapter) and is entitled to the financial benefits of the *ketubah*, while the liaison with a concubine was not formalized by a betrothal ceremony; nor was she entitled to any benefits of a *ketubah*.[60] The phenomenon of concubinage did not prevail in postbiblical times; the rabbis were opposed to it because it might lead to licentiousness.[61] By the same token, marriages registered only with civil authorities, and couples living together as husband and wife without either civil or religious ceremony, are prohibited by the *Halakhah*. The validity of such marriages as far as divorce procedures are concerned is dealt with in the section on divorce.

MANDATORY MARRIAGES

In several instances the Torah commanded that the man involved marry the woman, to wit:

1. *The Levirate Marriage:* Yibbum (Deuteronomy 25:5–10). If a man dies and leaves no child, one of his brothers—primarily, the oldest brother—is enjoined to marry the widow so that the child born out of the union will "establish a name for the deceased and his name will not be blotted out from Israel."[62] As pointed out by both Maimonides and Nachmanides, this was an ancient pre-Mosaic custom and included other relatives besides the brother.[63] Furthermore, the Torah realized that in most cases an enforced marriage was bound to be an unhappy one and therefore provided that if the brother-in-law did not want to marry the widow he was released from the obligation by the ceremony of *Chalitzah*, the removal of his shoe by the widow. Both talmudic and posttalmudic halakhists disagreed as to which procedure, *Yibbum* or *Chalitzah*, was preferable.[64] Generally, Sephardim ruled that *Yibbum* come first, whereas Ashkenazim ruled that *Chalitzah* come first. As I have pointed out, *Yibbum* has now become obsolete.

2. *The Defamer* (Deuteronomy 22:13–19). If a groom accuses his bride of having had intercourse with another during the period of betrothal[65] and the accusation is proved false, she remains married to him for the rest of his life; *he can never divorce her.* If he did divorce her, he is compelled to remarry her.[66] In addition, he is punished for defaming her by being

flogged and paying a fine of one hundred silver coins. No doubt, this scoundrel had changed his mind about marrying her and thought he would be able to get rid of her without having to pay her *ketubah*, and therefore he is obliged, as the Talmud puts it, "to drink from the vessel he had chosen," even though the vessel is no longer desirable.

3. *The Rapist* (Deuteronomy 22:28–29). If a man rapes a young unbetrothed virgin, he is penalized by having to pay a fine of fifty shekels and having to marry her: *he can never divorce her*. He also is obliged "to drink from the vessel he had chosen" to rape, even though the vessel is no longer desirable. In addition to the fine, he has to pay damages for having deflowered her and having caused her shame and pain.[67] These payments are made to the girl's father, for she is a *naarah*, a twelve-year-old still under her father's jurisdiction. The marriage is mandatory only as far as he is concerned; if either the girl or the father objects to the marriage, it does not take place.[68]

In defining rape, the Sages ruled that even if only the beginning of the sexual act was forced upon the woman against her will, but as the act continued she began to experience pleasure and wanted the act to continue, it is still considered rape. The explanation given is that the rapist forced the desire on her. In this connection the Jerusalem Talmud relates that a woman who was raped came to Rabbi Yohanan and asked if she could continue to live with her husband (a woman who committed adultery could not). The rabbi asked her if she enjoyed it at the end. She responded, "Suppose someone dipped his finger in honey and pressed it into your mouth on Yom Kippur, would it not initially be bad for you but in the end it would be sweet [and you would not be culpable]?" Rabbi Yohanan accepted her argument.[69]

4. *The Seducer* (Exodus 22:15–16). If a man seduces a young unbetrothed virgin, he is penalized by having to marry her in addition to paying her father damages for having deflowered her and having caused her shame. Since she had consented to the intercourse, he does not have to pay for having caused her pain; such pain is pleasurable.[70] Needless to say, if she or her father objects to the marriage, he does not have to marry her. In fact, the Sages so interpreted the relevant passages to imply that even if the seducer objects to the marriage, he is not obliged to marry her. Instead, he has to pay the fine of fifty shekels stipulated by the Torah.

DEFICIENT MARRIAGES

In all periods of Jewish history, almost all marriages were arranged by the young couple's respective fathers, who were obligated to see to it that their children be married. Thus Jeremiah, for example, charged the exiles in Babylonia, "Take wives for your sons and give your daughters to men" (Jeremiah 29:6). A problem arose when the father of a minor girl, too young to accept a proposal of marriage on her own, passed away. To protect such a youngster from sexual abuse, the Sages instituted that her mother or an older brother accept on her behalf a proposal of marriage. However, such a marriage, even though consummated by conjugal intercourse, was not legal as far as biblical law is concerned. Consequently, it could be terminated without a regular bill of divorcement (*get*). All that was necessary was for the girl, at any time before reaching the age of legal maturity, to say, "I do not want this man to be my husband." This kind of divorce was called *mi'un*, that is, not wanting.[71]

Furthermore, the Sages instituted rabbinically sanctioned

marriages for deaf-mutes, who, because of their incapacity, were assumed to be incapable of normal judgment and therefore incapable of effecting a biblically sanctioned marriage. Their wedding ceremony was conducted by means of sign language, and therefore they could terminate their marriage by a regular divorce given through sign language.[72] In deficient marriages an act of adultery, though prohibited, was not considered a capital offense.

Today these rules are no longer significant. We no longer marry off minor daughters, and deaf-mutes, who today receive special education, are no longer devoid of normal judgment and therefore are capable of establishing perfectly valid marriages. Nevertheless, it should be borne in mind that before our modern society these rulings were relevant.

INCESTUOUS MARRIAGES

The Torah commands, "None of you shall approach anyone that is near of kin to uncover their nakedness [a euphemism for sexual intercourse]," and proceeds to list the fifteen relatives included in the injunction (Leviticus 18:6–18). Even relatives through marriage—for example, the wife of a father's brother—are prohibited and remain prohibited even after the demise of the blood-related partner. An exception is a wife's sister; she is prohibited only as long as the wife is alive; after her demise her husband may marry her sister. Indeed, such a marriage was encouraged and not uncommon if she left young children; a sister would be a caring stepmother.[73] Another exception is a brother's wife. If someone dies without leaving an heir, his brother is enjoined to marry the widow. This is the *Yibbum* or levirate marriage mentioned above and which is now obsolete. Any marriage contracted between prohibited relatives is null and void, and any issue resulting from such a union is deemed a *mamzer*, an illegitimate child who may not marry a legitimate offspring.[74]

What may seem to be an anomaly is the fact that a man is forbidden to marry his aunt, but he may marry his niece. Indeed, the rabbis commended the man who married his sister's daughter.[75] Some have justified this anomaly by explaining that it is more appropriate for an older man to marry a younger woman than for a younger man to marry an older woman; ordinarily an aunt is older than her nephew, and therefore the Torah saw fit to prohibit a marriage between them.[76]

The Sages broadened the scope of incestuous marriages, adding several persons more remotely related. These are called *sh'niyot l'arayot,* women prohibited by a secondary degree of incest, and include, for example, a grandmother or a son's daughter-in-law. Such marriages must be terminated by means of a regular divorce because, biblically speaking, they are not incestuous.[77]

A question arose among posttalmudic authorities whether one might marry his stepsister, that is, his father married a woman who has a daughter from a previous marriage. Some would forbid such a marriage if the two were brought up together in the same household from childhood on.[78]

OTHER PROHIBITED MARRIAGES

As mentioned above, the Torah prohibited a child, male or female, born of an incestuous marriage, and thus stigmatized as a *mamzer,* from "entering the community of the Lord" (Deuteronomy 23:3), which the Sages interpreted as a prohibition to marry a Jew or Jewess born of a legitimate union.

Furthermore, if such a marriage was consummated, the offspring thereof also bears the status of illegitimacy. The Sages
sought to minimize the application of this barrier to marriage,
recognizing the seeming injustice of a child's having to bear
the harsh consequences of its parents' iniquity.[79] Thus they
ruled that a *mamzer* may marry a convert to Judaism, even
though their offspring would bear the status of illegitimacy.[80]
The Sages advised a *mamzer* to move to a community where
his deficient status is unknown, and we are not obliged to
reveal it. Once he or she has become assimilated in the community, all barriers to marriage to his or her children are
removed.[81]

The Torah also prohibited marriage of an Israelite to members of certain ancient nations, such as the Ammonites and
Moabites, "because they did not meet you with food and
water on your journey after you left Egypt, and because they
hired Bila'am . . . to curse you. . . . You shall not do anything
for their welfare or benefit as long as you live" (Deuteronomy
23:4–7).

This ruling created a crisis in Jewish life when David was
destined to become king of Israel. The Talmud describes the
crisis as follows: Doeg the Edomite (see 1 Samuel 21:8,
22:9–10) challenged David's legitimacy on the grounds that
he was a descendant of a Moabite woman (Ruth, chap. 4).
Abner replied, "We learned [i.e., in the Mishnah] that the
Torah only excluded the males, but not the females." This
teaching was challenged on various grounds, so the matter
was referred to the *Bet Ha-Midrash* (the academy of scholars).
The scholars of the *Bet Ha-Midrash* confirmed the ruling, "A
male Moabite, not a female Moabite [is excluded]." Doeg
continued to challenge the ruling until Amasa (see 2 Samuel
17:25) girded his sword and proclaimed, "Anyone who does

not accept this ruling will be pierced by the sword. I have a tradition from the *Bet Din* of Samuel the prophet that only a male Moabite is excluded, but not a female Moabite."[82]

Male Ammonites and Moabites were excluded from the community of Israel for all generations—*forever*. However, Edomites and Egyptians were excluded only to the third generation after accepting Judaism. "You shall not abhor an Edomite, for he is your kinsman [a descendant of Esau, brother of Jacob]. You shall not abhor an Egyptian, for you were a stranger in his land. Children born to them may be admitted into the community of the Lord in the third generation" (Deuteronomy 23:8–9). From this distinction between Ammonites and Moabites on the one hand, and Edomites and Egyptians on the other hand, the Sages learned an important lesson. The latter nations, even though they wanted to kill Israelites, attacked them only physically, whereas the former nations attempted to cause them to sin (see Numbers 25:1–2), teaching us that the one who causes us to sin is worse than the one who would kill us, for the former removes us only from this world, whereas the latter removes us from the world-to-come as well.[83]

These laws about the ancient nations were declared obsolete in talmudic times. Thus, it is related that a certain converted Egyptian appeared before the Sanhedrin and asked if he was permitted to marry a Jewess. After some heated discussion, it was finally ruled that ever since Sennacherib (eighth-century B.C.E. Assyrian king) came and transferred nations from their native lands and mingled them with other nations, one was no longer assumed to be a descendant of the ancient nations excluded by the Torah from the community of Israel.[84]

Another category of persons excluded by the Torah from marrying a Jewess is one whose testes are maimed or whose

privy member is cut off (Deuteronomy 23:2). The Sages
included in this category one whose ducts from which the
testes are suspended (i.e., the ducts that carry the semen) are
maimed (and no longer function). However, they also ruled
that these exclusions apply only to those who suffered these
injuries because of infliction by some sharp instrument, but to
one born with such impairment, or if it was brought about by
illness, the exclusion does not apply.[85]

If, as Maimonides maintains, one whose genitals are
maimed is excluded because "his intercourse would be of no
use or purpose [i.e., would produce no offspring]," then it is
difficult to explain the rabbinic distinction between one born
with the injury and one who suffered it by infliction. It must
be understood that the Sages generally did not base their
decisions on the rationale of the commandment,[86] and in this
particular case they felt that the denial to marry should not
apply to one whose impairment was not due to his negligence
or to human cruelty, but—as they phrased it—"to Heaven."
These laws apply today as well.

Special marriage restrictions were imposed by the Torah
for male members of the priestly family, *kohanim*: "They shall
not marry a woman that is a harlot or profaned, nor shall they
marry one divorced from her husband; for they are holy to
their God" (Leviticus 21:7). A harlot is the English version of
the Hebrew *zonah*, but the Sages have interpreted it to include
both a woman who has had sexual intercourse with a prohibited partner and a female convert to Judaism.[87] A profaned
woman, *challalah*, is a daughter of a union between a *kohen* and
one of the women prohibited only to *kohanim*, for example,
the daughter of a *kohen* married to a divorcée. The son of such
a union is a *challal* and has lost his status as a *kohen*. To the
prohibition of a divorcée, the Sages have added the woman

who has undergone the ceremony of *Chalitzah*.[88] The Torah also prohibited a man to remarry a woman who after he had divorced her, married another and the second marriage was terminated either by divorce or by the death of the husband (Deuteronomy 24:1–4). These prohibitions are not as severe as the prohibitions against incestuous marriages; they are not punishable by death, and if contracted by a betrothal ceremony, the marriage is valid, but the partners are urged to terminate their union by divorce.

<h3 style="text-align:center">INTERMARRIAGE</h3>

The Torah enjoins, "You shall not intermarry with them [the Canaanite nations mentioned in the previous verse], do not give your daughters to their sons or take their daughters for your sons; for they will turn your children away from Me to worship other gods" (Deuteronomy 7:3–4). This prohibition applies to any non-Jew, not only Canaanites, and any marriage contracted between a Jew and a non-Jew is null and void. And it is from this verse that the Sages derived the basic principle of Judaism that a child born of a non-Jewish mother, even though the father is Jewish, is deemed a non-Jew. Conversely, a child born to a Jewish mother and a non-Jewish father is deemed a Jew.[89]

The seriousness with which Judaism views marriage to a non-Jew was underscored by both prophet and spiritual leader at the time of the reestablishment of the Jewish state in the sixth century B.C.E. The prophet Malachi rebukes the people, "Judah has dealt treacherously and an abomination is committed in Israel and in Jerusalem; for Judah has profaned the holiness of the Lord and has married the daughter of a strange god" (Malachi 2:11). When Ezra the Scribe heard that

the people have taken the daughters of non-Israelites as wives
for themselves and their sons, "so that the holy seed is mingled with the peoples of the lands, he rent his garment and
mantle and plucked the hair of his head and beard and sat
down appalled" (Ezra 9:2–3). He then assembled the people,
"a very great congregation of men and women and children;
for the people wept very sore, saying, We have broken faith
with our God and have married foreign women" (Ezra
10:1–3), and they solemnly undertook to send away all the
wives and the children born of them. In subsequent generations until this very day, parents would sit *shivah*, mourning
the loss of a child who married outside the faith.

TEMPORARY RESTRICTIONS

The Sages instituted certain regulations limiting the period
during which a marriage could take place, primarily in order
to remove any doubts as to the paternity of a child born seven
months after the marriage. Thus a woman may not marry
until three full months have expired since she became a widow
or a divorcée.[90] Similarly, a proselyte woman has to wait three
months after her conversion before she may marry a Jew, to
make certain that the child she will bear is conceived after her
conversion.[91] The Sages also instituted that a man should not
marry a pregnant or nursing widow lest he deny her the
additional nourishment she requires and thus cause harm to
the infant.[92] A further restriction of the Sages is the case of a
katlanit, a woman who had been married to two men, each of
whom died and left her a widow; a third man is cautioned
against marrying her lest he suffer the same fate of her previous husbands.[93] Later authorities have found so many ex-
emptions to this restriction that it has practically become

obsolete.[94] More practical advice was given by the Sages when they said that a man should not marry a woman in whose family there is a history of epilepsy or leprosy (i.e., a hereditary disease). No doubt, this also applies to the other partner, namely, a woman should not marry a man afflicted with a disability.[95]

CONCLUSION

We have seen how fundamental a role marriage plays in the human species and how the *Halakhah*, based essentially on the talmudic exposition of biblical law, has defined its parameters. Judaism realizes only too well that it is within the framework of the family—created by marriage—that the traditions of its faith can best be preserved and transmitted to successive generations; hence the grave concern of contemporary spiritual leaders with the increasing phenomenon of family breakdown among Jews today, either through divorce and/or intermarriage. The ensuing chapters will describe how the Jewish people arranged and consummated marriages throughout their history, thus enhancing harmony and stability in family life. Perhaps with more knowledge of this tradition, Jewish couples can avoid some of the pitfalls of marriage that are prevalent today and can once again establish exemplary models of family stability and domestic tranquility.

CHAPTER 2

PRENUPTIAL AGREEMENT:
THE *TENA'IM*

Maimonides, in his Code of Jewish Law (*Mishneh Torah*), begins the Laws Concerning Marriage as follows:

> Before the giving of the Torah [at Sinai], a man would meet a woman in the marketplace; if he and she wanted to marry he would bring her inside his house, have intercourse with her between themselves [i.e., without witnesses], and she becomes his wife. As soon as the Torah was given, the people of Israel were commanded that if a man wanted to marry a woman, he first had to acquire her [i.e., he had to perform an act of acquisition described later] in front of witnesses and then she becomes his wife, as Scripture says, "If a man take a wife and cohabit with her [i.e., first take and then cohabit]."[1] (Deuteronomy 22:13).

Actually it was not so simple, neither before nor after Sinai. There were several preliminary steps before a marriage could be consummated. Over the centuries, despite the different

29

ceremonies accompanying each step and the different timing between them, these steps were more or less customary and were defined in legal terms. Even the names by which these steps were called differed from period to period, and it is essential for an understanding of their respective functions to be familiar with their nomenclature at a given period. We can distinguish four steps, each observed in its proper sequence, as follows: (1) matchmaking, (2) formal acceptance of the match, (3) betrothal, and (4) wedding ceremony. I shall discuss each in turn, with their respective Hebrew names.

MATCHMAKING

Matchmaking is the procedure whereby the respective parents of a prospective bride and groom first meet in order to discuss the advisability of their children marrying and to negotiate the terms, primarily financial, under which the marriage should take place.[2] Often, there is an intermediary to arrange such a meeting, either an acquaintance of the families or a professional matchmaker, who first meets the parents separately to suggest the match and to persuade the parties to get together.

The Torah refers to such a meeting between parents of the prospective bride and groom in the Book of Genesis. There we are told how Shechem, a Canaanite young man, fell in love with Dinah, the daughter of Jacob, and asked his father, Hamor, to get the girl for him as a wife. "Then Shechem's father Hamor came out to Jacob to speak to him." Dinah's brothers, who had heard that Shechem had raped their sister, came home from the field and were present at Hamor's proposal.

And Hamor spoke with them saying, "The soul of my son Shechem longs for your daughter. I pray you, give her to him for a wife and intermarry with us; give your daughters to us and take our daughters to you. You will live amongst us and the land will be open before you; settle, trade and take possession therein." And Shechem said to her father and to her brothers, "Let me find favor in your eyes and whatever you say to me I will give. Ask me ever so much dowry and gifts and I will give as you say; just give me the young lady to be my wife." (Genesis 34:1–12)

The Hebrew word that was translated "intermarry" is *hitchatnu*. It is the same term used in the admonition against intermarriage cited in Chapter 1 (p. 25), with the identical expressions, except it is in the negative: "Do not give your son to his daughter and do not take his daughter for your son." From this verb are derived the names for the various persons related by marriage. Thus, *chotein* is father-in-law, *chotenet* is mother-in-law, and *chatan* is son-in-law, but also refers to him on the day of his wedding, just as *kallah* is daughter-in-law but is also her designation on the day of her wedding. The in-laws themselves are called *mechutanim*,[3] and the wedding ceremony by which these relationships are established is called *chatunah*.

In talmudic times an Aramaic term was used for matchmaking; it was, and still is, called *shiddukhin*. A medieval commentator explains that this word, which basically means "tranquility," was used because "a woman finds tranquility in the house of her husband."[4] *Shiddukhin* is the negotiation, *shiddukh* is the match, and *shadchan* is the intermediary or the marriage broker. By the seventeenth century, marriage brokerage had become such an established institution among Ashkenazim that community officials fixed the broker's commission and outlawed unfair practices.[5] In Orthodox circles today it is the accepted practice to pay a substantial sum to the party who suggested the match, even if he or she is a nonprofessional.

In matchmaking, even more so than in commercial transactions, the advice of *caveat emptor* applies. The tendency among those who propose a match—especially the professional shadkhan—is to exaggerate the qualities of the suggested partner; therefore, the parties should be aware of possible misrepresentation or the withholding of serious disabilities that make the proposal unacceptable. Rabbi Yisrael Meir Hacohen, in his book *Guarding One's Tongue*, rules that disclosing such deficiencies of a suggested spouse to the prospective in-laws does not constitute a breach of the laws against *lashon ha-ra*, speaking evil of a person.[6] Furthermore, an eminent modern halakhist contends that it is a *mitzvah* to disclose such deficiencies in order to save the prospective bride or groom from falling into the trap of a disastrous marriage.[7]

What did the parents discuss? What were the subjects of the negotiation? The Talmud phrases it, "How much are you giving for your son; how much are you giving for your daughter?"[8] Shechem mentioned two monetary items: *mohar*, translated "dowry," and *mattan*, translated "gifts." There is no doubt that *mohar* was the bridal price that the father of the groom had to pay before his son could acquire the young lady as his wife, and so it is called to this day among Muslims. In fact, as is typical of the Hebrew language, the noun took a verbal form to signify the taking of a wife, as in the verse, "He [a seducer] must make her his wife [*yimharenah*] by payment of a bridal-price" (Exodus 22:15). However, we shall see later how and why the *ketubah*, or marriage contract, took the place of the *mohar*, which consequently fell into obsolescence.[9] In the *ketubah*, the transformed *mohar* is called *neduniah*, or dowry (in common parlance, *nadan*). The Sages advised the father of the bride to make property assignments in favor of the groom so that there would be many suitors for his daughter's hand.[10]

Mattan were exchanged soon after a verbal agreement was reached, though customs differed as to exactly when these gifts were exchanged; in some places the exchange took place before betrothal and in others afterward.[11] These gifts were called *sivlonot* in the Talmud, and the Sages discussed the legal problems regarding if and when one of the parties could reclaim the gifts if the other party decided to break off the agreement.[12] These gifts remain customary to this day, as in the giving of an engagement ring to the bride and the giving of a corresponding gift to the bridegroom. In recent times, European Jews call the understanding reached by the families a *vort*, a "word" or a verbal agreement, which is confirmed by a handshake.[13] In America such an agreement is called an *engagement*. (Bear in mind that engagement at this stage is only a verbal understanding before any religious ceremony has been performed.)

The Binding Character of a Verbal Agreement

Living up to one's word is a basic moral concept in Judaism. Even though a verbal commitment that concludes a certain transaction may not be legally binding, it is morally binding; as the Sages phrase it, "Your 'Yes' should be just, and your 'No' should be just."[14] This is true not only in commercial life; it is equally valid—and perhaps more so—in a verbal commitment to marry. This is vividly illustrated in a popular folktale alluded to in the Talmud[15] but related in full by Rabbi

Nathan ben Yechiel of Rome (c. 1035–1106) in his *Arukh*, as follows:

This is a tale of a young girl decked out in gold and silver ornaments going to her father's house and getting lost. By noon she became very thirsty; she saw a well with a rope hanging over it; she took hold of the rope and let herself down into the well. After quenching her thirst, she wanted to raise herself up out of the well but was unable to. She started to weep and cry out. A certain man passing by heard her cries; he looked down into the well but could not distinguish her features, so he asked, "Are you a human or a devil?" She replied, "I am a human." He asked her to swear to that, and she did. He then asked her what had happened to her, and she told him the whole story. He then said, "If I raise you up, will you marry me?" She said, "Yes." As soon as he raised her up he wanted to have intercourse with her, so she asked him, "Of what nationality are you?" He said, "I am a Jew from a particular town." She said, "I am also from a particular town, from a well-known family." She then rebuked him, "You are from a holy people chosen by God, and yet you wanted to act like an animal and have intercourse without a *ketubah* and betrothal ceremony. Come with me to my parents and I will become betrothed to you." They made a covenant with each other to marry. He asked, "Who will be a witness to this covenant?" At that moment a weasel was passing by, so she said, "Heaven and this weasel and this pit will be witnesses." Each then went their separate ways.

The young girl remained faithful to her pledge and refused all proposals of marriage, and to ward off all suitors she acted as if she were demented. He, however, soon forgot her, went to his hometown, and married another woman. His wife gave birth to a son, but a weasel strangled him when he was three months old. She then had another son; he fell into a pit and died. Whereupon she said to her husband, "If the children had died a normal death I would accept God's judgment, but dying so strangely, there must be a reason; tell me what you have done." He then revealed to her the whole story of his pledge. She divorced him, saying, "Go to the wife destined for you by God." He went to the young girl's town and inquired after her. He went to her father and told him the whole story, and the father agreed to marry her off to him. However, when he approached her, she—not recognizing him—started to act queerly as was her wont. He then told her the story about the pit and the weasel, and she assured him that she had remained faithful to their pledge. They became reconciled to each other, had children, and prospered. Concerning her, concludes the story, Scripture says, "My [God's] eyes are on the faithful ones of the land" (Psalm 101:6).

YICHUS, OR FAMILY PRESTIGE

Another consideration in these preliminary discussions, even before the usually controversial finances were discussed,[16] is what we call *yichus*, that is, family prestige acquired through distinguished forbears. Lineage was of great importance in biblical times, and families kept genealogical records called *megillat yuchasin*, as we see from the Book of Chronicles.[17] The Mishnah records that on the fifteenth day of the month of *Av* the maidens of Jerusalem danced in the vineyards[18] to attract young men for the purpose of marriage. They would say, "Young man, lift up your eyes and see whom you are choosing; do not look for beauty, look for family."[19] When Jews returned to *Eretz Yisrael* from Babylonia at the beginning of the Second Temple period, the spiritual leader at the time,

Ezra the Scribe, found it necessary to establish which families had retained their pure lineage during the Exile, and therefore could intermarry, and which had not, and therefore were restricted as far as marriage is concerned.[20] Pure lineage meant that there was no member of the family upon whom there was a suspicion that he or she was the offspring of an illicit union.

The Sages laid much emphasis upon having families preserve their genealogical distinction. They asserted that "the Holy One, blessed be He, would cause the *Shekhinah* [His Divine Presence] to dwell only among families distinguished by their pure lineage."[21] In many instances families would achieve this by arranging a match only with someone within the wider family circle. It is related that a man argued with his wife as to with whom they should arrange a match for their young daughter, he insisting that he be someone from his family, and she insisting that he be someone from her family. The wife was so insistent that the husband finally yielded to her wishes, whereupon they invited her relatives to dinner to celebrate the match. While they were eating and drinking, the husband's relative went up to the attic and betrothed the girl. The Sages decided that the betrothal was ineffective since it did not have the father's consent, essential in the betrothal of a minor girl. The assumption was that the husband did not go back on his word to his wife, an assumption based upon the verse "The remnant of Israel shall do no wrong and speak no falsehood" (Zephaniah 3:13).[22]

An example of how families were particularly careful that no tainted individual be permitted to marry within the family circle is recorded in the Mishnah.[23] A young girl of Ashkelon was at first rejected by the members of her extended family as a candidate for marriage because she had been taken by a non-Jew as security for a debt[24] and was probably sexually assaulted. However, witnesses came and testified that she had not been defiled by the non-Jew, and her status as a legitimate candidate for marriage was restored.

In talmudic times, families were very solicitous about their family's prestige and conducted a special ceremony called *ketzatzah*, or "breaking away," denouncing a member of the family who married a woman unbefitting their *yichus*. They would bring a barrel full of fruit, break it in the middle of the town square, and declaim, "Listen, O brothers of Israel; our brother married an unbefitting woman, and we fear that his children will mingle [i.e., marry] with our children. Come and help yourselves [of the fruit] as a token for coming generations that his children shall not be mingled with our children."[25] Priestly families in particular were discriminating before entering into any match; they would investigate four preceding generations of the prospective bride's family to make certain that it contained no discrediting person.[26] The Talmud relates that Rabbi Judah the Nasi went to Rabbi Hiyya's house to discuss arrangements for his son's wedding with Rabbi Hiyya's daughter. When it came to the writing of the *ketubah*, the young lady died. Rabbi Judah wondered, Is it possible, God forbid, that there was something defective in this match? He investigated and found out that he was a descendant of one of King David's wives, whereas Rabbi Hiyya was a descendant of Shimi, a brother of King David.[27] Thus fate intervened to prevent an inappropriate match.

All this is not to say that Judaism is indifferent to woman's physical beauty. One sage was so bold as to say, "A woman was created only for beauty," though he hastened to add, "A woman was created only to bear children."[28] It is related that once a man who was being pressed to marry his sister's daughter vowed not to have anything to do with her because

she was ugly. So the family took the girl into the house of
Rabbi Yishmael and beautified her. Then Rabbi Yishmael said
to the young man, "My son, is this the young lady whom you
vowed to reject?" He replied, "No," whereupon Rabbi Yishmael released him from his vow. At that moment Rabbi
Yishmael wept and said, "The daughters of Israel are pretty; it
is the poverty that makes them ugly." When Rabbi Yishmael
died, continues the Mishnah, the daughters of Israel lamented
him, saying, "Daughters of Israel! Weep over Rabbi Yishmael. Thus does it say concerning Saul, 'Daughters of Israel!
Weep over Saul who clothed you in crimson and finery, who
decked your robes with jewels of gold' " (2 Samuel 1:24).[29]

We begin to discern a change in the concept of *yichus* in
talmudic times, and it has persisted to this day. The Mishnah
avers, "A *mamzer* [of dubitable lineage] who is a scholar is
more important than an ignorant High Priest."[30] It is related
that Rabbi Yohanan, head of the academy in Tiberias (second
half of the third century C.E.), wanted one of his students,
Ze'iri, to marry his daughter, but the latter was reluctant; he
felt that his family's *yichus* was superior to that of Rabbi
Yohanan's family. One day, as they were traveling together,
Rabbi Yohanan said to Ze'iri, "What do you think? My
teaching is kosher but my daughter is not kosher!"[31] However, to this day *yichus* plays an important part in arranging
matches, especially among *chasidim* and in particular among
their spiritual leaders, the "rebbes."

There was another consideration adopted by chasidic families that inhibited certain *shiddukhin*. A medieval pietist, Rabbi
Yehudah Ha-Chasid, in his will cautioned his children against
a *shiddukh* if the prospective bride's name was the same as that
of the groom's mother, or if the groom's name was the same as
that of the bride's father.[32] Sometimes, in order to overcome

this obstacle, an additional name was given to the prospective bride or groom. Rabbis to this day argue whether Rabbi Yehudah Ha-Chasid's testament is to be generally observed or may be disregarded.[33]

KOLLELIM: MARRIED MEN STUDYING TORAH

Another tradition from talmudic times, which is quite resurgent today in Orthodox circles, is for the parties to agree that the groom, instead of working to provide a livelihood for his wife and subsequent children, enter a *kollel* (an institution for married men for the exclusive study of Talmud), leaving financial support to others. The support of such students was so highly regarded by the Sages that even the most prominent among them would visit various communities to gather funds for such a purpose. An example of this high regard is found in the Jerusalem Talmud, where it is related that Rabbi Hiyya bar Ba, outstanding disciple of Rabbi Yohanan, went to the town of Homs in Syria and was given money by the townspeople to distribute to orphans and widows, but he went and distributed the money to scholars studying Torah.[34] In talmudic times, the groom would invariably leave his newly acquired wife for an extended period in order to study Torah in some out-of-town academy.[35]

Perhaps the most extended period of absence from a wife in order to study Torah was that of Rabbi Akiva. At the suggestion of his young bride, Rachel, he left her for a period of twelve years in order to study Torah. The Talmud relates that when he returned home he heard an elderly gentleman remonstrate with Rachel, "How long will you be like a widow while your husband is alive!" She responded, "If he would listen to me, he would remain studying for another twelve years." Whereupon Rabbi Akiva said, "Since she is giving me permission, I shall do so," and he studied for another twelve years. When he returned home the second time, bringing with him twenty-four thousand students, Rachel ran to greet him and kissed his feet. When Rabbi Akiva's students wanted to push her away, apparently not knowing who she was, he said, "Leave her be; what both you and I possess [i.e., knowledge of Torah] is due to her."[36]

This felicitous relationship between Rabbi Akiva and Rachel, despite such an extended absence, was unique and was not recommended by the Sages for other scholars. Indeed, such prolonged absences of husbands from their wives, it was pointed out, could lead to tragic circumstances. Thus, it is related that Rabbi Rechumi, a disciple of the Amora Rava, would come home from the house of study once a year, on the eve of Yom Kippur. One year he was so engrossed in his studies that he failed to come home. His wife, who was eagerly anticipating his annual visit, became so distraught when he failed to arrive that she became depressed and began to cry, for which Rabbi Rechumi was punished by Heaven. Another wife, whose husband had been away for twelve years and was not expected at home was so shaken emotionally when she spied him that she fell into a coma. Fortunately, the story ends, she was subsequently revived. Another rabbi's experience demonstrates that prolonged absence from home also estranges a father from his children, who grow up during his absence, and he fails to recognize them.[37]

Today the husband invariably lives at home, studying in a local institution. In either case, the bride must agree beforehand that her husband study in a *kollel*. This means that the parents have to undertake to support the young couple while the husband is not earning a livelihood. In Eastern Europe this undertaking was called *kest*[38] and usually was for a period of two years. Support in such cases is provided for not only by the parents but by the institution in which the husband is studying, namely, the *kollel*, and by the earnings of the wife, who in Europe might be a storekeeper or a seamstress, while in America and Israel most probably a teacher.

PARENTS AND CHILDREN

Up until now I have mentioned only the parents' role in matchmaking, except in the case of Shechem, who intruded on the discussion of the betrothal. What about the son and daughter in the Jewish tradition; did they play any active role in the discussion? Furthermore, did the son and the daughter meet beforehand and express their wish, if not to the match itself, at least that their parents should enter into matrimonial negotiations on their behalf? The fact of the matter is that in most cases up until modern times the children did not see each other, or even know of each other, until the parents reached an agreement, after which the children were informed that they were matched up to be married.

An important ruling in this connection was derived from the matchmaking negotiations for Rebecca, the daughter of Bethuel, to marry Isaac, the son of Abraham. After an agreement was reached between Eliezer, who represented his master Abraham, and Rebecca's mother and brother Laban,[39] they said, " 'We will call the young lady and ask her opinion.' They called Rebecca and said to her, 'Will you go with this man?' And she said, 'I will go' " (Genesis 24:57–58). From this precedent the Sages ruled that "a girl is not to be married without her consent."[40] This is confirmed by the talmudic injunction, "It is forbidden for a man to betroth his daughter

while she is a minor; [he must wait] until she grows up and
says, 'This is the person I want [to marry].' "[41]

Unfortunately, circumstances in the Middle Ages did not
allow for such restriction. Thus *Tosafot* comments:

> However, now that we are accustomed to betroth our daughters
> even when they are minors, it is because every day the Exile
> overwhelms us [with its frequent expropriations and expul-
> sions], and if at the moment one can provide a dowry for his
> [minor] daughter, perhaps later he may not be able to provide,
> and his daughter may remain a spinster for the rest of her life.[42]

Rabbi Moshe Isserles (sixteenth-century Poland) confirms
this practice of early marriages among Ashkenazim.[43] It was
even more common among oriental Jews to marry off minor
daughters. As recently as one hundred years ago, the rabbi of
Baghdad, Yosef Chayyim, complained that the mothers
would begin to talk about marriage to their very young
daughters. He said, "This is ridiculous and childish and will
result in harm to the girl." He also cautioned against being
persuaded by an aggressive *shadkhan* who may misrepresent
the qualities of the prospective groom.[44]

PARENTS VERSUS CHILDREN

It seems that in Italy and the Balkans, young men enjoyed
considerable freedom in the selection of their mates, but not
so in Germany and Poland.[45] There, fathers would agree to
marry off their grown daughters without their prior consent,
and in some cases a father would impose his will upon his
daughter and insist that she marry someone not to her liking.

More instances are known in which a daughter expressed a desire to marry a certain individual but the father objected for reasons of his own, and her desire was frustrated. In strict Orthodox circles it is still the parents who decide, and the children accept the match as a matter of course. The *Shulchan Arukh*, however, rules that a son is not obliged to listen to his father if the father objects to the girl his son wants to marry.[46]

Typical of such parent–children problems is one recorded by a twentieth-century European rabbi, whose opinion was solicited in a case in which a young man from a strict Orthodox family fell in love and wanted to marry a girl whose parents were Reform Jews, and his father objected. The rabbi, after hearing that the girl promised to observe the dietary laws, advised the father that rather than object to the marriage, he should welcome the young lady and encourage her to be an observant Jewess.[47]

A more difficult problem to solve and rather common today arises when a young man falls in love with a non-Jewish girl (or vice versa, which is less common) and wants to marry her on condition that she convert to Judaism. The usual reaction of parents when first confronted with the situation is to attempt to dissuade the son from marrying her on the grounds that even after conversion the different backgrounds will inevitably lead to serious clashes jeopardizing the marriage. If the son is adamant in his desire to marry and if the girl avers her sincerity in adopting the Jewish faith, parents will cease to object and indeed will welcome her into the family circle. Rabbis, however, differ; some will agree to such conversion and subsequent marriage, while others will refuse to accept candidates for conversion motivated by marriage. In regard to a couple already living together, the preponderant rabbinic opinion is to convert the non-Jewish partner.[48]

Person-to-Person Matchmaking

The life-style in modern urban society has brought about
some novel means of matchmaking. There is now a considerable increase in the number of persons called "singles," bach-
elors and single women in their thirties and forties, as well as
widowed and divorced men and women, many of them
seeking mates. For these, the traditional parental family-
to-family approach to marriage is not suitable. Instead, there
has developed (necessity is the mother of invention) a person-
to-person approach made possible through various agencies.
Both commercial bureaus and public service organizations,
such as community centers and synagogues, arrange mass
meetings of singles, affording them the opportunity of
meeting mate-seeking individuals of the opposite gender,
with the hope that liaisons leading to marriage will follow.

As in so many other aspects of modern life, the computer
has come to play an important role in matchmaking. Marriage
bureaus, upon application of a mate-seeking individual, will
enter into the computer his or her salient physical characteristics—age, height, weight, color of hair, and so on—cultural
and religious interests, and what he or she considers desirable
in a mate. From these data, the bureau is able to find and
recommend compatible partners. Newspapers and magazines
also serve in person-to-person matchmaking. A mate-seeking
individual places an "ad" in the "personals" column of the
journal, with a brief description of his or her qualities and the
type of mate being sought, anticipating a response that eventually will lead to marriage.

The Sages underscored the need for *shiddukhin* or inter-
family discussion to be held prior to any act of betrothal that
solemnizes the relationship. Indeed, Rav (Abba Arikha, head

of the academy in Sura, Babylonia) would punish with lashes anyone who betrothed a woman without prior *shiddukhin*.[49] Because of its importance, the Sages permitted *shiddukhin* negotiations (no doubt including financial arrangements) on the Sabbath.[50]

The Talmud refers to *shtarei pesikta*, writs of stipulation in which the financial terms of the *shiddukh*—how much each of the parties agreed to give to the young couple—were documented, but then argues the possibility that these were writs of betrothal, and the agreements made at the time of the *shiddukhin* became binding by word of mouth without being documented.[51] Some *Rishonim* (medieval *poskim*) distinguish between agreements made at the time of the betrothal, which do not require a written document or a *kinyan* (a symbolic act such as the transfer of an article, usually a kerchief), and agreements made long before the betrothal.[52] Maimonides states that the scholars of *Sepharad* (oriental communities) would confirm financial undertakings, including those made at *shiddukhin,* by means of a *kinyan*, and this became the universal custom.[53] In Ashkenazi communities, a ban (*cherem*) would be pronounced excommunicating anyone who reneged on a prenuptial agreement.[54]

Tena'im

In the Talmud there is no mention of a formal festive gathering to celebrate the *shiddukhin* agreements. A survey of the posttalmudic literature will reveal scant reference to any formal ceremony at the signing of *tena'im*—the conditions under which two parties agree to the marriage of their children—until the late sixteenth to early seventeenth century. A *responsum* of Rabbi Shlomo ibn Adret (Rashba, thirteenth-century Spain) describes "the *kinyan* at a *shiddukhin*, a large gathering of men and women, the bride sitting on a chair, and they took the *kinyan* [i.e., the symbolic article] in the presence of the bride, then the *chazzan* [cantor or sexton] would get up and announce that so-and-so engaged his daughter to so-and-so."[55] Rabbi Jacob Moellin (Maharil, fourteenth- to fifteenth-century Germany), in describing the wedding ceremony in his community, states that "they would bring the *ketubah* and the *tena'im* to the *chuppah*," but he does not describe any *tena'im* ceremony.[56] Mention is also made of a custom to write two *tena'im*, one written at the time of the agreement and another at the time of the *chuppah*.[57] When we come, however, to the commentators to the *Shulchan Arukh*, one generation after its publication, we find a discussion among them as to which type of vessel is broken at a *tena'im* ceremony, a glass goblet as at the betrothal ceremony, or—to differentiate it from the one used at the betrothal—a pottery dish. Those who insisted on the latter explain the difference: Broken glass can be repaired, signifying that a marriage broken by divorce can be repaired through remarriage, whereas pottery once broken cannot be repaired, indicating that a *tena'im* agreement should never be broken. "Better have the couple go through a wedding ceremony and then be divorced, rather than break a *tena'im* agreement."[58] This formalization of a *shiddukhin* ceremony was due to the shifting of the betrothal to the wedding ceremony, and it now included a festive gathering and the signing of a document. This is the ceremony of *tena'im*, the second event leading to the consummation of the marriage.

Since the *tena'im* ceremony is a substitute for the shifted betrothal, any feast held in conjunction with it would be in the same category as the betrothal feast, namely, a *se'udat mitzvah*, a feast held in honor of a religious ceremony. Thus, many pious scholars who restrict their attendance at public dinners to a *se'udat mitzvah* would attend a betrothal feast and by extension to a *tena'im* celebration.[59] On the other hand, the Talmud rules that even though one may betroth a woman during *Chol Ha-Mo'ed* (the intermediate days of a festival) lest someone else betroth her before him, it is not permissible on those days to make a betrothal feast, for it would be mingling the celebration of the festival with a personal celebration, which is forbidden.[60] By the same token, some post–*Shulchan Arukh* authorities—again an indication that *tena'im* celebrations were not customary before the late sixteenth century—did not sanction them during *Chol Ha-Mo'ed*. Similarly, the same rule applies to those periods of partial mourning, such as the "three weeks" from the seventeenth of *Tammuz* to Tish'a B'Av. In other words, *tena'im* agreements are permissible but festive celebrations in honor of them are not permissible.

By now, the *tena'im* ceremony has become fixed. The two mothers are called into the room where the *tena'im* document was signed, and it is read aloud. Whereupon the mothers take the earthenware dish they have been holding and smash it, and the assembled call out *"Mazal tov."*

THE *TENA'IM* DOCUMENT[61]

The *tena'im* document, topped by a decorative *"Mazal Tov"* (Good Luck), begins with an inscription in rhymed prose:

> May it rise and sprout like a watered garden[62]
> May the good God pronounce the union good;
> Who finds a wife finds a good thing and wins the
> favor of the Lord. (Proverbs 18:22)

Who declares the end from the beginning. (Isaiah 46:10)

May He give a good name and a remainder. (2 Samuel 14:7) To these words of condition and covenant spoken and stipulated between these two parties: On the one part Mr. _____ of _____ (city of residence), who stands on behalf of his son the groom _____ ; and on the second part Mr. _____ of _____ , who stands on behalf of his daughter the bride the virgin _____ . First of all, the aforementioned groom will marry for *mazal tov* the aforementioned bride in a betrothal and *chuppah* according to the law of Moses and Israel; and they shall neither sequester nor conceal one from the other any sums of money wherever held, but shall control them in equal portions; they shall live together in peace, love, brotherhood, and companionship for the length of many days. We asked her [if she agrees] and she said yes [see p. 41]. The aforementioned Mr. _____ obligates himself to provide for his son the agreed-upon sum in cash and in raiment for the Sabbath and Festivals and weekdays as befits his honor and corresponding to the value of the dowry gifts to the bride. Mr. _____ obligates himself to give his daughter the bride a dowry, the value of which was agreed upon, also alimentary support for the young couple as agreed upon, in cash and in raiment for the Sabbath and Festivals and weekdays as befits her honor. The payment of the dowry shall be made at the time agreed upon [usually before the wedding ceremony]. The wedding, for *mazal tov* and in a propitious hour, shall take place at the time agreed upon. The bride's father will pay the emoluments for the officiating clergy [usually a trio: the rabbi, the cantor, the sexton, see p. 91]. All the above was accepted by both parties to confirm and establish a fine of half the value of the dowry to be paid by the party who cancels to the party who fulfills. The guarantors of this agreement: from the groom's part, Mr. _____ ; from the bride's part, Mr. _____ . The parties agree to reimburse the guarantors for any loss they may incur. AND WE MADE A *KINYAN* [symbolic confirmation of agreement] with the parties on all that is stated and written above with a vessel fit for a *kinyan*, this being neither an *asmakhta* [presumptuous forfeiture][63] nor a sample form AND EVERY-THING IS FIRM AND ESTABLISHED

DONE in _____ (city) on the _____ day of _____ (month)

TESTIFIED BY (witness's signature) WITNESS

TESTIFIED BY (witness's signature) WITNESS

For further confirmation the parties have affixed their signatures.

CANCELLATIONS

We have already mentioned the seriousness with which a *tena'im* agreement was regarded, in addition to the penalties for unilateral cancellation stipulated therein. Nevertheless, the law recognized that if certain defects in one party became known to the other party only after the agreement was signed, the latter has the right to cancel the agreement without incurring any penalty. If, for example, a father entered into an agreement on behalf of his daughter without having previously advised her and she subsequently rejects the *shiddukh* and refuses to go to the *chuppah*, the father is not liable. If a serious physical defect or illness became disclosed afterward, the other party may cancel.[64] Furthermore, if either prospective bride or groom committed immoral acts prior to the wedding, or even if some taint in one of the families became known—for example, the brother of the bride was an apostate Jew—the *tena'im* may be broken.[65] Where there is justification for the nullifying of the agreement, the expensive gifts that were exchanged must be returned.[66]

What happened to the betrothal—new considerations causing it to be postponed—happened eventually to the *te-

na'im. Since changed circumstances during the interval between it and the actual wedding might lead to second
thoughts by either party, and the penalty for breaking the
agreement is so severe, the *tena'im* in most cases has now been
shifted to moments before the wedding. It does seem rather
supererogatory to sign an agreement that a wedding shall take
place at a certain time when all preparations for the wedding
are complete, all the guests are assembled, and the young
couple is ready to go to the *chuppah.* As far as the financial
obligations assumed by both parties in the *tena'im* are concerned, these can well be included in the original nuptial
document, the *ketubah,* the only difference being that whereas
in the *tena'im* the obligations are assumed by the parents, in the
ketubah they are assumed by the groom himself.

No matter what brought about an agreement to marry—a
spontaneous falling in love, a casual encounter, a parent-
to-parent *shiddukh,* or a person-to-person search—if the
agreement is to be fulfilled, sanctioning their living together
as husband and wife, the couple must go through a wedding
ceremony. In the Jewish tradition, to become religiously as
well as legally binding, the ceremony must be conducted in a
manner regulated by the *Halakhah.* But first, the prenuptial
agreement must give way to a nuptial agreement, a formal
contract, spelling out the conditions under which the parties
enter the marriage, including the mutual obligations, duties,
and responsibilities undertaken by them. This contract is the
subject of the next chapter.

CHAPTER 3

THE NUPTIAL CONTRACT: THE *KETUBAH*

THE *KETUBAH*[1]

There is a Hebrew expression that an object, or even an idea, "puts on a form and takes off a form" but intrinsically remains the same. This is what has happened to the *ketubah* (plural, *ketubot*) in the course of history, from biblical times to the present, changing its wording from period to period and locale to locale but essentially remaining the document that spells out the mutual obligations of the partners to marriage. These changes have led to a basic difference of opinion among halakhic authorities as to its origin and authenticity, some maintaining that it is *d'oraita*, that is, of biblical provenance and legal force, and others maintaining that it is *d'rabbanan*, that is, a regulation instituted by the Sages.[2] To this day, some *ketubot* add the word *d'oraita* if the bride is a virgin, to denote that the basic sum due the wife is due by virtue of biblical law;

others deliberately omit it, refusing to recognize any biblical force to its stipulations.[3]

I have discussed earlier (p. 32) the biblical *mohar*, the bridal-price paid by the groom's family. Some of the Sages, as well as some classical commentators, understood this *mohar* to be the equivalent of the *ketubah*.[4] Though so far no such actual document dating from the First Temple period has been found, several *ketubot* from early Second Temple days have been found and published.[5] A statement in the Talmud discussing the changes that have taken place in the nuptial agreement prior to Simon ben Shetah (c. 120–60 B.C.E.) clarifies how the *mohar* was transformed into the *ketubah*. It reads as follows:

> At first they would write [in the *ketubah*] 200 zuz[6] for a virgin and 100 zuz for a widow, but they would grow old and not marry, so they [the Sages] instituted that the sum should be deposited in her [the bride's] father's house; yet when the husband would be angry with his wife he would say to her, "Go to your *ketubah*" [i.e., go back to your father's house, thus divorcing her on impulse], so they instituted that the sum should be placed in her father-in-law's house [i.e., with her husband]—the rich would put it into baskets of silver and gold, the poor into copper containers—and still when he would be angry with her he would say to her, "Take your *ketubah* and get out," until Simon ben Shetah came and instituted that he [the groom] should write, "All my possessions are liable for your *ketubah*."[7]

We can see here the following development: In ancient times, in the biblical period, it was the accepted procedure that if one wanted to marry a woman he would have to pay, either in cash or in kind, a sum of money before the wedding.[8] This is evident from the verse obligating the seducer of a virgin to "pay a bridal-price for her to be his wife," that is to say, he is obligated to marry her and therefore he has to pay the bridal-price. However, the verse continues, "If her father refuses to allow him to marry her, he shall pay a sum equal to the customary bridal-price for virgins" (Exodus 22:15–16), that is, he has to pay a penalty for the seduction.[9] In Deuteronomy the Torah specifies the penalty a rapist has to pay to the bride's father, fifty silver shekels, in addition to the obligation to marry her (22:28–29), and the Sages inferred that this sum also applies to the seducer.[10]

In the Second Temple period, when money and goods were scarce, men were unable to pay the bridal-price and consequently could not marry. Therefore, it was decided that the bridal-price need not be paid before the wedding; rather, the groom should write a document—the prototype of the *ketubah*—in which he promised to pay the money at some future time. Since the fifty silver shekels prescribed by the Torah had been replaced by other coins, this regulation also instituted that the minimum sum to be stipulated should be two hundred zuz for a virgin and one hundred zuz for a non-virgin,[11] with, of course, the option of adding to this sum if he could afford it. This additional sum was called *tosefet ketubah*.

Added was a clause that stipulated that the sum would become due "when you become married to another," that is, when you become permitted to marry another, either when you are divorced or widowed.[12] At the same time it was ruled that a token sum, even as little as the cheapest silver coin or its equivalent in goods, be given to the bride at betrothal, a token of the bridal-price.[13] However, it was found that this regulation was not enough to encourage marriages. This time it was the women who were the reluctant partners; a mere document pledging a future payment without a concrete surety did not

satisfy them. So it was further instituted that the groom
should set aside a precious household item equal in value to
the sum stipulated in the *ketubah* as surety.[14] This still did not
satisfy the women, since in a moment of anger the husband
could summarily dismiss them together with the surety. Finally came Simon ben Shetah, who instituted that all the
husband's property be liable for the sum pledged, and consequently the wife need not worry that in case of divorce or her
husband's death she would be left penniless. On the other
hand, since the sum would have to be paid upon divorce, the
husband would think twice before divorcing her. As the
Talmud phrases it, "The *ketubah* was instituted so that it
would not be easy for him to divorce her."[15]

TERMS OF THE *KETUBAH*: STATUTORY OBLIGATIONS

Simon ben Shetach's regulation was by no means the last.
Two generations later, a generation and two after the destruction of the Second Temple in the year 70 C.E., the Sages of the
Mishnah, the *Tanna'im*, expanded the scope of the *ketubah* to
define in detail the mutual obligations and rights assumed by
bride and groom upon marriage. In fact, they ruled that
certain basic obligations are mandatory even if not spelled out
in the nuptial document, "for they are a condition of [imposed
by] the court," that is, the Supreme Court or Sanhedrin of the
time, and therefore many of them are no longer specified in
the *ketubah*.[16] However, the obligation of the husband to
provide for his wife's alimentary support (*mezonot*) and re-
spectable raiment is written out to this day.[17] Correspondingly, the wife is obligated to perform specified household
duties, depending on the number of domestic servants the
husband can afford. He must pay for his wife's medical ex-

penses, for the ransom demanded by her captors, and for the funeral expenses upon her demise.[18]

There were also statutory obligations of the husband's estate if he predeceased his wife, primarily her right to remain in the family residence and be supported until she marries or is paid the full amount of the *ketubah*.[19] In general, these terms reflect the talmudic statement, "The Sages were considerate of the daughters of Israel."[20]

Another statutory obligation of the husband's estate arose out of the phenomenon of polygamous marriages, apparently not too uncommon in talmudic times. In such marriages, a *ketubah* was drawn up for each wife, the sums stipulated therein depending on the particular dowry given by the father and any other agreements reached between the parties. To enable each woman to leave to her children the patrimony that she had brought to her husband upon marriage and which accrued to his possessions upon her demise, a standard clause provided that upon the husband's death her sons would inherit their mother's *ketubah* in addition to inheriting their share in their father's estate together with the sons from another wife.[21]

THE DOWRY (*NEDUNIA*)

An integral part of the *ketubah* was the total value of the cash and household goods that the bride brought from her father's house, namely, the dowry (in Aramaic, *nedunia*, "gift"), which the groom acknowledged to have accepted. There were many different customs over the years as to the evaluation placed on the *nedunia* and written in the *ketubah*. The Mishnah records that the cash, since it could be used by the groom for a profitable enterprise, was acknowledged by him to be one-third more than its actual value; the household goods, since their value would depreciate through wear and tear, would be acknowledged at one-fifth less than their actual value.[22] When these items became collectible, account was taken of the inflated or depreciated values written in the *ketubah*. In later times, the value placed on the dowry was inflated in order to enhance the prestige of the bride. Maimonides sums up the situation as follows: "In all these matters, the principal factor is the local custom, provided it is a custom widely accepted in that province."[23]

The Sages ruled that the minimum dowry for a poor bride is fifty zuz and must be provided for by the community if she is an orphan. Indeed, it was, and still is, considered a great *mitzvah*, called *hakhnasat kallah*, to enable young men and women of limited means to establish a home. This *mitzvah* is included in those philanthropic deeds for which "one enjoys the fruits thereof in this world, and the principal thereof remains in the world-to-come [i.e., in life hereafter]."[24] The directives given by the Talmud to the trustees of the local charity fund are: If both a male and a female orphan seek assistance in being married, the female has priority, "for the embarrassment [of remaining single] is greater for the woman than for the man." Furthermore, he or she must be provided with an apartment, furniture, and household utensils, and then a spouse.[25] If a father dies and leaves young girls, the *ketubah* provides that they have to be supported from the estate until they marry, and their dowry has to be paid from the estate, a sum proportionate to the father's wealth. Correspondingly, the groom must bring into the household a sum equivalent to the value of the dowry, plus any additional amount agreed upon. In the Middle Ages, communities were concerned with the inequity of a situation caused by the death of a wife within a year or two of the marriage. Since according to biblical law the husband inherited all his wife's property,[26] with the marriage of such short duration it was not right that the dowry remain in the husband's possession, so regulations were instituted that in such an event the dowry be returned to the wife's family.[27] From time to time communities would also define the basic amount due the woman (the two hundred zuz) in local coin and relative to its economic value.

Technically, the *ketubah* is a promissory note issued by the husband to the wife, and she has the right to sell it. However, its payment is conditional upon the husband predeceasing or divorcing her. If she predeceases her husband, the note loses its entire value. Thus, the purchaser of a *ketubah* is taking a gamble, and therefore it is sold at a considerable discount. And just as a lender may cancel a loan, so may the wife, if she so desires, cancel her *ketubah*. In fact, if she agrees to her husband's selling all his property and leaving her without any surety, it is assumed that she is canceling her *ketubah*.[28]

NONSTATUTORY STIPULATIONS

In addition to those terms of the *ketubah* fixed by rabbinic law, the parties could add conditions of their own, financial and otherwise, and in their own language. An example from the days when the Temple still stood in Jerusalem is recorded in the Talmud, whereby a groom undertook to pay for the offerings that his wife had been obligated to bring to the *Bet Ha-Mikdash* before the marriage.[29] Another interesting provision is recorded in the Jerusalem Talmud, whereby bride and groom agree that the party who refuses conjugal relations is to be fined a sum of money.[30] Since the *ketubah* is a legal contract, its terms enforceable in a court of law, its text has to be scrutinized in the event of a claim based on it. An interesting example of such scrutiny, which helped legitimize a peculiar custom of the ancient community in Alexandria, is also recorded by the rabbis.[31] The people of Alexandria would betroth their women long before the wedding, as was the custom in all communities up until the Middle Ages. When the time came for them to go to the *chuppah*, other men would come and take the brides away and marry them.[32] The rabbis at the time wanted to declare their children *mamzerim*, that is, issue of an adulterous marriage, since a betrothed woman is considered married. Hillel the Elder, however, asked them to bring their mothers' *ketubah*, and he saw in them the phrase "when you go to the *chuppah* you will be my wife," indicating that they did not want the betrothal to effect married status until they actually went to the *chuppah*. Before that moment, the bride was still free to marry another and, hence, if another married her, their children would be legitimate.

Other stipulations in talmudic times dealt with property arrangements. Generally, the property—comprising movables, immovables, and non-Jewish slaves—that the bride brought into the household was divided into two categories. The first was designated *nikhsei melug*, "profit-taking property." It remained the property of the wife; if it increased in value the gain was hers, and if it decreased in value, the loss was hers. The husband, however, was entitled to the income derived from it (the profit was designated *peirot*, "fruits"). Technically speaking, she had the right to sell the property, but the Sages instituted that the husband could cancel the sale so that he could continue to enjoy the fruits thereof. Upon dissolution of the marriage through death of the husband or divorce, such property would revert completely to her control. Thus *nikhsei melug* were also referred to as "property entering and going out with her."[33] The Mishnah rules that where the groom waives in writing his right to the fruits of his wife's property, the agreement is binding.[34]

The second category of goods brought by the bride as part of the dowry was designated *nikhsei tzon barzel*, "iron-sheep property."[35] These were subject to an iron-clad agreement that the husband, accepting all responsibility for the goods, could utilize them to engage in business for himself, with the understanding that they or their equivalent value as stipulated in the *ketubah* had to be returned to the wife upon dissolution of the marriage. Thus, any increment in the value of the property would be the husband's; any decrease would be his loss.[36]

Typical of other nonstatutory conditions often included in *ketubot* in oriental countries were that the groom undertake not to marry another woman, and that he would not sell any of her property without her consent. If the couple married in *Eretz Yisrael*, he would stipulate that he would not move outside of Israel (in some *ketubot* he even stipulated that he would not take her farther than Damascus) without her consent, and that if he had to travel some distance he would make prior arrangements for her alimentary support during his absence.[37]

THE *KETUBAH* DOCUMENT

A custom that developed in the Middle Ages, then grew out of style in the nineteenth and twentieth centuries, is now being revived. This is the artistic illumination of sacred texts, and the *ketubah* is no exception. Invariably topped by some biblical verse extolling the virtues of marriage in large decorative

letters, surrounded by pictorial representations of nature,
framed in colorful borders, the *Ketubah*, which is essentially a
prosaic legal document, often becomes a treasured work of
art, displayed in museums and published in expensive coffee-
table productions. This is perfectly in accordance with the
rabbinic exhortation to beautify the *mitzvot*,[38] and the *ketubah*,
being an integral part of the *mitzvah* of marriage, is no exception. Today, even more so than previously, attention is given
to a beautiful calligraphy of the text.

The essential text reads as follows:

On the _____ day of the week, the _____ day of
the [Jewish] month, in the _____ year anno mundi, in the
city of _____ WE (the undersigned) are witnesses that
(groom's name), son of (his father's name), of the family,
_____ , said to this virgin[39] [Sephardim insert: beautiful
graceful gazelle] (bride's name), daughter of (her father's name)
of the House of (family name), Be thou my wife according to the
law of Moses and Israel and I will [Sephardim: with the help of
Heaven] work and honor and provide food and clothing as is the
custom of Jewish men in truth, and I will give you the dower of
your virginity 200 silver zuzim which is coming to you [outside
of Israel: by the Torah] and your food and your clothing
and your other needs[40] as is the universal practice; and so did
_____ this virgin desire to be his wife and this is the
dowry which she brings from her father's house[41] both in silver
and in gold and in jewelry and in clothing and in household
utensils and in bedroom facilities, all of which our groom accepted in the value of 100 refined silver coins and he desired and
added from his own another 100 refined silver coins correspondingly, making a total of 200 refined silver coins. AND thus
did _____ the son of _____ declare, The surety
for this *ketubah* and this dowry and this additional sum I accept
upon myself and my heirs after me to be paid from the most
desirable of my possessions and acquisitions that I possess under

Heaven and that I may acquire in the future, both immovable and movable property, all are surety to pay from them this *ketubah* and this dowry and this additional sum from me and even from the cloak on my shoulder during my lifetime or after my death from this day onward, and the surety and stringency of this document our groom _____ the son of_____ has accepted upon himself in accord with the stringency of all *ketubot* and additional sums customary among daughters of Israel, done in accord with the regulations of our Sages and not as an *asmakhta*[42] or standard form, AND WE HAVE MADE A KINYAN [a symbolic act of agreement] from _____ the son of _____ our groom to _____ the daughter of_____ this virgin on everything that is written above with an article[43] proper for making such contracts, AND EVERYTHING IS FIRM [Sephardim: AND CLEAR] AND ESTABLISHED

DECLARES (signature) WITNESS
DECLARES (signature) WITNESS

[In Israel they add: And I the groom also agree to all the above and sign on the above day (signature of groom).][44]

It should be noted that in talmudic times, when the economy was based almost exclusively on agriculture, the *ketubah* would be collected only from immovable property, though we are told that in one community it was also collected from rental money.[45] However, in the immediate posttalmudic period, when there was a trend toward urbanization and a mercantile economy, the *geonim* instituted that the *ketubah* could be collected from movable property as well, and so it has remained to this day.

Timing and Signing of the *Ketubah*

The *ketubah* is invariably written just before the betrothal. However, since it includes a statement that the groom has betrothed the bride, technically speaking, the *kinyan* and the signing by the witnesses should be done after, and not before, the betrothal. Since today the bride and the groom are already standing under the *chuppah* for the betrothal, the *kinyan* and the signing should take place under the *chuppah* during the wedding ceremony. Indeed, this is the practice insisted upon by some officiants. However, for purposes of convenience it has become customary in many communities for the *kinyan* and signing to be done before the bride and groom go to the *chuppah*, that is, before the betrothal, though the *ketubah* is not handed over to the bride until after the betrothal.

Since the *ketubah* is evidence that the bride has been married, its dating must correspond to the actual day in which the betrothal takes place, and therefore the *kinyan* and the signing should be done on the day stated in the *ketubah*. According to the Jewish calendar, a change in date occurs at nightfall, and therefore if the date is of daytime, the *kinyan* and signing should be done before nightfall. However, the Talmud already recognizes that often the writing of the *ketubah* may take longer than expected, and by the time the witnesses have to sign it is already nighttime and a day later as far as the Hebrew date is concerned. It was therefore ruled that as long as the signing took place right after the writing was completed, the *ketubah* is valid.[46] Many weddings are performed after nightfall; in such case the date recorded in the *ketubah* is one day later than the corresponding English date.

In accordance with the verse "The fathers shall not be put to death for the children, neither shall the children be put to death for the fathers" (Deuteronomy 24:16), the Sages ruled that close relatives of parties involved in court cases—even relatives of the judges—cannot serve as witnesses.[47] They are also disqualified to sign a document if a relative is a party to the contract, which applies to the *ketubah* as well. The *Halakhah* specifies the following relatives disqualified as witnesses: parents, children, brothers, uncles, in-laws, first cousins. Also disqualified are minors (under thirteen), various transgressors of Jewish law—for example, non-Sabbath observers and professional gamblers—and women, whether related to the parties or not. Such persons should not be asked to serve as witnesses for the *ketubah*.

Loss of *Ketubah* Rights

The Sages ruled that certain women lose their claim for the payment of their *ketubah* if they are divorced because of their misbehavior. A woman who transgresses "the law of Moses and Judaism"[48] and deceives her husband thereby (for example, she feeds him nonkosher food saying that it is kosher, or she claims that she is not a *niddah* [menstruant], thus allowing him to have sexual intercourse with her, but it is found out that she was a *niddah* at the time), or a woman who acts immodestly, forfeits the amount stipulated in her *ketubah*.[49] Furthermore, for each week that a woman denies her husband his conjugal rights she is penalized by reducing a certain amount from her *ketubah*. If she persists in her obdurate behavior until the entire amount of her *ketubah* is canceled, she is divorced without receiving any payment whatsoever.[50]

Claims and Counterclaims

Much of rabbinic legislation concerning the *ketubah* deals with disputes arising from its financial terms. One of the major disputes in biblical and talmudic times was the claim of a widow or divorcée that she was a virgin at the time of her marriage and therefore is entitled to two hundred zuz (she claims she lost her *ketubah*). The husband, on the other hand, or his heirs claim that she was a nonvirgin (*be'ulah*) at the time and is entitled to only one hundred zuz.[51] Generally speaking, a woman had to swear an oath in court that she had not seized any assets or received any monies due her from the *ketubah* before she could collect.[52] In some cases, if she did not submit a claim for a period of twenty-five years after it became due, it is assumed that she had waived her rights for payment.

In modern times, in Western countries in which Jews generally resort to the local civil courts rather than to rabbinic courts in financial matters, the *ketubah* no longer serves as a legal contract. In fact, no local currency is specified therein, so couples usually have a notary draw up a civilly recognized marriage contract to regularize their financial obligations.[53] In the State of Israel today, the total sum of the *ketubah* is stated in local Israeli currency and is a legal obligation.

Now that I have described the *ketubah* and examined practically all aspects of its contents, we proceed to the next step in the marriage process, the betrothal.

CHAPTER 4

THE BETROTHAL:

KIDDUSHIN

And I will betroth you forever;
I will betroth you with righteousness and justice
and with kindness and mercy;
And I will betroth you with faithfulness;
Then you shall know the Lord. (Hosea 2:21–22)

TERMINOLOGY

It is clear from Scripture that as early as in biblical times, two procedures were followed in order to establish a marital union. Thus we read, in connection with preparations for combat, "The officers shall speak to the people. . . . Any man who has betrothed a woman but has not yet taken her, let him go and return to his home, lest he die in battle and another man take her" (Deuteronomy 20:7).[1] For a better understanding of these procedures, we must examine the Hebrew terms as they

are used in the Bible, since they have received different interpretations both in the Talmud and later in common parlance.

The word that has been translated "betrothed" is *aras* in the
original.[2] From another verse in Deuteronomy, it is evident
that on the one hand, after this act of betrothal the woman is
considered married, but on the other hand the marriage is not
yet consummated, for she is still a virgin. The verse reads, "If
there be a young woman who is a virgin betrothed unto a
man, and a man find her in the city and lie with her, you shall
take the two of them out to the gate of that city and stone them
to death. . . . the man because he violated his neighbor's wife"
(Deuteronomy 22:23). Apparently, she is still living in her
father's house,[3] waiting for the time for her fiancé to come and
"take her" to his own domain, at which time she passes from
betrothed status to complete wifehood. Scripture does not
provide at either of these procedures a description of a particular ceremony, leaving it to local custom and folkways.

Two things should be noted here. First, only in those books
of the Bible written after the return from the Babylonian exile
(end of sixth century B.C.E.) has the term now commonly used
for marrying, *nasa* (from which we derive the commonly used
term for marriage, *nissuin*), been substituted for the previous
term, *lakach*.[4] (Actually, *nasa*, in one of its several meanings,
denotes an action similar to *lakach*.)[5] Second, the term *lakach*,
which the Bible uses for the final step of marriage, has been
transferred by the Sages to the prior step, the betrothal,[6] and
the final step they now call "entering the *chuppah*." This latter
term will be explained in the next chapter.

THE HALAKHIC DEFINITION OF BETROTHAL

Once the Sages removed "taking a woman" from its literal
meaning and defined it as betrothal, they had to define the

procedure—call it ceremony—of "taking." In doing so, they used a form of the verb *kanoh*, the biblical verb for purchasing,[7] for they regarded the act of betrothal as a "purchasing" or acquisition of a woman for the purpose of marriage. Thus, the very first ruling in the tractate that deals with the laws of marriage, tractate *Kiddushin*, states, "A woman *niknet* [is acquired] in three ways." The rabbis of the Talmud, the *Amora'im*, in their opening discussion of this first ruling ask, "Why is this [commercial-sounding] term *niknet* used, when in practically all other rulings of the Mishnah—as well as in subsequent rabbinic discussion—the term *mekadesh* [consecrates] is used for betrothing?" And the answer given is, because one of the three ways of betrothing—and as we shall see, the commonly used way—namely, the giving of money by the groom to the bride, is inferred from the similarity of the biblical expression for betrothal, *lakach*, to the biblical expression for purchasing, as we find in Abraham's purchase of the Cave of Machpelah from Ephron the Hittite (Genesis 23:13).[8] Since the act of purchasing is also expressed by the verb *kanoh* (Leviticus 25:14), the Sages used the term *niknet*, a form of *kanoh*.

Once the Sages substituted the term *mekadesh* for betrothal, they rarely used the term *aras* or the inferred term *kanah* for the act of betrothal. They instituted the standard formula for the groom's proposal, "Behold, you are *mekudeshet* [consecrated] unto me," and from now on the term *kiddushin* takes precedence over the term *eirusin*. In fact today this latter term in common parlance—except for halakhic discussion—signifies affiancing, or what we call "engagement," which does not have the binding character of *kiddushin* and does not confer the status of even partial wifehood.

The Sages were quick to explain why they called betrothal *kiddushin*: "He [the groom by his act of betrothal] prohibits her [the bride] to the whole world [except himself, of course] like *hekdesh* [an article consecrated to the Holy Temple, which is prohibited for any use other than as an offering to God]."[9] *Arusah*, a derivative of the biblical *aras*, is still used in all halakhic writings to designate a woman who has been betrothed but has not yet been taken to the *chuppah* for the completion of the marriage.

Nor has the concept of *kanoh* in betrothal been forgotten. The Sages ruled that according to biblical law, a daughter of a non*kohen* betrothed to a *kohen* may eat of the *terumah* heave-offering—forbidden to nonpriestly branches of the Jewish people—because it says, "If a *kohen* buy any person *kinyan caspo* [the purchase by his money], he may eat of it" (Leviticus 22:11); this includes a betrothed woman, for she was "purchased" with her fiancé's money.[10] It should, however, be emphatically clear that this acquisition by the groom is not that of the bride's person; she is by no means a chattel. It is the acquisition of certain rights to her property and earnings and supervision over her vows.[11]

It seems to me that the Sages adopted the term *kiddushin* for betrothal to make sure that people should not follow the example of the Alexandrians mentioned earlier (p. 58), who assumed that betrothal does not constitute wifehood since the betrothee does not as yet live with her fiancé. People would now understand that even though the bride is not living with her husband—indeed, he is forbidden by rabbinic law to have intercourse with her—she, like a wife, is consecrated to him and is prohibited to everyone else.

THE BETROTHAL CEREMONY

Since the betrothal confers upon the bride the status of a married woman, it is essential that it be performed strictly in accordance with all halakhic requirements. In fact, the Talmud asserts, "One who does not know the rules of *kiddushin* and *gittin* [divorces] should not be involved in conducting them."[12] To ensure that this is obeyed and that everything is done properly, many communities instituted that betrothal and wedding ceremonies be conducted only by the rabbi of the community or someone officially designated by him.[13]

Basically, if a man approaches an unmarried woman and in the presence of two witnesses hands her a coin or an article worth a perutah[14] or more with a proposal of betrothal, and she accepts it, she is betrothed. The Sages were quite flexible in assessing the value of the article given her. It may not necessarily be a concrete object; even if he undertakes to do something that provides her an enjoyment worth a perutah, it is considered a valid gift. Thus, for example, if she says, "Give so-and-so a loan and I will be betrothed to you," it is valid.[15] Furthermore, if he is an important person who in deigning to receive a gift gives the donor tangible enjoyment, she becomes betrothed by his accepting a gift from her.[16] However, to prevent any casual spur-of-the-moment betrothal, which the parties are liable to regret, numerous regulations over the course of time and in many different localities were instituted by the local authorities standardizing betrothal procedures. For example, a *minyan* of ten adults, including the parents— or, in lieu of the parents, an older relative—must be present. These regulations are in addition to the basic rules laid down by the *Halakhah*. At least two qualified individuals must witness the ceremony. Because many relatives unqualified to serve as witnesses are usually present and witness (i.e., observe) the ceremony, two qualified persons must be singled out to serve as witnesses to the exclusion of all others present.[17] The proposal made by the groom must be in a

phraseology clear and unmistakable to the bride, and therefore a standard formula has been instituted. It is in Hebrew
and says, "Behold you are consecrated unto me with this ring
in accord with the law of Moses and Israel." (If the bride does
not understand Hebrew, it should be translated for her.) It is
essential that the bride accept the proposal of her own free will
and not under duress. The Talmud rules that even though a
sale made because of a threat to the seller is valid, a betrothal
made under a threat is invalid. "He acted improperly [by
forcing her to accept], therefore the Sages acted improperly
[i.e., not strictly according to law] and nullified his act of
betrothal."[18] After the talmudic period, halakhic authorities
were reluctant to nullify *ab initio* betrothals conducted contrary to community regulations and would instead demand
that the groom divorce his unwilling bride by means of a *get*.[19]

Betrothal is a *mitzvah*, it is the prelude to the basic *mitzvah* of
producing progeny. Therefore, it must be sanctified by pro-
nouncing over it a benediction:

Blessed are You, O Lord, our God, King of the Universe, Who
has sanctified us by His commandments and has commanded us
concerning incestuous marriages and has prohibited to us our
betrothees[20] and has permitted to us those married to us by
chuppah and *kiddushin*, Blessed are You, O Lord, Who sanctifies
His people Israel by *chuppah* and *kiddushin*.

Such benediction must be preceded by a blessing over a cup of
wine (*kos shel berakhah*), which is drunk by the groom and the
bride. Originally, it was the groom who pronounced the
blessings, for he is performing the *mitzvah*; however, in order
not to embarrass those who may not know the blessings, it is
the officiating rabbi who pronounces them.

THE BETROTHAL RING

Tractate *Kiddushin* begins, "A woman is acquired in three ways . . . with money, with a written document, and with intercourse. With money, Bet Shammai say, with a dinar or an article worth a dinar; Bet Hillel say, with a perutah or an article worth a perutah." The Mishnah then proceeds to give the value of a perutah, the cheapest copper coin, in terms of the currency then in use.[21] Though the universal custom today, for Jews and non-Jews alike, is for the groom to give the bride a ring, this was not always so in Jewish custom. No mention of a ring for this purpose is found in the Bible or Talmud. (In talmudic times, rings were worn by both men and women and were used as personal seals.)[22] The Talmud mentions many other articles, some of which might have actually been used for betrothal and some theoretical. Most prominent among these articles is a cup of wine, which seems to reflect a common practice in those days.[23] Interestingly, this usage seems to have been prevalent in North Africa in the fifteenth century[24] and in Yemen in recent times.[25] Possibly, this cup was also broken by the groom right after the betrothal.[26]

There are scattered references to the use of the ring in certain localities in the period of the *Geonim*, not in Babylonia but in Palestine.[27] In the Middle Ages, the use of a ring became widespread in Ashkenazi communities, but not in Moslem countries.[28] A codifier of the *mitzvot* from medieval Provence explains the use of a ring "because it serves as a constant reminder on her hand that she is married and must be faithful and subservient to her husband."[29] Rabbi Moses Isserles codifies the custom in his notes to the *Shulchan Arukh*, attributing its use to a statement in a kabbalistic work that it symbolizes some mystical "encompassing light."[30] Later commentators speak of a gold ring, though a ring of any precious metal, such as platinum, is halakhically acceptable.

The *Halakhah* set a restriction on the use of a ring: it must be without a precious stone. The true value of a gem is known only to an expert jeweler, and the bride might be misled into thinking that the gem being offered her is worth much more than it actually is. Furthermore, since it is the groom and not the bride who has to make the formal proposal and give the valuable article, a double-ring ceremony with its exchange of rings and proposals is halakhically improper.[31] It is, however, halakhically proper for the groom to use a borrowed ring, provided the lender knows it is going to be used for the betrothal.[32]

The custom is for the ring to be placed on the index finger of the bride's right hand, the finger most easily extended and visible. (After the ceremony, she may place the ring on whichever finger she wishes.) If she is wearing gloves, some rabbis may insist that she first remove the glove before accepting the ring, though this is not an absolute requirement of the *Halakhah*. Then the *ketubah*, which attests that the betrothal ceremony has been performed, is read aloud so that the public is made aware of the newly established union. It is customary to honor a distinguished guest, usually a rabbi, with the reading. Then the groom hands over the *ketubah* to his bride, which she then hands over to her mother for safekeeping. It is forbidden for a married woman to remain with her husband without a *ketubah*; therefore, if it is lost, a new one must be written.

At the time when the betrothal was still separate from the wedding, this concluded the ceremony, which then was celebrated with a feast, a *se'udat mitzvah*, a celebration of a religious event (see p. 47). After the feasting, the groom returned to his home and the bride to her father's house to await the final step that would sanction their living together in complete union as husband and wife. A virgin bride was given twelve months in which to prepare her trousseau from the day the groom said that he wants to marry her.[33] If she is very young and wants to wait longer, her wish is granted.[34]

BETROTHAL BY MESSENGER

The Mishnah rules that betrothal can be effected not only by a person-to-person proposal but also by an agent of either the bride or the groom, or even of both. The Talmud, however, discourages such impersonal betrothals, stating that it is forbidden for a man to betroth a woman before he has seen her, lest he find something repulsive about her.[35] Apparently, if he has seen her beforehand and found her to his liking, there would be no objection, if circumstances make it convenient, to have the betrothal made via an agent. The Mishnah also discusses the case of a man who asked his friend to betroth a certain woman on his behalf, but the friend betrothed her to himself. The betrothal to the latter is valid even though he acted dastardly. In this connection the Talmud relates that a certain pious man went to betroth a woman for his son but betrothed her to himself, the excuse being that the woman's family refused to have her betrothed to the son but were willing to have her betrothed to the father.[36]

CONDITIONAL BETROTHALS

A betrothal may be made upon a certain condition. If the condition is fulfilled the betrothal takes effect; if it is not, the betrothal is null and void *ab initio*. Even if the condition was

that the husband would not be required to support his wife
and she agreed, the betrothal takes effect and he does not have
to support her. However, if the stipulation was that he would
deny her her conjugal rights, it does not have to be fulfilled,
for "it is a condition contrary to what is written in the Torah"
(Exodus 21:9). Judaism frowned upon "marriages of convenience" entered into for some ulterior consideration. Even
though alimentary support is also prescribed by the Torah,
since it is a question of money the rule is that a person has the
right to forego a monetary obligation due him. If a husband is
free of the obligation to support his wife, she keeps for herself
all the money that she earns from her labor.[37]

A condition discussed in detail in the Talmud is that the
betrothal be dependent upon the approval of the father, even
if he is not present at the betrothal and was not consulted
beforehand. If the father was later apprised of the betrothal
but remained silent, expressing neither approval nor disap-
proval, the question is, Is silence considered approval? Or
suppose the father passed away before being asked about the
betrothal, do we assume that he would have approved if he
had known, or do we not?[38] These thorny questions were not
theoretical in times past and can even be a matter of judicial
concern today.

MISREPRESENTATION

If a man proposing betrothal to a woman represents himself as
enjoying a certain status—for example, that he is a scholar—
and later it is proved that he lacks that status, the betrothal is
null and void. Similarly, if he represents himself as owning
certain property and later it is found out that he does not own
it, the betrothal is of no effect. A curious exception to this

rule—one that reflects the basic attitude of Judaism toward the sinner—is that of a man who represents himself to be a righteous person but actually is thoroughly wicked. In this case the betrothal is not invalid, for it may be assumed that just before the betrothal he had thoughts of repentance.[39]

If a condition of betrothal was not expressed verbally, but after the betrothal one of the parties says, "I thought he or she was such and such a person and that is why I consented to the betrothal," the betrothal is valid even if the person does not fit the expectations, for the general rule is, "Words of the heart—i.e., words thought but not verbalized—are not words." The only way to cancel such a betrothal is through divorce.[40]

All of the above cancellations of a betrothal apply when the conditions of the betrothal were not met before the wedding takes place. If the wedding took place—that is, the marriage was consummated by intercourse—and the conditions were not repeated just before the wedding, the assumption is that the conditions were waived, for "a person does not indulge in intercourse wantonly," that is, with the possibility that the intercourse is extramarital.[41] However, even if the conditions of the marriage were expressed just before the marriage, and after intercourse it was found that the conditions were not fulfilled, the rabbis were reluctant to declare a marriage void *ab initio* and would ask the husband to divorce his wife with a regular bill of divorcement (a *get*).

The Status of the Betrothed Woman

The status of the *arusah*, the betrothed woman, in the period between her betrothal and her entering the *chuppah*, is anomalous and very irregular. On the one hand, she is under the control of her father, and he enjoys the proceeds of her earnings. If she is raped or seduced, the monetary penalty is paid to him; if she is divorced or widowed, he receives the payment of her *ketubah* and even her betrothal money.[42] (Of course, all these rulings in favor of the father apply only to a minor daughter, until she reaches the age of twelve and a half; afterward she herself is the recipient of all these payments.) On the other hand, she is considered a married woman; to sever the relationship, she requires a *get,* a bill of divorcement similar to that required of fully married woman. A clear example of the anomaly of her status is seen in the following ruling: "A betrothed young woman, both her father and her husband annul her vows; if the father annulled but the husband did not, or the husband annulled but her father did not, her vow is not annulled."[43] The Sages were divided as to whether a *kohen,* who may not render himself unclean by contact with a corpse other than that of a close relative, may or may not render himself unclean with the corpse of his betrothee.[44] Rashi explains the *arusah*'s situation as follows: "*Eirusin* [betrothal] constitutes doubtful *Nissuin* [marriage]; maybe she will eventually be married, maybe not."[45]

The *arusah* 's anomalous situation led to different customs in ancient Palestine. In Judea, the bride and groom were brought together during the betrothal period "so that he should be familiar with her." Since this contact might lead to intercourse, they first pronounced the blessings usually recited under the *chuppah,* "for a bride without a blessing is forbidden to her husband like a *niddah* [menstruant]."[46] Furthermore, the assumption that intercourse would take place was so strong that later, after the *chuppah,* the groom could no longer claim that she lost her virginity through someone else. In the Galil, however, such meetings were banned and intercourse before the *chuppah* was interdicted, and anyone who violated the ban was subject to corporal punishment. To strengthen the ban, it was incorporated in the blessing preceding the betrothal ceremony with the words, "Blessed are You . . . Who has forbidden our betrothees to us." A parallel concern remained in some postmedieval communities, where a ban was placed on a meeting of the couple in the period between the *tena'im* and the *chuppah*. Interestingly, the reason given for this is that familiarity before the *chuppah* might lead to contempt.[47]

The Mishnah mentions three ways of betrothal. I have discussed only the first, betrothal by money or valuable article. The other two, betrothal by a document and betrothal by intercourse, need not be described here, for they were rarely used. The Talmud mentions that Rav administered a lashing to anyone who betrothed a woman with intercourse,[48] but there is no evidence that this was any more than a rare occurrence. There is, however, evidence, apparent from the many community regulations against them, that many betrothals were irresponsible, hasty, and impulsive, and occasionally even frolicsome.[49] There was a period in recent times when elopements were fairly common, in some cases to avoid the expense of a large formal wedding, but in many more to avoid parental displeasure. In such cases, the rabbi called on to solemnize the couple's union must first ascertain that there was no halakhic impediment to their joining. The thrust of both rabbinic legislation and folk custom was to emphasize the sanctity of marriage and its importance for the continuity of Jewish tradition. We shall see in the next chapter how these goals were expressed in the different ways in which Jewish weddings were conducted.

CHAPTER 5

THE *CHUPPAH*:
THE WEDDING

King Solomon made himself a palanquin
  of the wood of Lebanon,
He made the pillars thereof of silver,
  the top thereof of gold,
  the seat of it purple,
The inside thereof being inlaid with love
  from the daughters of Jerusalem.
Go forth, O ye daughters of Zion
  and gaze upon King Solomon,
Even upon the crown wherewith his mother has crowned
  him in the day of his wedding,
And in the day of the gladness of his heart.

(Song of Songs 3:9–11)

Perhaps in no other event has custom and folkway inter-mingled with legal procedure as in the wedding. It would require painstaking research to separate the absolute halakhic requirements—the absence of which renders the ceremony in valid—from the ancillary customs that have become part and parcel of the ceremony in all communities and therefore have acquired halakhic sanction, and further to take note of the procedures that are of purely local character and therefore may be ignored in other quarters. Also, it would require a separate volume to review all the customs at Jewish weddings over the course of Jewish history and settlement. I can do no more here than review the more significant customs as they evolved over the centuries, leading up to the more established practices followed today. Just bear in mind that today the betrothal (*kiddushin*), which has already been described in the preceding chapter, is the first part of the wedding ceremony under the *chuppah*.

The *chuppah* is too significant an occasion to be approached without a series of preliminary preparations. I have already described the major preliminary steps: *shiddukhin* and *tena'im*, which usually take place months before the wedding, and the writing of the *ketubah* and the betrothal, which now take place right before the wedding. But there are a host of matters that require serious attention in advance before a couple can proceed to the *chuppah*. Perhaps the earliest advance preparations for a wedding took place in the town of Betar in ancient Judea. There the custom was that when a boy was born, a cedar would be planted, when a girl was born, a cypress would be planted, and when the children married, branches from the two trees would be cut to fashion a *chuppah*.[1] My discussion of preparations will be less fanciful and more practical, beginning right after the agreement to marry has been reached. The first decision that has to be made is when the wedding is to take place.

TIMING THE WEDDING

Not every day in the week, nor every week in the year, is it permitted to conduct a wedding ceremony. Weddings on

Sabbaths and Festivals, including their intermediate days (*Chol Ha-Mo'ed*), are prohibited.[2] An interesting exception to a Sabbath wedding occurred in sixteenth-century Poland, when Rabbi Moshe Isserles (known by his acronym, Rema) conducted a *chuppah* on Friday night, well into the Sabbath. The circumstances were as follows: A wedding for an orphan girl who was being married off by her uncle was scheduled for Friday afternoon. An argument erupted between the uncle and the groom about the amount of the dowry, and before it was settled it was two hours after the onset of *Shabbat*. In order not to embarrass the bride were the wedding to be put off until after the Sabbath, the Rema decided to go ahead and perform the ceremony, which in itself does not involve the violation of any biblical law.[3]

There are several periods of mourning during the year when weddings are proscribed. Sephardim do not conduct weddings for the nine days preceding and including Tisha B'Av, the day of mourning after the destruction of the *Bet Ha-Mikdash* (the Holy Temple in Jerusalem), while Ashkenazim proscribe weddings for the three weeks preceding Tisha B'Av.[4] It would be unseemly to conduct weddings on the other two prescribed fast days, Tzom Gedalia (the day after Rosh Hashanah) and Asarah B'Tevet. As for the period of mourning known as *Sefirah*,[5] occurring between the festivals of Passover and Shavuot, the rulings as to which days during this period weddings are not permitted are so numerous and conflicting that one cannot put down a definite ruling, and the couple must depend on the opinion of the officiating rabbi. However, all Ashkenazim agree that Lag B'Omer, the thirty-third day of the counting of the *Omer*, is a permissible day. It should be noted that in exceptional circumstances—for example, if the groom is going to be conscripted into the army—a rabbi will sanction the holding of a wedding during *Sefirah*, particularly if it is after Lag B'Omer, when the Sephardim do not have any restriction. Custom has also ruled out weddings on Purim and the ten-day period between Rosh Hashanah and Yom Kippur (*Aseret Yemei Teshuvah*), though the *Halakhah* does not specifically proscribe them.

Those who are inclined to follow various omens will prefer to have weddings during the first half of the lunar month when the moon is waxing, rather than during the second half when the moon is waning.[6]

In different eras and localities, certain days of the week were preferred for the holding of weddings. Thus, the first Mishnah in tractate *Ketubot* states, "A virgin is married on a Wednesday . . . so that if the groom would have a claim that he found his bride not to be a virgin [and suspected of having had intercourse with another during the betrothal period] he could bring it to court, which convened on Thursdays."[7] A Babylonian *Amora* qualifies this ruling and says that now any day of the week is appropriate, since the court can be convened on any day. The Talmud goes on to say that because the (Roman) governor insisted on his right to deflower the bride (*ius primae noctis*), weddings were held on Tuesdays in order to confuse him. From further discussions, it seems that weddings were also held on Fridays, though this was discouraged lest it lead to a violation of the Sabbath (the feast for a Friday wedding was held on Friday night).[8] There was another reason weddings on a Friday were discouraged. Many talmudic authorities ruled that one may not deflower a virgin on Friday night, for the rupturing of the hymen would cause blood to flow, an act included among those prohibited on the Sabbath.[9] The choice of day also had to do with the blessings for fertility that the Creator gave to the fish (Thursday) and man (Friday) (Genesis 1:22, 28).[10] In Ashkenaz (Germany and later Eastern Europe) the custom developed to have weddings on Fridays for economic reasons: one could combine the Friday night Sabbath meal with the wedding feast.[11] Thus, we can well understand the choice of Sundays in Western countries, when most guests are free to attend.

An important consideration in choosing an appropriate day for the wedding is the menstrual cycle of the bride; if at all possible, a wedding should not be held when the bride is a *niddah*.[12] To avoid such a circumstance, it is customary in many traditional circles for the bride and groom to avoid seeing each other during the week preceding the wedding, lest the excitement cause the bride to menstruate.[13] It is also customary for the bride's mother and future mother-in-law to escort her to the *mikveh* (ritual bath) before the wedding in preparation for the nuptial night. This should be done not more than four days before the wedding.[14]

PRACTICAL PREPARATIONS

Sufficient time before the wedding has to be allowed for the bride to outfit herself and for the wedding feast to be prepared. I have already mentioned (p. 73) the lengthy time that was required in talmudic times for a bride to prepare her trousseau. Then, ready-to-wear outfits were not available; dresses and linens were invariably made at home. But even with our sophisticated economy, if the wedding is going to be formal, sufficient time must be allowed for dressmakers to complete the gowns for the bridal party. As for the preparation of food for the wedding feast, its importance did not escape the attention of the Sages. The atmosphere in the house while preparing the food was so joyous that as soon as the preparations began, the phrase "Joy is in His Abode" was added to the Grace after Meals (*birkat ha-mazon*).[15] The activity was so intense (who dreamt then of freezers and refrigerators, or professional caterers) that Saturday night weddings were banned lest preparations would begin before nightfall, which would inadvertently violate the holiness of the Sabbath.[16] Today, with our modern means of conserving food, we do not ban Saturday-night weddings provided the hour set for the ceremony is late enough to allow sufficient time after sundown for the last-minute preparations.

The importance of the food for the wedding feast is underscored by a ruling necessitated by a tragic circumstance. The ruling reads as follows: "The bread was baked and what had to be slaughtered was slaughtered and the wine was mixed,[17] and the father of the groom or the mother of the bride died; the deceased is removed to another room, the bride and groom are brought to the *chuppah*; [after the ceremony] the groom performs the initial intercourse[18] and then separates himself from the bride. [After the deceased is buried] the seven days of feasting are observed[19] and after them the seven days of mourning. This applies only if it is the groom's father or the bride's mother who passed away, for [in their absence] no one else would bother themselves [to prepare other food if the food already prepared were to go to waste]." The ruling also provides that if the prepared food could be sold, and with the money other food can be prepared, the wedding is postponed until after the period of mourning.

From this ruling we learn two important lessons. First, once a date has been fixed for a wedding, it should not be postponed unless there is a very compelling reason. Thus, if the grandparent of the bride or groom died just before the wedding, it should not be postponed. (The participation of mourners at a wedding is governed by the laws of mourning.) Second, a bride or groom is not allowed to marry within thirty days after the passing of a close relative.[20] If a man's wife dies, he should not remarry until the Three Festivals have gone by. However, if she left young children he may remarry earlier in order to have someone take care of the children.[21]

THE "*UFRUF*"

Among Ashkenazim the groom is called up to the reading of the Torah—usually the *maftir* or final portion—on the *Shabbat* before the wedding, while among Sephardim this custom is followed on the *Shabbat* after the wedding. In medieval Ashkenaz, though no longer observed today, a special *haftarah* (portion from the Prophets) was chanted in honor of the groom, beginning with the verse, "I greatly rejoice in the Lord, my whole being exults in my God, for He has clothed me with garments of salvation, wrapped me in a robe of victory. Like a bridegroom adorned with a priestly diadem, and like a bride bedecked with her finery" (Isaiah 61:10). Upon concluding the chanting of the *haftarah*, the groom is pelted with nuts and raisins thrown by the women from the gallery, symbolizing prosperity for the new couple.[22] After the prayer service, the friends are invited by the groom's family to an elaborate *Kiddush*. In traditional circles the bride does not go to the synagogue on the *Shabbat* before the wedding, but stays at home in the company of her friends. However, she does go to the synagogue on the *Shabbat* after the wedding and is then given a place of honor in the women's section.

A FAST DAY

Custom dictates that bride and groom fast on the day of their wedding.[23] Again, this custom dates from late medieval Ashkenaz. Two reasons are advanced for such solemnity on the eve of great rejoicing. One finds its basis in a statement of the Jerusalem Talmud[24] that all the sins of a groom are pardoned; thus for him, and for the bride as well, it is like Yom Kippur, the Day of Atonement. Hence, not only do they fast, but in the afternoon prayer (*Minchah*) before the wedding they recite the *al chet*, the confession for sins, as is recited by all on the Day of Atonement. The second reason is a pragmatic one; since wine is usually drunk at a meal, the couple fasts to make sure that they are sober under the *chuppah*. If the *chuppah* is held during the day, they may eat right after the ceremony even before nightfall; if the *chuppah* is conducted well after nightfall, they may eat before the *chuppah* shortly after sunset.

There are minor holidays during the year on which the supplication prayer for pardon, *tachanun*, is not recited. On most of these days bride and groom are exempted from fasting. They are Rosh Chodesh (the first of the month in the Jewish calendar), the day following a festival (*Isru Chag*), the fifteenth day of *Av*,[25] the fifteenth day of *Shevat* (the New Year for Trees), the eight days of Chanukah, the two days of Purim, and Passover eve. Most recent *poskim* agree that even on the days they do not fast they should recite the penitential prayers.[26]

THE PROCESSION

It is time now for the bride and groom to go to the place set for the wedding ceremony. In times gone by, they were usually escorted from their respective homes by their families and a large following of friends and neighbors through the streets of the town to the wedding site. Wine would be drawn through tubes and roasted kernels of grain and nuts would be thrown in front of the couple as symbols of good luck.[27] In some places, we are told, the custom was to have a rooster and a hen in front of the procession, signaling the couple to be fruitful.[28] Perhaps a modern metamorphosis of this ancient custom is the garlanding of the automobile and the blatant tooting of its horn as the bride and groom are being driven to the wedding hall.

Thus began the general rejoicing enhancing the happiness of the couple. These processions were so important that the Sages ruled that students of the Torah might interrupt their studies to join the procession, and a funeral procession must give way to the parade escorting bride and groom.[29] This was part of the *mitzvah* of *hakhnasat kallah*[30] and *le-same'ach chatan ve-kallah* (to make the groom and bride rejoice), included by Maimonides in the general commandment, "Love your neighbor as yourself."[31] Special customs were observed at the bridal procession to indicate that the bride was a virgin (if that were the case).[32]

In medieval Germany the wedding procession first escorted the groom to the courtyard of the synagogue with torches and a band of musicians; then they went back to the bride's house to escort her to the groom. When the couple met, the assembly threw kernels of wheat on them and shouted, "Be fruitful and multiply."[33] In many descriptions of weddings we find that the bride was seated in a special settee surrounded by her attendants and the female guests, while the groom was escorted to the groom's room to be welcomed by the menfolk.[34] It was here that the *ketubah* was written, after which the groom was escorted to the bride to draw the veil over her face.[35] The assembled then invoked over her the blessing that Rebecca's family gave her before she left to meet her groom, Isaac: "Our sister, may you grow into thousands of myriads" (Genesis 24:60). This is reminiscent of the custom of the *hinumah* (veil or curtained litter) in talmudic times, which indicated that the bride is a virgin.[36] Other customs mentioned in the Talmud are the placing of a tiara with a picture of Jerusalem engraved on it on the bride's head, and a garland of myrtle on the groom's head. There is also the custom of drumming on a tabour before the groom, a rite that persisted in medieval France.[37]

Another custom dating from talmudic times and codified in the *Shulchan Arukh* is the placing of some ashes on the groom's forehead as a remembrance of the Temple's destruction.[38] A custom from medieval Ashkenaz, persisting today in traditional circles, is to clothe the groom with a *kittel*, a white robe. Originally, a white garment was a symbol of the pardon of sins,[39] and as I mentioned earlier, the wedding day is a Day of Atonement for the bride and groom. However, postmedieval commentators see in it a symbol of burial shrouds to remind the groom of his mortality and thus induce him to repent of his sins.[40]

Now the groom is ready to be escorted to the *chuppah*, to be followed by the bride and her retinue. An ancient custom provided that the groom and bride be escorted to the *chuppah* by *shoshvinim*, best friends, and in the Talmud this custom is ascribed to the Almighty Himself, Who acted as a *shoshvin* for Adam and Eve.[41] It should be noted that the function of these *shoshvinim* in talmudic times—persisting in oriental communities in the Middle Ages—was much more than escorting the groom to the *chuppah*. These best friends would bring both

cash and delicacies to the wedding to help the groom cover the
expenses. Actually, these were not construed as mere gifts but
as a type of loan, in that the groom would be required to
reciprocate with similar donations when the friends married.
In the event that the groom did not reciprocate, he could
actually be sued for the amount he had expended.[42]

Today, the tradition of escorts has been preserved in
Western countries with a best man for the groom and a maid
of honor for the bride. However, in traditional ceremonies the
respective parents act as the escorts (called *unterfeurer* in Yiddish), though in chasidic circles the two fathers escort the
groom and the two mothers escort the bride, eliminating any
other attendants as being "goyish," or imitating the Gentiles.
The tradition also provides that the escorts carry lit candles
while proceeding to the canopy. If grandparents are attending
the wedding, they are usually invited to stand under the
chuppah during the ceremony. The groom always precedes the
bride to the canopy, and when she reaches the canopy she
walks around him, followed by the mothers, three times,
complying with the verse in Jeremiah, "A woman surrounds
a man" (31:22) and symbolizing the three betrothals binding
God and His people Israel (Hosea 2:21–22).[43] The bride is
then stationed to the right of the groom[44] and the ceremony
may begin.

THE *CHUPPAH*

Before continuing with the ceremony, let us first examine the
chuppah. What exactly is it, and what is the halakhic significance of "entering the *chuppah*"?[45] Literally, the *chuppah* is a
covering or canopy, but from the halakhic point of view it can
be something else. It is in effect any procedure in which the

bride is transferred from her father's house (and in the case of
a minor, from her father's control) to the domain of her
husband. But this procedure varies according to circumstance, local custom, and rabbinic interpretation. In talmudic
times, for example, if the bride did not live in the same city as
the groom and had to travel to his place of residence for the
wedding, if the groom sent an escort to meet her en route, as
soon as she was handed over to the groom's escort for the
completion of the journey, she technically entered the *chuppah*
and became his wife.[46] Centuries later and in a different clime,
Rabbi Asher ben Yehiel (fourteenth century) reports that in
Ashkenaz the custom was to make an *aperion* (canopied couch)
for seating the groom and bride, which is called a *chuppah*.[47]

Some poskim insist that *chuppah* is not the ceremony under
a canopy but the closeting together after the ceremony of the
bride and groom in complete privacy, which is called *yichud*.
According to this opinion, it is required that after the public
ceremony under the canopy, the couple retire to a private
chamber (*cheder yichud*) in order to complete the marriage. It is
customary to have some food in the *cheder yichud* so that the
young couple can eat their first meal together in privacy, as
they would in their own home. Since this *yichud* marks the
actual union, it must be witnessed by two individuals who
observe them enter the chamber. The minimum time for them
to be closeted together is not specified by the *Halakhah*, and it
can be anywhere between five and ten minutes.[48] Other
poskim maintain that bringing the bride and groom together
under a canopy is sufficient, and *yichud* afterward is not required. Generally, Ashkenazim follow the former opinion,
whereas Sephardim follow the latter. Sephardim customarily
spread a *tallit* (prayer shawl, usually a newly acquired one
given by the bride's father) over the heads of the bride and

groom, and this constitutes the *chuppah*. This is reminiscent of the gold-braided *tallit* used as a *chuppah* in talmudic times.[49] Ashkenazim add that the canopy be held up by four posts, representing the home to which the groom will be taking his bride.[50] Most Ashkenazim also follow the requirement to conduct the *chuppah* "under the canopy of heaven"—namely, outdoors—to signify the wish that the couple be blessed with progeny as numerous as the stars in heaven,[51] though other sources indicate that the *chuppah* was usually held in the synagogue.[52]

THE OFFICIATING RABBI

I have mentioned (p. 69) that one who does not know the rules of marriage and divorce should not be involved in conducting them. To ensure that this is so, it has become standard practice, codified in the *Shulchan Arukh*,[53] that only the rabbi of the community conducts the wedding ceremonies held in his community, even if a senior colleague happens to be present. In fact, he is entitled to be remunerated for this service, an emolument considered part of his salary. By the same token, if a wedding is held in a synagogue, it is the prerogative of the rabbi of the synagogue to conduct the ceremony, though he may, upon request of the parties, yield his privilege to an invited colleague without necessarily waiving his right to the emolument. It has become customary at the wedding of a *yeshivah* student to invite his *rosh yeshivah* to be the *mesader kiddushin*, namely, the officiant at the betrothal part of the ceremony. At many weddings the officiating rabbi delivers a message to the bride and groom at the beginning of the ceremony.

In addition to the rabbi, at most formal weddings a cantor also participates. He opens the ceremony by chanting the following words of welcome: "Who is mighty above all; Who is blessed above all; Who is great above all; Who is distinguished above all; may He bless the groom and the bride." If a parent of the bride or groom is deceased, the cantor may chant the *el maleh rachamim* memorial prayer in memory of the departed parent, though many do not observe this. Incidentally, it is customary for the bride or groom whose parent is deceased to go to the parent's grave before the wedding and "invite" him or her to the wedding. A talmudic source mentions a rather bizarre custom of erecting a canopy over the coffin of a deceased bride or groom and suspending from it fruits or vegetables that have not reached their edible stage.[54]

BIRKAT CHATANIM: THE WEDDING BENEDICTIONS

After the reading of the *ketubah*, marking the transition from the betrothal (*kiddushin*) to the marriage (*nissuin*), another cup of wine is handed over to the officiating rabbi. The benediction over the wine serves as an introduction to the six benedictions that the Sages instituted for the wedding ceremony.[55] They are chanted only if a *minyan* of ten adult males (including the groom) is present; if a *minyan* cannot be assembled, only the final blessing is recited. It is customary to distribute the honor of reciting one or more of the benedictions to chosen guests. Where there is an officiating cantor, the final blessing is reserved for him.

The following is the English version of the benedictions, which are chanted in the original Hebrew:

1. Blessed are You O Lord, King of the Universe, Creator of the fruit of the vine.
2. Blessed are You O Lord, King of the Universe, Who created everything for His glory.

3. Blessed are You O Lord, King of the Universe, Who is the Creator of man.

4. Blessed are You O Lord, King of the Universe, Who has formed Adam in His image, in the image of the likeness of His form, and has provided for him out of his very self [from his rib] an everlasting structure [a wife, Eve]; Blessed are You O Lord, Who is the Creator of man.

5. May the barren woman[56] greatly rejoice and be glad with the ingathering of her children in her midst with happiness; Blessed are You O Lord, Who makes Zion happy with her children.[57]

6. May You make abundantly happy the beloved companions [bride and groom] as You made happy the one You formed in the Garden of Eden in the East;[58] blessed are You O Lord, Who makes groom and bride happy.

7. Blessed are You O Lord, King of the Universe, Who has created rejoicing and happiness, groom and bride, joy and song, delight and pleasure, love and brotherhood, peace and companionship. Soon, O Lord our God, may there be heard in the cities of Judah and in the streets of Jerusalem the voice of joy and happiness, the voice of groom and bride,[59] the voice of grooms' jubilation from their *chuppah* and youths from the feast of their singing; blessed are You O Lord, Who makes happy a groom with the bride.[60]

The chanting of the benedictions concluded, a glass is placed under the groom's foot. He steps on it and breaks it,[61] thus bringing the ceremony to a close. The assembled guests cry out "*Mazal tov*" to the newly wedded couple and their parents, after which they proceed to the dining hall for the wedding feast.

THE WEDDING FEAST

To join a wedding feast and make the bride and groom happy is a *mitzvah*, and even distinguished scholars would attend and participate in the festivities.[62] The Talmud relates that Rabbi Judah bar Ilayi would take a myrtle branch and dance before the bride, saying, "Beautiful and gracious bride." This paean to the bride was established by Bet Hillel and has continued to be sung at Jewish weddings to this day. Another talmudic sage would dance in front of the bride while juggling three myrtle branches. Still another went so far as to take the bride upon his shoulders and dance with her, though he did not sanction his students to do so. We are told that in the West (*Eretz Yisrael*) they sang in front of the bride, "Neither eye-blue, nor rouge, nor hair-dye, yet she is a graceful doe."[63] A recent custom is to sing in front of the bride (Proverbs, chap. 31), extolling the virtues of a Woman of Valor.

As time went on, there was a gradually increasing insistence on less contact between the sexes. Though earlier halakhic authorities had permitted guests to glance admiringly at the bride, later authorities ruled that this was improper.[64] The leading Babylonian *Amora'im* of their time (early fourth century), Abbayei and Rava, would set up barriers between the sexes at weddings in order to prevent their mingling.[65] The pietistic *Sefer Chasidim* of twelfth-century Ashkenaz ruled that we do not say at the Grace after Meals (*Birkat Ha-Mazon*) the special phrase *she-ha-simchah bi-me'ono* (in Whose abode there is joy) if the men and women can see each other, for there is no happiness for the Almighty where there might be impure thoughts. Today it has become *de rigueur* in strict Orthodox circles to arrange separate seating for men and women at wedding dinners, and mixed dancing is absolutely taboo.

A reverse development, from stringency to leniency, has taken place with respect to the playing of music at weddings. After the destruction of the Temple the Sages banned music at festive occasions, but posttalmudic authorities ruled that the ban does not apply to weddings, which are a *simchah shel mitzvah*, a religious rejoicing.[66] In sixteenth-century Eastern Europe we find that even non-Jewish musicians were hired to play at weddings on the Sabbath.[67] Another feature of these weddings was the *badchan*, the jester, who recited in a light mood rhymed verses in praise of the bride and groom.

In many communities the parents invited all the members of the community, a special boon for the poor inhabitants. However, as the list of invitees became larger and larger, and the food and the entertainment became more and more expensive, many fathers put themselves into debt. Besides, it was considered unseemly for Jews living among non-Jews to celebrate too ostentatiously, lest it arouse jealousy.[68] As a result, many communities adopted regulations restricting the number of guests and musicians.[69] In recent times, several chasidic spiritual leaders have found it necessary to caution their adherents against extravagant expenditures for weddings.

Certain special procedures with respect to the Grace after Meals (*Birkat Ha-Mazon*) have been instituted for the conclusion of the wedding feast. Two cups of wine are placed before the person chosen to lead in the *Birkat Ha-Mazon*, one for the *Birkat Ha-Mazon* itself[70] and one for the *Birkat Chatanim*, which were chanted under the *chuppah* and now are to be repeated. After summoning the guests to join in the *Birkat Ha-Mazon*, the leader recites a brief rhymed poem that begins with the words *d'vei haser*. This is the English version:

> Remove all ache and anger too,
> And then the mute in song will praise;
> Guide us in the paths of righteousness,
> Accept the blessings of the sons of Aaron.[71]

To the usual phrase "Let us bless our God" is added *she-ha-simchah bi-me'ono*, "In Whose abode there is joy."[72] During the *Birkat Ha-Mazon* the leader is holding the first cup of wine. At its conclusion he places that cup on the table and takes in hand the other cup, over which are chanted the *Birkat Chatanim*, the six benedictions that were chanted under the *chuppah* after the reading of the *ketubah*. (The first benediction chanted under the *chuppah*, the one over the wine, is left here for the last benediction.) Again, one or more persons may be given the honor of chanting one or more of the benedictions, each honoree holding the cup while chanting. This being accomplished, the leader takes the first cup and recites the blessing over wine (*borei p'ri ha-gafen*). He then pours some wine from each cup into a third cup, drinks from it, mixes the wine from the two cups, and hands them over to the bride and groom to drink from them. Though the feast and the blessings are now over, the dancing and singing are not; they continue as long as the guests have the energy and the desire to continue.

THE SEVEN FESTIVE DAYS

The Torah commands, "If a man marries a woman new to him, he shall not go out to the army . . . he shall be free one year for his home to make happy the woman he has married" (Deuteronomy 24:5). Based on this verse, the Sages ruled that for twelve months after the marriage, one recites the phrase *she-ha-simchah bi-me'ono* at a special meal held in honor of the bride and groom.[73] However, the *Shulchan Arukh* rules that today, in this era of Exile, when our happiness is mitigated by our sorrow, we recite the phrase only at a meal held within seven days after the wedding.[74] Indeed, the rule is that for seven days following the wedding the groom is not allowed to go out to work; he must remain all the time with his new bride in order to make her happy.[75] These days are known as "The Seven Days of the Feast," and at every meal at which the bride and groom are present the *Sheva Berakhot*, the seven benedictions that were recited under the *chuppah*, are to be recited at the end of the meal, following the procedure mentioned above. However, they are recited only if there are guests present who did not participate in any previous celebration of the wedding. On *Shabbat* the benedictions are recited even if no new guest is present; the Sabbath itself is a new guest. The festive meal is so important that the Sages ruled that if held during the Festival of Sukkot, when it is obligatory to eat all meals in the *sukkah*, this meal could be held outside the *sukkah*, which is too small to accommodate all the guests.[76]

The great joy that was manifested at Jewish weddings was not only in order to make the bride and groom happy, and thus enhance their love for each other, but was also an expression of the joy of the Jewish community in the establishment of another Jewish family that hopefully would contribute to the continuity of the Jewish people. The vicissitudes of Jewish life in the Diaspora, the persecutions and pogroms that decimated large numbers of Jews, made every Jewish family a precious asset that had to be encouraged and cherished. In the next two chapters I shall try to show how the teachings of Judaism with respect to family life nurtured a tradition of domestic devotion and mutual respect between husband and wife, ensuring the stability of Jewish families.

CHAPTER 6

THE JEWISH WIFE

Who has found a wife has found happiness
And has won the favor of the Lord. (Proverbs 18:22)

Enjoy happiness with a woman you love
All the fleeting days of life that have been
    granted you. (Ecclesiastes 9:9)

Twice in the benedictions chanted in honor of the bride and
groom we invoke for them the blessings of the Lord, "Who
makes bride and groom happy." Indeed, the wish most commonly expressed at weddings is that the young couple find
happiness in their married life together. If they find happiness—which implies contentment, satisfaction, fulfillment—
there is the assurance that their union will be a *binyan adei ad*,[1]
an everlasting structure. However, we also wish the young
couple "*Mazal tov*," good luck. Is then happiness a matter of
luck, of chance, or is it dependent upon the partners them-

selves, upon their approach and behavior toward each other? In other words, does a married couple *find* happiness, or are they supposed to *seek* it. Is happiness a matter of fortuitous circumstances or a result of a serious effort to create it?

From more than one statement in the Talmud it is apparent that the Sages understood that happiness in married life must be achieved, and that it can be achieved through proper behavior and attitude. They aver that, "He who loves his wife as himself, and honors her more than he honors himself, concerning him Scripture says, 'You will know that all is well in your tent' " (Job 5:24).[2] Furthermore, it seems that the Sages put the onus on the husband, the one more liable to upset domestic harmony. Thus, they caution a husband to be very careful in the way he speaks to his wife, "for her tears are frequent and she is easily offended"[3]; and they reiterate, "A man should never impose excessive fear upon his household, but when giving instructions should speak softly."[4] They also advise that a man should always be diligent in honoring his wife, "for the blessing of a household is due to the wife."[5] Indeed, when the Torah speaks of a man's household it is referring primarily to the wife; and the *Tanna* Rabbi Yose called his wife, "my house."[6] Honoring a wife meant providing her with the proper finery, cosmetics, and jewelry, though in keeping with the husband's financial circumstances. This was done especially on festivals on which there is a special *mitzvah* to rejoice and make one's wife rejoice as well.[7]

Words of caution against a husband's domineering attitude were all the more necessary in view of the subservient attitude a wife was told to adopt toward her husband. Maimonides sums it up as follows: "The Sages commanded the woman to honor her husband to excess, and she should fear him; all her actions should conform to his wishes, and she should regard him as a minister or a king."[8] We shall see that this subservience is a reflection of the *Halakhah*, the norm in Jewish life as propounded by the Sages of the Talmud.

THE HALAKHIC STATUS OF THE MARRIED WOMAN

According to the Torah, the woman is placed under the protection of the man and is consequently under his control, which in rabbinic parlance is called *reshut*. When a child is born it remains in the *reshut* of its father until it reaches legal adulthood. For a female child this means that a father may marry off his daughter to whomsoever he wishes until she reaches the age of puberty that is, twelve and a half.

In ancient times, when bondage was in practice, a father could sell his minor daughter as an indentured servant, but then her master or his son was obliged to marry her (Exodus 21:7–9). Upon marriage she was transferred from her father's *reshut* to her husband's *reshut* and remained there even after adulthood.

In the married state, a woman's primary obligation is to her husband. This is reflected, for example, in the obligation to honor one's parents. Thus the Talmud teaches, "Both men and women are obliged to honor their parents; however, men are able to fulfill the obligation but not women, for the *reshut* of others [i.e., their husband's] is upon them." Hence, if at the same time both mother and father ask a child to give them a drink of water, the rule is, "Leave your mother's honor and honor your father first, for both you and your mother are obligated to honor your father."[9]

In the seventeenth century a halakhic authority suggests a modification of these rulings. Shabbatai ben Meir Hakohen (Shakh, 1621–1663) states, "It seems that if the husband does not insist [that his needs come first], she is obliged to honor her parents no less than a son."[10] No one doubts that today, even in traditional families, a woman enjoys more freedom from her husband's control than in previous generations. But even today, if a wife gives undue attention to her parents' needs at the expense of attention to her husband's reasonable needs, and provokes thereby his overt displeasure, it may lead to the breakdown of the marriage, a most undesirable consequence.

By the same token, a husband's attention to his wife's needs must take precedence over his concern for his parents. Thus the Torah asserts, "Hence a man leaves his father and his mother and clings to his wife" (Genesis 2:24). By no means, however, should this leaving be construed as forgetting or neglecting one's parents. Husband and wife must understand and even encourage their spouses' concern for the welfare of parents, and they should not look with disfavor on the visits of their spouses to their parents' home. The Mishnah records the custom of young brides' returning to their parents' home to celebrate the first festival after their marriage. The Talmud explains that this postnuptial visit will give them the opportunity to tell their parents how well received they were in the home of their in-laws.[11] Also requisite to domestic harmony is the reciprocal understanding on the part of the parents that the primary concerns of their married children are to their spouses.

WOMEN'S EXCLUSION FROM RELIGIOUS RITUAL[12]

The role of the wife in the home she shared with her husband was also affected by her special religious status as defined by the *Halakhah*. In accordance with their exposition of Scripture, the Sages ruled that women are exempt from those positive *mitzvot* of the Torah that have to be performed at a fixed time (*mitzvot aseh she-ha-zman gerama*), though there are several exceptions to this rule.[13] Many commentators have explained this ruling on the grounds that a woman's primary obligation is to her husband's needs, with which the fixed-time *mitzvot* might interfere. Thus Jacob Anatoli (thirteenth-century France–Italy) writes, "If a woman were to occupy herself performing a *mitzvah* at a fixed time, her husband would be without a helpmate at that moment and this would lead to quarrels between them." From a more modern perspective, Samson Raphael Hirsch (nineteenth-century Germany) explains this exemption as a recognition of woman's superior religious sensitivity, and therefore she is not obliged to observe as many *mitzvot* as a man. He adds, "Men's loyalty to Torah is tested by their many occupations and requires frequent reminders, the *mitzvot* of a fixed time; not so women, whose life-style [their occupation with household duties] subjects them to less challenges to their faith."

There is much disagreement among the *poskim* as to the extent of women's participation in many rituals. Though the ruling was that women are exempt from positive fixed-time *mitzvot*, the Talmud relates that a few outstanding women in the biblical period did observe them. Michal, daughter of King Saul, put on *tefillin* (phylacteries), and the prophet Jonah's wife observed the festival pilgrimage.[14] Although women are technically exempt from the *mitzvah* of "laying on the hands" on a sacrificial offering, some Sages permitted them to perform the ritual "in order to please the women."[15] In the Middle Ages we find women voluntarily accepting upon themselves the obligation to perform several *mitzvot*.[16] Yet the rabbis are divided as to whether they may recite the blessing preceding the performance of the *mitzvah*, Sephardim generally ruling that they may not, while Ashkenazim say that they may. Though the Talmud expressly includes women in the *mitzvot* of reading the *Megillah* on Purim and kindling the candles on Chanukah, some *poskim* insist that women's obligation is inferior to that of the men.[17] According to the basic rule of the *Halakhah*, women are obliged to recite *Birkat Ha-Mazon*, the Grace after Meals. However, we find that women in the Middle Ages did not observe this *mitzvah*; the justification for this noncompliance is based on a certain phrase in the prayer that does not apply to women.[18]

WOMEN'S KNOWLEDGE OF TORAH AND JUDAISM

If we were to judge from the song of Deborah (Judges, chap. 5) and the prayer of Hannah (1 Samuel 2:1–10), we might assume that women in biblical times were quite literate. However, it could equally be assumed that Deborah and Hannah were exceptional, and that women in general were not literate. For talmudic and posttalmudic times, we do not have to speculate very much; much more information concerning women's literary ability and knowledge of Judaism is available. The background to any understanding of the extent of their knowledge is the rabbinic ruling that women are exempt from the *mitzvah* of teaching their children Torah, and consequently that they themselves are exempt from the *mitzvah* of learning Torah (*Talmud Torah*).[19] Nevertheless, they receive a reward for assisting the menfolk to perform the *mitzvah*, "in that they bring their children to school, and wait till their husbands return—after some absence from home— from the academy."[20] Maimonides sums up the rabbinic attitude to women's study as follows:

> A woman who studies Torah receives a reward, though not as great as the reward received by a man since she is not commanded to study. . . .However, even though she receives a reward, the Sages commanded that one should not teach his daughter Torah, because the minds of most women are not suited for learning, and because of their poor understanding they interpret the words of the Torah as trivial.[21] . . . This is so only with respect to the Oral Torah [rabbinic teachings], but as for the Written Torah [the Bible, particularly the Pentateuch], one should not teach it to her in the first place, but if one did it is not as if he were teaching her nonsense.[22]

As a consequence of this ruling, schools of learning were established for boys and young men,[23] but not for girls, for whom household duties and wifely obligations were deemed sufficient.[24] However, it cannot be said that women were totally ignorant of Torah. We find that some women were more knowledgeable than their husbands, a fact that disturbed the rabbis. They pronounced a curse on the man whose wife had to recite for him the *Hallel* on festivals and the *Birkat Ha-Mazon* after meals.[25] They also ruled that a woman, though she knows how to read from the scroll of the Torah, may not be called up to read a portion in the synagogue, "because of the honor of the congregation."[26] Women did attend Friday-night lectures given by the rabbis,[27] and some exceptional women were knowledgeable of rabbinic discourse and were able to teach young students.[28]

For centuries traditional Jewry followed the rabbis' negative attitude toward women's learning and made no provision

for the formal education of girls. All that women knew of
Jewish ritual and observance was learned by observing the
practice of their parents and the customs of the community in
which they lived. The Sages entrusted to the women three
mitzvot in particular that involved the home and family[29]:

1. *Challah*, the separating from the dough of the portion
   assigned to a *kohen*.[30] Subsumed under this is the preparation of all food for the family in compliance with the laws
   of *kashrut*.[31]
2. *Niddah*, observance of the laws that prohibit intercourse
   between husband and wife during her menstrual period.[32]
3. *Hadlakat Ha-Ner*, kindling of candles in honor of *Shabbat*
   and *Yom Tov*.[33] Daughters learned at home certain basic
   prayers recited in the home, such as *Modeh Ani* upon rising
   in the morning, *Keriat Shema* before going to sleep at night,
   and blessings before eating such as *Ha-Motzi*, but did not
   learn much more.

In the women's section in many synagogues, where most of
the women were unable to follow the prayers being conducted by the men, there was a woman leader who recited the
prayers out loud for their benefit.[34] Translations of the *siddur*
(prayer book) into the vernacular were published primarily
for women, who could not read or understand the Hebrew.
Special emotionally laden prayers called *Techinot* (supplica-
tions) were devised in Yiddish for women to recite on special
occasions. A popular Yiddish digest of the weekly Torah
readings with the classical commentators, called *Tzenah
U-Renah*, afforded Ashkenazi women a cursory familiarity
with the *Chumash* (Pentateuch) and rabbinic homily.[35] For
Ladino-speaking Jews, a more elaborate survey of rabbinic

lore based on the Torah readings, called *Me'am Lo'ez*, was written by Yaakov Kuli of Kushta (Constantinople, 1685–1732). Many women must have garnered some acquaintanceship with rabbinic lore while listening to the weekly review, usually held on Saturday afternoons, of their sons' studies with the fathers. Knowing only these bits of Torah knowledge, the bulk of Jewish women were excluded from the breadth and depth of talmudic studies, which were the daily intellectual nourishment of Jewish boys and young men.

WOMEN'S EDUCATION TODAY

Time and tide wait for no one. The changes that were taking place in society could not have been ignored by the spiritual leaders of the Jewish community. In the early twentieth century, when secular education became widespread and Jewish girls were sent to public schools, rabbis began to question the traditional practice of no formal Jewish schooling for girls. No less a strict halakhist than the saintly Chafetz Chayyim, Rabbi Yisrael Meir Hakohen of Radun, Poland, conceded that Rabbi Eliezer's negative attitude toward women's studying Torah was tenable only in previous ages, when children did not question the practices of their elders. Today, he argued, since non-Orthodoxy is rampant, if girls are not taught the fundamentals of Judaism, their defection from tradition is an imminent possibility.[36] Thus the needs of the hour demanded the establishment of Jewish schools for girls, a demand first met in Poland with the founding of the network of *Bet Yaakov* schools.[37] The more traditional amongst the Orthodox still refuse to open the entire field of Jewish knowledge to girls; they confine girls' studies to *Chumash* (the Pentateuch) and the *mitzvot* that women are obliged to observe, ruling out for them the study of Mishnah and Gemara. But as girls began to taste the fruits of knowledge, and especially as women in Western countries began to assert their independence more aggressively, the scope of instruction for girls became broader and deeper. Thus, we find today the young women at the Stern College for Women of Yeshiva University studying Talmud and Jewish philosophy in addition to the sciences and liberal arts. In Israel today, there are several institutes devoted exclusively to women studying the classic Jewish texts, especially Talmud, in depth. Another area opened recently to women in Israel, hitherto denied them because of their limited knowledge of rabbinic law, is that of advocate in the religious courts. No longer are women willing to accept the rabbinic stigma that *nashim daatan kallot*, that women's ability to understand the intricacies of Jewish law is limited and deficient. This increasing familiarity of women with Judaic studies has opened up another area of common interest between husband and wife, strengthening the bond of companionship and compatibility.

WOMEN AND THE SYNAGOGUE

Regular thrice-daily prayer in the synagogue became the norm in Jewish life after the destruction of the Second Temple. It is a moot question whether women attended the synagogue regularly in talmudic times, and if they did, whether they sat in a separate section now known as the *Ezrat Nashim*.[38] The Mishnah rules that women are obliged by the *Halakhah* to pray, the Gemara supplying the rationale; to wit, "Prayer is supplication for God's mercies," which women are in need of as much as men.[39] This ruling notwithstanding, women played a negligible role in the synagogue, neither

conducting the prayers therein nor taking part in its adminis-
tration. Women were not counted in the *minyan* (quorum) of
ten worshipers necessary for certain "sacred" prayers and the
public reading of the Torah;[40] nor did women amongst themselves constitute such a *minyan*.[41]

For women, the very attendance at synagogue at certain
times, for example during their menstrual period, even in their
own segregated section, was problematic. Though there was
no definite halakhic ruling barring them from the synagogue
at that time, they themselves felt that attendance was inappropriate. Typical among the differing customs reported by the
poskim are the following: Rabbi Meir Hakohen (late thirteenth-
century Germany) reports that "women would on their own
enhance their piety by refraining from entering the synagogue
during their menstrual period."[42] Rabbi Israel Isserlein
(fifteenth-century Germany–Austria) ruled that women may
enter the synagogue on the High Holydays to pray even
during their menstrual period, on the grounds that to deny
them that privilege at a time when everyone else is in the
synagogue would cause them distress and shame.[43] Rabbi
Joseph Karo (sixteenth-century Safed) reports that "our
women do not refrain from entering the synagogue."[44] Rabbi
Yosef Chayyim of Baghdad (nineteenth century) writes,
"During a woman's menstrual period it is forbidden for her to
stop praying or reciting benedictions. However, she should
not go to synagogue while a menstruant. Nevertheless,
during the months of *Elul* and *Tishri*, which are Yamim No-
ra'im [days of awe], she may go to synagogue even while a
menstruant."[45] A more contemporary Ashkenazi *posek*, Rabbi
Yisrael Meir Hakohen, though preferring to have women
pray at home, concedes that in his country (Lithuania) women
do attend the synagogue.[46]

Several prayers were problematic for women. According to the *Halakhah*, the benediction (*Birkat Ha-Gomel*) recited after recovery from illness or deliverance from a dangerous situation—or even after traveling overseas—must be recited in the presence of ten men, which makes it quite uncomfortable for a woman. The *poskim* are divided as to what she should do. Some excuse her from reciting the benediction on the grounds that it is incompatible with modesty, while others say that her husband should recite it on her behalf, though this does not take care of the unmarried woman or widow. A recent *posek* cites an opinion that a woman should recite it in the presence of ten women and one man.[47]

One of the benedictions recited by men in their morning prayers praises God "for not having made me a woman,"[48] decidedly inappropriate for women. Instead, women recite, "for He has made me according to His will." The ceremony celebrating a boy's having reached the age of obligation to observe the *mitzvot*, namely his *Bar Mitzvah*, is the calling him up to the reading of the Torah in the synagogue for the first time in his life. Since this was inappropriate for a girl's reaching the age of obligation,[49] it was not customary to celebrate a *Bat Mitzvah*. Recently, however, due to the introduction of Torah-learning for girls and the general assertion of feminine equality, latter-day *poskim* have sanctioned the celebration of a *Bat Mitzvah*, but not in the synagogue.[50] In Conservative, and needless to say in Reform, synagogues, a *Bat Mitzvah* is called up to read the *Maftir* (concluding Torah reading portion) and *Haftarah* (section from the Prophets) and may deliver a message to the congregation. In some Orthodox synagogues congratulations are extended to the *Bat Mitzvah* from the pulpit, and she may be called upon to deliver a *d'var Torah* (a lesson from Scripture) at a *Seudah Shlishit* held in the synagogue hall. Recently, a custom has arisen even in modern Orthodox circles to celebrate the birth of a baby girl at a home gathering called *Simchat Bat*, Rejoicing of a Daughter.[51]

THE WOMAN'S SOCIAL AND LEGAL STATUS

Outside the synagogue, in the home and in public affairs, the attitude of the Sages toward woman's role was somewhat ambivalent. Balancing the charge of her intellectual inferiority and emotional instability were many expressions of homage and recognition of her innate wisdom. Noting a similarity in the letters of the word *vayiven* in the verse "And the Lord God fashioned into a woman the rib" (Genesis 2:22) and in the word *binah*, which means understanding, the Sages asserted that God blessed woman with more understanding than man.[52] Though she is disqualified to serve as a witness in court—with some exceptions—or as a signatory to legal documents such as a *ketubah*, her testimony that the food she is serving is kosher is as valid as that of a man's. If on returning home from some distant place she testified that her husband had died there, her testimony was accepted and the court would permit her to marry another; though if it was later established that her testimony was false, she was subjected to very dire punishment.[53] On the one hand, she could collect her *ketubah* only from the poorest assets of the estate, on the grounds that "more than a man wants to marry, a woman wants to marry"[54]; on the other hand, she would receive certain preferential treatment in collecting it "because of finding favor" in the eyes of men.[55] In accordance with a ruling of Maimonides, women were excluded from holding public office, and even in modern times many rabbis ruled that they could not vote in elections held for public office.[56]

Nevertheless, in the State of Israel today women have both the right to vote and the right to hold public office.

One comprehensive rabbinic statement confirming women's equality with men in the eyes of the Torah is the talmudic exegesis of the verse "These are the judgments you shall place before them" (Exodus 21:1): "Scripture here has rendered woman equal to man with respect to all the laws in the Torah."[57] This statement refers particularly to monetary judgments; a woman who owns property is subject to all the rights and obligations of ownership. Subsequent rabbinic legislation restricted this equality in great measure. When the Sanhedrin was reconstituted in the Galilean town of Usha after the defeat of Bar Kochba, a regulation (*takkanah*) was adopted that transferred to the husband control of his wife's property; she could not sell it without his consent, and he enjoyed all the income therefrom. (Not everybody was happy with this regulation. Rabban Gamaliel commented, "We are ashamed of these new regulations.")[58] A woman was also declared equal to man as far as punishment for transgressions was concerned.[59]

Notwithstanding these regulations, we find that in the course of time women engaged in various commercial enterprises. Many women were the breadwinners while their husbands studied Torah. The Talmud lays down certain rules concerning women who conducted their husbands' affairs, either selling his merchandise or managing his estate.[60] Much later in Jewish history we find two exceptional women, one a Sephardi and the other an Ashkenazi, who were able to manage their husbands' extensive enterprises. Donna Gracia Nasi (Venice, 1510–1569) not only engaged in widespread commercial activities but also simultaneously conducted diplomatic negotiations on behalf of her coreligionists who were expelled from Spain. A century later in Germany, Glueckel of Hameln (1645–1724) was able to carry on her husband's financial affairs after his death while raising a large family and writing her famous memoirs.

THE DEMANDS OF FEMININE MODESTY

Another basic approach of the Sages to women is based on their interpretation of the verse in Psalm (45:14), that a woman's honor is indoors, in the home, reducing her appearance in public to a minimum. One opinion in the Talmud holds that a husband does not want his wife to appear in court, as it would be a violation of her modesty.[61] Maimonides sums up the rabbinic attitude as follows: "It is shameful for a woman to go outside her home continually; and her husband should not let her go out more than once or twice a month when necessary, for the beauty of a woman is to stay in the confines of her home"; he then cites the verse from Psalm 45:14. Furthermore, he rules that a woman is immodest if she goes to market without wearing a veil, as do other women, even though her hair may be covered by a kerchief.[62] Another ruling, however, did not allow a husband to keep his wife from visiting a house of mourners or attending a wedding feast unless he charged that the people there were promiscuous.[63]

The Hebrew term for modesty, applied to both conduct and dress, is *tz'niut*, and its common application to feminine modesty is seen in the popular inscription on women's tombstones, *ha-ishah ha-tz'nuah*, "the modest woman." Halakhic authorities in all ages dealt with the parameters of female modesty as far as her dress was concerned: how much exposure of her flesh was considered *ervah*, nakedness, in the presence of which sacred passages could not be recited.[64]

Some granted flexibility in this ruling, depending on the dress customary in a particular place. Exposure of a married woman's hair was considered immodest; in some communities women even went to the extreme of removing all the hair from the head immediately after marriage. In some Ashkenazi communities women are able to preserve some of their external beauty by wearing a wig (*sheitel*), which served as the required head covering. Sephardim, as well as many Ashkenazim, still insist on a kerchief covering all the hair, though they would not put uncovered hair in the category of *ervah* today since so many women, Jewish as well as Gentile, walk around in public without any head covering.

Feminine modesty was praised by the Sages, especially when it was adhered to even within the confines of the home. It is related about a woman whose name was Kimchit that she had seven sons, and each of them was successively appointed to serve as the High Priest. When asked why she merited such distinction she replied, "I swear that even the beams in my house did not see my hair uncovered; nor did the walls see the hem of my robe."[65]

The Talmud also pronounced the voice of a woman to be in the category of *ervah*, interpreted by most halakhists to refer to the singing voice, thus banning men from listening to a female chorus or even an individual singer.[66] Various *responsa* have dealt with the question of whether such a ban applies also to a woman's singing over the radio or television or from a recording. In all these matters there is a wide divergence of both opinion and practice, stretching from one of leniency to one of stringency.

Ancient standards of modesty have persevered in our own times, and the tendency in traditional circles is to be more rather than less stringent, no doubt a reaction against the general permissiveness in modern society. I have already mentioned (p. 94) the separation of men from women at wedding dinners amongst the strict Orthodox, even though *poskim* of two generations ago found no objection to mixed seating.

Considerations of modesty dictate the segregation of the sexes not only on the adult level; even boys and girls as young as elementary-school age must be separated in school according to a *responsum* by the late Rabbi Moshe Feinstein.[67] In the *Bet Yaakov* schools, girls are taught very early the importance of modest dress, the proper length of the sleeves and the skirt. Many Orthodox leaders today oppose mixed youth-group activities, though the late Rabbi Yehiel Yaakov Weinberg sanctioned them.[68] One cannot deny, however, that the rigid standards of talmudic and medieval times are not enforced in all their aspects among the strict Orthodox, as we see young ladies from these traditional homes go out daily to offices and shops to join the general work force.

Let it be clear that what has been discussed heretofore are some of the halakhic rulings that have defined the legal position of women in Jewish society. They do not, however, necessarily reflect the high esteem in which the Jewish woman was regarded by the man. Her modesty, her devotion to her husband and children, even her innate understanding of practical matters, were sincerely praised. Though the "*eshet chayyil*" of Proverbs portrays an ideal woman, its verses were sung by the husband in honor of his wife every Friday evening as he saw the glow of the Sabbath candles and the spotless white cloth on the table all set for the Sabbath meal. Angels also, it is said, accompany a person on *Shabbat* evening on his way from the synagogue to his home, and when they enter and find the candles kindled, the table set, and the bedspread laid out, they say, "Please God, may such sacred beauty endure."[69]

The celebration of the Sabbath in the bosom of the family residence, etched in poetry and painting, has contributed immensely to the stability of the Jewish family. Even children pulled away by the allurements of the street recharge their feelings of family closeness by returning to the warmth of the Friday-evening meal, graced by the *Kiddush* wine, the special loaves of bread (*challah*), and the special dishes prepared and served by a doting mother. Festivals also have countered the centrifugal forces of nature by bringing together the scattered members of the family for joint celebration. This is evident even today, when tradition is no longer as compelling as it used to be, in the widespread observance of the *Seder* service on the first night of Passover, which from its very beginning was designed as a family celebration and a protection of the Israelite homes (Exodus 12:3, 13).

The Sabbath is welcomed both as a queen and as a bride,[70] and the queenliness and the bridal freshness alight on the wife, kindling a flame of desire in her husband. His paean of praise is an expression of true love, coming to fulfillment in the more intimate aspects of Jewish married life, which is the subject of the next chapter.

CHAPTER 7

THINGS BETWEEN HIM AND HER: CONJUGAL RELATIONS

The Sages say, "Everyone knows why a bride enters the nuptial chamber; however, for anyone who mouths obscene words, even though he may have been destined for good fortune, his fate is reversed to misfortune."[1] The intimate relations between a husband and wife were traditionally cloaked under a veil of utmost privacy, euphemistically categorized in the Talmud as *devarim she-beino le-beinah*, "things between him and her."[2] Conjugal relations and sexual intercourse were never a seemly topic for public discussion or parlor conversation. Nevertheless, for the sake of defining the halakhic and moral standards of these matters, the Sages spoke clearly and unabashedly. In Chapter 1 (p. 11) I have already pointed out Judaism's recognition of sexual intercourse as a normal and desirable activity of married couples, which consequently has enabled the observers of Jewish ritual to avoid the pitfalls of excessive prudery and suppression of legitimate discussion. The Bible and Talmud are frank about sex, and the study of these texts was never confined to scholars alone. Every Jew is required to study the fundamentals of Jewish religious law, including those sections that deal with our sexual behavior as human beings.

Furthermore, modesty in normal conversation must not lead to a deviation from the truth. A story is told in the Talmud about a city called Kushta, the Aramaic word for truth. This city had the unusual good fortune that all its inhabitants lived to a ripe old age, and this because they always told the truth. It so happened that a man from another city married a woman from Kushta and came to live there. In due course they were blessed with two children. One day, while the woman was washing her hair, a neighbor wanting to visit with her came to the house and knocked on the door. The husband opened the door and, when told by the neighbor the purpose of her visit, said that his wife was not at home, because he felt that it was not proper to say that she was washing her hair.[3] Because of this deviation from the truth, based on an exaggerated sense of modesty, his children died young, and the townspeople asked him to move out of their community, which told the truth even about intimate matters.[4]

In order to expound the laws concerning conjugal relations (more particularly, those defining the situation that renders a woman a *niddah* [menstruant] and consequently prohibited sexually to her husband) the Sages had to have a knowledge of female anatomy. Such knowledge is best obtained by examining a female, something that ordinary considerations of modesty preclude. However, if such examination is made purely for professional purposes—as in the case of a medical trainee or halakhic instruction—it is permissible. Such an

instance is recorded in the Talmud. Shmuel of Pumbeditha
(third-century Babylonian *Amora*) was both talmudic authority and physician, and in order to become familiar with
the female anatomy for purposes of Jewish law, he examined
his female slave and then gave her four zuzim for embar-
rassing her.[5] We have no record of other talmudists who
permitted themselves such liberty; they usually obtained their
information from physicians.[6] It should be noted that the
rabbis of the Talmud were quite accurate in their description
of the woman's reproductive organs,[7] though the same
cannot be said of many posttalmudic authorities.[8] Today,
with advanced methods of illustration and with religious
gynecologists versed in Talmud, rabbis called on to respond
to inquiries concerning these matters are well equipped to
base their responses on the physical facts as well as on the
halakhic literature.

REGULATING CONJUGAL RELATIONS

Frankness may be a virtue in studying the *Halakhah* governing
conjugal relations, but in the actual practice of these relations
it has its curbs and limitations, with modesty a definite virtue.
Hence, it is not given to us to describe in detail how Jewish
husbands and wives generally behaved in this aspect of their
married life.[9] However, it may be assumed that they were
influenced by the guidelines given in the rabbinic literature, of
which there is no shortage and no concealment. There are two
sections in the *Shulchan Arukh* that deal with these intimate
matters,[10] with exhortations culled from statements found in
scattered places in the Talmud. They emphasize at the very
beginning the desirable approach to conjugal intercourse,
namely, a sense that one is engaging in a sacred duty.[11] Hence

lewd remarks, even just between husband and wife, are highly objectionable. Though intercourse is a sacred duty, it should be limited to appropriate frequencies and is not to be indulged in—as the Talmud puts it—"like hens." To make sure that scholars reduce the frequency of their marital intercourse, it was instituted that anyone who had had a seminal emission had to first immerse himself in a *mikveh* before reciting certain prayers.[12]

Maimonides was quite forthright in warning people against excessive indulgence in sexual activity. He asserts, "Excessive intercourse causes premature aging, bodily weakness, dimness of eyesight, bad breath, falling hair and teeth, much pain. Wise physicians say that one in a thousand die from other causes, while a thousand die from excessive intercourse."[13] Nachmanides explains the command "You shall be holy" (Leviticus 19:2) as an exhortation against, among other undesirable habits, overindulgence in sex.[14] Accordingly, the Mishnah lays down a schedule of frequencies appropriate to one's vocation.[15]

Furthermore, conjugal relations should be engaged in only by mutual consent; a husband has no right to force himself on an unwilling wife.[16] If she is reluctant, he should speak to her tenderly to arouse her desire. By the same token, if the wife finds her husband averse, she must not be too forward and outspoken in demanding that her sexual needs be satisfied; rather, she should employ subtle feminine wiles to arouse his desire.[17] One sage cautioned his daughters to act modestly in their husbands' presence and to avoid any personal habit that might make them repulsive in their husbands' eyes.[18] At the same time, he advised them how to increase their husbands' passion during intercourse. A husband, on the other hand, must be cognizant of his wife's sexual desires and be ready to satisfy them, especially before he leaves on a journey.[19]

Intercourse is a matter "between him and her" and must be withheld from public knowledge and prying eyes. Indeed, a loudmouthed woman whose voice when discussing her intimate relations with her husband is heard by her neighbors is to be divorced.[20] Intercourse should never be engaged in outside the privacy of the home,[21] and then only at night in the dark with no one else—even young children able to talk—in the same room. If the wife is asleep or in a drunken stupor, or if the husband is inebriated, intercourse is forbidden. The Sages maintain that it is permissible for the husband to engage in the sexual act in any position he desires, though the pious person will do so only in the normal position, that is, with the male above the woman.[22]

Intercourse should be an expression of love between the two partners, with no thoughts of others intruding.[23] It is related of a certain pious individual that during the day, when he was out in the field working, his wife wore filthy clothing, but when he came home she wore clean clothing. When asked by the rabbis to explain this conduct, he said, "When I am away she wears filthy clothing so that no stranger should gaze upon her; when I come home she wears clean clothing so that I should not gaze upon another woman."[24] In general, all relations between husband and wife must be based on mutual love and respect, the best guarantee of a happy married life. Thus the Sages aver, "Who loves his wife as himself, and respects her more than himself, concerning him Scripture says, 'You will know that all is well in your tent; when you visit your wife you will never fail'" (Job 5:24).[25]

TAHARAT HA-MISHPACHAH: JEWISH FAMILY PURITY

The divine wisdom of the Torah, in mandating the laws about a woman during her menstrual period, has taught Jewish husbands and wives how to inculcate this mutual love and respect so essential for marital happiness. The basic rule is laid down in the Written Law, the Pentateuch, as follows: "Do not come near a woman during her menstrual uncleanness to uncover her nakedness" (Leviticus 18:19), a ban against sexual intercourse during a woman's menstrual period. In earlier verses Scripture distinguishes between a woman who has a discharge of blood "at the time of her impurity," that is, at the time of her regular menses, and a woman who has a discharge of blood "for many days not at the time of her impurity." The former is designated a *niddah*,[26] and for her the rule is "she shall remain in her impurity seven days" (Leviticus 15:19). The latter is designated a *zavah*, and for her the rule is "when she becomes clean of her discharge she shall count seven days and after that she shall be clean" (Leviticus 15:28). As we shall see later, in talmudic times it was accepted that every woman, whether having a regular period or not, is considered a *zavah* and under the more stringent ruling of having to wait seven clean days before resuming conjugal relations. Furthermore, she becomes clean—and may resume conjugal relations— only after immersion in a *mikveh*, a pool of water collected according to certain rather complicated rules.[27] These rulings have been amplified in the Oral Law by the Sages of the Talmud and their successors, the halakhic authorities in every age, the *poskim*.

From the halakhic literature, it is apparent that these laws were generally observed despite the restraints imposed on the sexual urge and the difficulties in performing the ritual of immersion. It is related that a heretic remonstrated with Rabbi Kahana, "You [i.e., the rabbis] maintain that a *niddah* may be alone with her husband [and yet refrain from intercourse]; how is it possible for a flame to be close to chaff and the chaff doesn't ignite!" Rabbi Kahanah responded, "Scripture testifies that even if 'hedged about with lilies' [Song of Songs 7:3], Jews do not break through the barrier [i.e., the Torah's admonition against intercourse with a *niddah*]."[28]

THE RATIONALE FOR THE LAWS OF FAMILY PURITY

The basic reason for the Torah's banning of sexual intercourse during a woman's menstrual period was given by the *Tanna* Rabbi Meir.[29] He explains, "Because if a husband is with her constantly he will come to loathe her, therefore the Torah said that she should be unclean for seven days [only later was it increased to approximately twelve days] and thus she will become endeared to him as at the moment she entered the nuptial chamber." Someone paraphrased this idea by remarking that these laws make for a new honeymoon every month.

At the same time, these laws reflect a profounder understanding of the nature of sexual intercourse, that it is not simply a physical act but involves some very basic emotions. We are so constituted by nature that these emotions stimulate reactions in our bodies that affect the very mechanics of intercourse. The emotion of love interacts with physical stimuli, producing responses in our bodies that prepare us for the sexual embrace. Without this desirable emotional climate, without a feeling of love shared by both partners, intercourse becomes a sterile unsatisfying experience that can warp one's future attitude toward sex and create a host of psychological difficulties in married life.

It is well known that individuals vary a great deal in the intensity and expression of their emotions. Just as some people are more temperamental than others and respond more readily to an affront real or imagined—what our Sages call "easy [or hard] to anger"—so some respond to a sexual stimulus more rapidly than others. Generally speaking, a male's tempo of reaction to such a stimulus is much more rapid than that of a woman's, and being more easily aroused, the husband is more eager for consummation than his wife.[30] She, on the other hand, needs more time to be able to respond wholeheartedly to her husband's attentions, and not only more time but more gestures of affection, such as the bringing of a gift or a verbal expression of love. Because of these natural differences, there is a need for adjustment in married life so that the responses of husband and wife will be more or less mutual. In addition, there is much evidence that these laws are hygienic and contribute to one's soundness of body as well as of mind. Many medical experts have testified that the incidence of cancer of the genitalia of both male and female is much less among those who observe the laws than among those who do not observe them.[31]

The laws of family purity, which bespeak continence and self-control at certain times, help considerably in attaining this adjustment. They impress upon the husband the first requisite for establishing a happy and satisfying relationship with his wife, namely, respect for her feelings. He has no right to impose himself upon her merely because of *his* feelings; he has to ascertain that she feels the same way. He will begin to understand that a woman's emotional pattern is cyclical, with alternate periods of elation and depression. When she has her menstrual period she is not only physically weary but emotionally at a low ebb, unable to respond eagerly to her husband's desires. This is the time of the month when she requires privacy, and she tends to withdraw from physical intimacy. And this is precisely the time for which the Torah has prescribed separation and suspension of physical contact. Here the Torah has laid the foundation for a happy marriage, when a man learns to respect the peculiar needs and feelings of his wife. At the same time, the wife has her responsibility in the process of adjustment; during this period she must display an understanding of her husband's masculine reactions and refrain from acts that might unduly arouse her husband's passion. Thus, the Sages instituted a whole series of regulations designed to reduce the ordinary familiar contacts between them.[32] They may not sleep together in the same bed, even if they are both clothed and do not touch each other.[33] That is why in traditional Jewish homes there are always twin beds in the master bedroom.

In this connection, the Talmud relates in the name of Elijah (who visited the Sages from time to time) that a certain student who had studied a great deal of Torah under many scholars had died young. His wife took his *tefillin*, went around to various schools of learning, and said to the scholars, "It is written in the Torah 'for it is your life and your length of days' [Deuteronomy 30:20]; my husband studied so much Torah, why did he die so young?" No one could answer her.

> Once I [Elijah] was her guest, and she told me the whole story. I asked her, "My daughter, while you were a *niddah*, what was his relationship with you?" "God forbid," she said, "He didn't touch me even with his little finger." "How was he with you during your seven clean days?" She replied, "He ate with me and drank with me and slept with me with our bodies touching, but he never considered having intercourse." I then said to her, "Blessed is God Who does not forgive anyone acting contrary to Torah, which says, 'You shall not *approach* a woman in her menstrual uncleanness' [Leviticus 18:19]."[34]

Other restrictions were even more extreme, banning all physical contact. Even when the wife is ill, the *Shulchan Arukh* rules that the husband may not tend to her while she is a *niddah*, even if he is a physician he may not take her pulse. However, the Rema (Rabbi Moshe Isserles) advances a more lenient opinion and records that the custom is to permit physical contact when necessary. Already in talmudic times, some extreme restrictions gave way to more reasonable considerations. We are told that the Sages at first felt a woman should not use cosmetics or wear pretty dresses during her menstrual period lest she tempt her husband, until Rabbi Akiba argued that she would become ugly in his eyes and he might divorce her, so the ban was removed.[35] At other times, as I have mentioned earlier, she must display for him affection in order to encourage him in the performance of his conjugal duties.

Tevilah: Immersion in a *Mikveh*

It is the ceremony of *tevilah*, the immersion that follows the period of separation, that serves best to illustrate the Torah's attitude toward the intimate aspects of married life. By prescribing a ceremonial act before one is permitted to enjoy conjugal relations, it has raised sexual intercourse from a mere animal indulgence to a consecrated act. It should be clear that *tevilah* is a religious ritual, a symbol and a reminder of the place of sex in marriage as well as a line of demarcation between ritually clean and ritually unclean. Since its purpose is not bodily cleanliness—though such cleanliness is a prerequisite for undergoing the ceremony—no ordinary bathing can take its place. Like any other religious ceremony, it is defined by the *Halakhah*; otherwise it loses its sanctity. Maimonides has explained this in his concluding remarks to the Laws of Cleanness.

It is clear and apparent that the laws of purity and impurity are scriptural decrees and not among the rules that are established by human reason. This is true also of the law of immersion [to cleanse oneself after an impurity], since such impurity is not mud or excrement that is removed by washing. Rather, it is a scriptural decree and depends upon the person's intention [to cleanse himself]. It also serves as a symbol: Just as the intention to become ritually clean by immersion renders the immersion effective even though it has not effected any change in the person's body, so a person, through a sincere intention to purify himself from spiritual impurities—such as sinful thoughts and false opinions—by immersing himself in the waters of wisdom renders himself pure.

MIKVEH: THE RITUALARIUM

One of the basic requirements of a kosher *mikveh* is that the water be gathered in it by natural and not by artificial means. This is a token of the naturalness that should prevail in the relations between husband and wife, a normal response to mutual feelings of love and respect, and an understanding of the sacredness of the marriage bond. The observance of the law of immersion, until recent times, was never a pleasant or easy chore. In the days of the Second Temple, the Sages took drastic measures to promote the use of the *mikveh* because its waters, not being changed often enough, would become fetid, and people began to doubt its cleansing character.[36] Centuries later, in medieval Egypt, religious authorities again found it necessary to take drastic measures to ensure observance because women would pour water (a makeshift shower) in place of immersion in a *mikveh*.[37] A perennial problem arose from the halakhic ruling that the immersion had to take place after sunset, and going to the *mikveh* in the dark was quite frightening and even hazardous. In fact, some *Amora'im* in Babylonia permitted immersion during the daytime because of the dangers involved in nighttime immersion, provided it was the day after the time of the prescribed immersion.[38] Nevertheless, despite these and other difficulties, observant women throughout all ages displayed unusual fortitude and religious devotion in fulfilling all the halakhic requirements under most difficult circumstances, such as immersion in very chilling waters or having to travel great distances to reach the *mikveh*.

Today, observing the *mikveh* ritual has become a much more pleasant task. Modern ritualariums maintain high standards of cleanliness and provide several ancillary facilities and equipment, such as showers and hair driers. What remains for the religious leaders today is not the taking of drastic measures to enforce observance—as if that were effective—but promoting observance by enlightening instruction and explanation of its significance for domestic happiness.

DOMESTIC HARMONY: *SHALOM BAYIT*

I have mentioned the basic differences in the emotional natures of men and women, which the laws of family purity help resolve. In addition, there are the general differences in temperament and outlook to which a married couple have to adjust in order to maintain a harmonious relationship. The Sages aver, "Just as the facial features of persons do not resemble each other, so their opinions do not resemble each other."[39] Thus, it is inevitable that these differences will lead to argument and dissension. Even in jealousy and suspicion there are different degrees and reactions that can upset domestic harmony and endanger the stability of the marriage. The Talmud illustrates a wide divergence of these reactions with two examples: Most men are not jealous if they see their wives speaking with neighbors and relatives, whereas others lock their wives in the house when they go out.[40]

To combat frequent dissension in the home, the Sages have emphasized the importance of helping quarreling spouses achieve domestic harmony, known in Hebrew as *shalom bayit*, "peace in the home." Indeed, one version of the Mishnah that cites several acts of philanthropy adds "the bringing of peace between husband and wife."[41] Even God Almighty deviated from the truth in order to preserve domestic harmony between Abraham and Sarah. She said, "My master [husband] is old," but God told Abraham that she said, "I am old" (Genesis 18:12, 13).[42]

An illustration of the importance of this objective is seen in the following anecdote. Rabbi Meir was accustomed to lecture every Friday evening in the synagogue in Hamta. There was a certain woman who attended these lectures. One Friday evening Rabbi Meir spoke longer than usual, and by the time the woman returned home the candles were extinguished. Her husband asked her, "Where were you?" She said, "I went to listen to the lecture." He responded, "I swear you cannot enter the house until you spit in the face of the lecturer." Rabbi Meir became aware of this and pretended that his eye was sore. He announced that anyone who knew how to treat an eye sore should come forward. The woman's neighbors advised her to go and pretend that she could treat the eye sore. Rabbi Meir prompted her to spit in his face seven times and told her to tell her husband, "You told me to spit once, and I spat seven times." Afterward, Rabbi Meir's disciples asked him how he had allowed himself to be abused in that manner, so he told them, "Meir's honor is no greater than his Creator's. If God's holy name, written in holiness, may be erased in order to bring peace between husband and wife, how much more so may Meir's honor be abused for that purpose."[43]

Rabbi Meir was referring to the biblical law of the *Sotah*, the woman suspected by her husband of committing adultery. The procedure included writing on a scroll a curse with the divine name and then erasing it with sacred waters, which were then given to the woman to drink (Numbers 5:11–31).

DOMESTIC VIOLENCE

There is a statement in the Talmud that people generally learn bad habits from their neighbors instead of learning good habits.[44] Unfortunately this was borne out in the phenomenon of wife beating, as reported by the historian Salo Baron. He wrote, "Wife beating, *in imitation of their German neighbors*, seems to have spread among the Jews of medieval Germany to a sufficient extent to constitute a problem, and Rabbi Meir of Rothenburg proposed the Draconian penalty of cutting off the guilty husband's hand."[45] However, a careful reading of Rabbi Meir's *responsum* does not justify the impression that this ugly phenomenon was widespread, for he wrote therein, "One deserves greater punishment for striking his wife than for striking another person, for he is enjoined to respect her. *It is not the way of our people to beat their wives as the nations do*; God forbid that a Jew should do such a thing."

Rabbi Meir also quotes Rabbi Paltoi Gaon's ruling that if a husband constantly quarrels with his wife, it is grounds for divorce, and if a live-in mother-in-law causes the quarrels, she should be moved to some other place.[46] In this connection, Rabbi Moshe Isserles writes, "A man who beats his wife is committing a sin . . . for it is not the way of Jews to beat their wives; it is a non-Jewish practice."[47]

THE MODERN FAMILY VERSUS THE TRADITIONAL FAMILY

The vast majority of Jewish people today live in an open society and are more exposed than ever to the influence of their non-Jewish neighbors. This has affected their attitude toward family life, among other things. A professor of the law faculty of the Hebrew University who has written extensively on marriage law makes the following distinctions between the modern family and the traditional one. The latter encompasses a large number of relatives, whereas the former is a "nuclear family," concerned almost exclusively with the husband and wife and minor children. In the traditional family there is a division of responsibility and allocation of specific duties, whereas in the modern family the tendency is for the partners to share equally in the family responsibilities. In addition, in the traditional family the head of the family, invariably the husband, plays a more authoritative role; in the modern family, more significant than the legal aspects are the understandings arrived at by common consent of the two partners.[48] An indication of the latter is the recognition given by the *Knesset*, the parliament of the State of Israel, to the common-law marriage.

On the other hand, the *Knesset* has shown its recognition of the importance of preserving the Jewish family in its traditional form by assigning to the rabbinic courts, whose decisions are based upon the *Halakhah*, exclusive jurisdiction in matters of marriage and divorce. The standard procedure in these courts in any petition for divorce is first to attempt to restore *shalom bayit* and preserve the family. To combat the growing incidence of family breakdowns, various extralegal organizations have been founded in order to assist quarreling couples in overcoming their differences. There is even "pre-

ventive medicine" in this social area, with organizations
reaching out to affianced couples to guide them in the proper
attitudes that make for a happy marriage.

A most important factor in maintaining domestic harmony
comes with the birth of a child.[49] I have mentioned earlier (p.
8) the rabbinic understanding of the verse "therefore . . . cling
to his wife, and they shall be one flesh" (Genesis 2:24) that the
one flesh is the child born of the union. It is the fruit of the
husband and wife's love, the treasure they both cherish, the
ever-present living token of their marriage. In becoming
parents, husband and wife now share a common responsibility of rearing their child and all subsequent children. The
traditional stability of the Jewish family was due in large
measure to the seriousness with which Judaism regards the
upbringing of offspring. In the next chapter, I review the
relationships between parents and children, shaped by the
mandates of the Torah and their actual practice in traditional
homes.

CHAPTER 8

THE JEWISH FAMILY:
PARENTS AND CHILDREN

For I [God] have known him [Abraham] that he commands his children and his household after him that they keep the way of the Lord to do righteousness and justice. (Genesis 18:19)

THE FATHER AS TEACHER

The distinguishing feature of the Jewish people, beginning with their first ancestor the Patriarch Abraham, has been the transmission of their religious tradition from father to son. In Abraham's time, this tradition was summarized in the general moral principles of righteousness and justice,[1] but by the time his descendants had become a numerous people and had experienced the revelation of God's word at Sinai, the tradition comprised a copious series of both ritual and ethical mandates.[2]

Time and time again parents were enjoined by the Torah to transmit this tradition to their children, not only its mandates, its do's and don'ts, but also the historic experiences of their forefathers. They were commanded to make known to their children two experiences in particular: the Exodus from Egypt and the Revelation at Sinai. For the first, it is said, "You shall tell your son on that day [of Passover] saying, 'This [Passover ritual] is performed because of what the Lord did for me when I went out from Egypt' " (Exodus 13:8). We fulfill this injunction by conducting the elaborate ritual of the *seder*, the festive meal on the first night of the Passover Festival.[3] The main feature of the *seder* is the involvement of the children; without their participation we cannot perform the *mitzvah* in its entirety.[4] For the second experience, the Torah commanded "You shall make known to your children and your children's children the day you stood before the Lord your God at Horeb" (Deuteronomy 4:9–10).

These two events were singled out from the many other historic events we are commanded to remember because they are unique in all of human history, underscoring the uniqueness of the Jewish People as the Chosen People. We read:

> Inquire now about the early days that were before you, ever since God created man on earth, from one end of the heavens to the other, has anything as great as this ever happened, or has there been anything like it? Has any people heard the voice of God speaking from the midst of the fire as you have heard [at Sinai] and survived? Or has God ventured to come and take to Himself one nation from the midst of another by trials, by signs and wonders, by war, by a mighty hand and an outstretched arm and awesome power, as all that the Lord your God did for you in Egypt before your very eyes? [Deuteronomy 4:32–34]

These two events are the twin pillars of Jewish identity, of the Jewish people as a nation and of their religious faith.

Judaism's tradition is transmitted by teaching, as we read, "These My words you shall impress upon your heart and soul . . . and you shall teach them to your children" (Deuteronomy 11:18-19), and this is repeated again and again (Deuteronomy 4:9, 6:7). This is why Maimonides begins his codification of the laws of *Talmud Torah*, studying the Torah, not—as we expect—with the obligation of every Jew to study Torah but with the obligation of the father to teach his young son. Maimonides adds, "Just as a person is obligated to teach his son, so is he obligated to teach his son's son" citing Deuteronomy 4:9.[5] Thus, the role of the father was defined in Judaism primarily as that of teacher.

The importance the Sages imputed to teaching Torah to children and children's children is seen in the following anecdotes related in the Talmud. Rabbi Yehoshua ben Levi was accustomed to listen every Friday to his grandson review the weekly Torah portion. Once he forgot and entered the bathhouse in Tiberias, assisted by his disciple Rabbi Chiyya bar Ba. He suddenly reminded himself about his grandson's lesson and left the bathhouse without his cloak. When his disciple expressed his surprise at such haste, Rabbi Yehoshua said to him, "Chiyya, my son, is it of little importance to you that he who listens to the portion from his grandson is as if he had heard it from Sinai, as is written, 'You shall make them known to your sons and grandsons . . . the day you stood before the Lord your God at Horeb.' "[6] Rabbi Chiyya himself would not eat breakfast before first teaching his grandson, and Rabbah bar Huna would not eat breakfast before first taking his grandson to the schoolhouse.[7]

A Public School System

It was this *mitzvah* of teaching Torah to children that led to the establishment of a public school system in every Jewish community. The Talmud records,

> Truly this man is remembered for his good deed—his name is Yehoshua ben Gemala—for if not for him the Torah would have been forgotten in Israel. In the beginning, a child who had a father would be taught by his father; one who had no father would not learn Torah, for the verse "You shall teach them to your children" [Deuteronomy 11:19] was understood to imply that only you yourselves [i.e., fathers] shall teach. So it was instituted that teachers of young children would be employed in Jerusalem, in accord with the verse "Out of Zion shall go forth the Torah and the word of the Lord from Jerusalem" (Isaiah 2:4).[8] As yet, however, who had a father was brought to Jerusalem and taught, but the one who had no father was not brought to Jerusalem and hence did not learn Torah; so it was instituted that teachers be employed in every province for teenage students, who if incurring the wrath of their teacher would rebel and leave. So finally Rabbi Yehoshua ben Gemala instituted that teachers be employed in every province and in every city for children who entered the school at the age of six or seven.[9]

By the Middle Ages it became customary to take children to school (called *cheder*, "room") at the age of three, where they would be given some honey as a symbol of the sweetness of Torah. From certain midrashic statements we learn that they would begin their lesson in Torah not with *Bereishit*, the beginning of the Torah, but with *Vayikra*, the beginning of the Book of Leviticus, which deals with the laws of sacrificial offerings. The reason for this rather strange custom is explained in the *Midrash* as follows: "Why do they begin teaching children the Book of Leviticus and not *Bereishit*? Because children are pure [i.e., innocent] and sacrifices are pure [i.e., render purity]; let pure ones study pure things."[10]

In Jewish communities today, parents who wish to fulfill their obligation to provide proper schooling for their children in their religious tradition have several alternatives. Either they send them to a nondenominational public school, where the children spend most of the day learning secular subjects, and then send them to an afternoon Hebrew school (or even, more limited, to a one-day-a-week Sunday school), or they can send them to a Jewish day school, where they learn both secular and religious subjects. Experience has shown that in the afternoon Hebrew school, which usually meets only three days a week, the knowledge of Judaism gained is quite superficial, and invariably the child's Jewish education is not continued after the elementary stage. Consequently, there has been a decided increase in the number of Jewish day schools that provide continuing education through the high, or secondary, stage. Here the children obtain a sufficient grounding in their Jewish studies to enable them to carry on and deepen their interest in Judaism in subsequent years. The major problem today is the fact that many—all too many—Jewish children are allowed to grow up without any religious education whatsoever.

The father's role of teacher was not completely usurped by the schoolteacher. Indeed, it remained the father's obligation to begin teaching his son several years before the latter reached school age. The ruling set down by the Sages is, "As soon as the child knows how to speak, his father teaches him Torah and the *Shema*." To learn "Torah," in this context, is to recite the verse "Moses commanded us Torah, a heritage of the congregation of Israel" (Deuteronomy 33:4); to learn

"*Shema*" is to recite the verse "Hear O Israel, the Lord is our God, the Lord is One" (Deuteronomy 6:4). Thus every morning, as soon as the child is awake, the father asks him to repeat these verses.[11] To these verses was added the prayer that every Jew is obliged to recite every morning upon awakening: "I give thanks to You, Living and Eternal King, that you have returned to me my soul with mercy; great is Your faithfulness" (*Modeh Ani . . .*). This is followed by the verse from Proverbs (1:8), "Listen my son to the instruction of your father, and do not forsake the teaching of your mother."

The Honor Accorded a Teacher

With the establishment of a school system, especially for the older students who studied in a *Bet Ha-Midrash*, or academy, the teacher assumed an importance greater than that of the father. The Sages taught, "If a man and his father and his teacher were in captivity, he [the son] is to be ransomed before his teacher and his teacher before his father."[12] Similarly,

> To return his and his father's lost property, his comes first; his and his teacher's lost property, his comes first; his father's and his teacher's, his teacher's comes first, for his father brought him into this world, whereas his teacher who taught him wisdom [i.e., the Torah] brings him to life in the world-to-come. If both his father and his teacher were bearing a burden, he first relieves his teacher and then relieves his father.[13]

One Sage went so far as to assert that "the reverence for one's teacher should be as great as the reverence for [God in] Heaven."[14]

THE PARENTS' NATURAL ROLE

Of course, the Torah recognizes the natural role of the father as biological begetter of the child, obligating him to be its provider and protector.[15] This role is so fundamental in the relationship between the two that it became the symbol of God's Providence over the children of Israel. We read, "Is He not your father Who begot you; fashioned and established you . . . He found him in a desert land. . . . Surrounded him and gave him understanding, watched over him as the pupil of his eye" (Deuteronomy 32:6–10). The father is also a symbol of mercy over his children, as we read, "As a father has mercy over his children, God has mercy over those who revere him" (Psalm 103:13).[16] And just as we regard the Almighty as our father, so He regards us as His children, as is written, "You are sons to the Lord your God" (Deuteronomy 14:1).[17]

The mother also is the teacher of her children, as we read in Proverbs (1:8): "Do not forsake the teaching of your mother." True, the Sages have downplayed the role of the mother as teacher. They exempted her from the *mitzvah* of teaching Torah to her children,[18] restricting her part in their formal education to bringing them to the schoolhouse.[19] However, they do not deny her decisive role in establishing the religious status of her offspring. In rulings that at first glance seem paradoxical they determined, on the one hand, that a child born of a non-Jewish father and a Jewish mother is Jewish, even to the extent that such a child may be appointed an official of the Jewish community, for "since his mother is an Israelite we regard him as being "from among your brothers" (Deuteronomy 17:15).[20] On the other hand, it is the father's tribal status—*kohen* or Levite or Israelite—that determines the child's tribal status, in accordance with the ruling "The father's family—and not the mother's—is considered family."[21] Hence, all the special rules governing *kohanim* (the priestly tribe) devolve upon a child born of a *kohen* father and an Israelite mother.

Herein lies the recognition by the Sages that each parent has a distinctive role in the rearing of their children, as a consequence of their respective biological experience in the process of procreation. This distinction between mother and father is reflected in the different intensity of the emotional attachment of parents to their children and children to their parents. Thus the Sages explain why in the commandment to honor father and mother, the father is mentioned first (Exodus 20:12), while in the commandment to revere mother and father, the mother is mentioned first (Leviticus 19:3):

> It is perceived by the Creator that a son honors his mother more than his father, for she chastises him by words [i.e., and not by corporal punishment, as the father does] and therefore attention was first called to honoring one's father; and it is perceived by the Creator that a son reveres his father more than his mother because his father teaches him Torah; therefore revering one's mother was mentioned first.[22]

The deeper emotional attachment of mother to child, reciprocated by the child, has moved the prophet to employ it as the symbol of God's attachment to His people Israel, as we read, "Will a woman forget her offspring, from having mercy over the son of her womb; even if these will forget, I [God] will not forget you [Israel]" (Isaiah 49:15). The particular role of the mother is to comfort her children when they despair, as it is written, "As a mother comforts her son, so I will comfort you" (Isaiah 66:13).

A FATHER'S RIGHT OVER HIS SON'S LIFE

Among the ancient Canaanites, a father could dispose of his son's life by offering him up as a sacrifice to the gods, a practice that Israel was strongly admonished not to follow (Deuteronomy 12:31, 18:10).[23] In fact, many commentators maintain that the story of the *Akedah,* in which Abraham was commanded by God to offer up his son as a sacrifice, but at the last moment a voice from Heaven said, "Do not raise up your hand against the lad" (Genesis, chap. 22), was a declaration that God does not want—indeed, He abhors—child sacrifice.[24]

Among the ancient Greeks and Romans a father had the power to condemn his child to death, a right known as *ius vitae necisque.* The Torah ruled out this power of the parents and transferred it to the courts in the case of "a stubborn and rebellious son who does not listen to his parent's voice" (Deuteronomy 21:18–21); only the court may condemn him to death. The Sages explained this harsh judgment on the grounds that such a wayward son undoubtedly would end up being a bandit and a murderer: "better punish him before he commits the murder than after." However, they curbed this power of the courts by putting so many qualifications that it could never be exercised.[25] What remained for the father was the right—indeed, the obligation—to administer corporal punishment to a wayward child.

QUESTIONS OF MATERNITY AND PATERNITY

Notwithstanding the up-to-date equipment in our modern hospitals, there still occurs the rare instance of newborn babies' being switched, leading to both heartbreak and litigation. The classic example of babies switched at birth is the case brought before the judgment of King Solomon as described in the Book of Kings, though in this case the mix-up was deliberate (1 Kings 4:16–28). One of two babies born in the same room to two harlots died, and each woman came before the king and claimed, "My son is the one alive, and hers is the one who died." The king ordered that they bring a sword and sever the live child in half, so as to give one half to each claimant. Whereupon the true mother, having mercy on her child, said, "Give her the child and do not kill him," while the other woman said, "Sever him so that neither of us will have the baby." Thus, King Solomon in his wisdom was able to determine the true mother.

The *Halakhah* discusses several cases of switched babies. Two women, one the wife of a *kohen* and the other the wife of a Levite, gave birth together, and it had to be established which baby was the child of the *kohen* and which of the Levite. Analogously, one child was born to the wife of a man of pure lineage and another to the wife of a *mamzer*, and it had to be established which child was of pure lineage and which of tainted lineage. There is also the case of a woman who gave birth to twins, and it had to be established which child was the firstborn. In all such cases we rely on the testimony of the midwife, provided it was given before she left the room in which the children were born; if given after she left the room, she lost her credibility. (In general, a woman's testimony is invalid.)[26]

In a case of establishing which child is the firstborn, the Talmud rules that the mother's testimony is accepted if given within seven days of the child's birth, not afterward. As for the father, his testimony is valid at all times, a ruling based on the verse dealing with one who has two wives, one a loved one and the other unloved. It reads, "He must acknowledge as firstborn the son of the unloved wife and allot him a double portion of all that he possesses" (Deuteronomy 21:17). Thus, it is understood that his acknowledgment is the determinant. The Sages are divided as to whether a *kohen*'s testimony is accepted if he testifies that his son was born to a divorcée, thus disqualifying him from the priesthood.[27] As we shall see, this ruling has serious ramifications.

If a couple is married and living together and the woman gives birth, the assumption is that even if the woman committed adultery, it is the husband who is the father of the child.[28] If, however, the husband claims that the child is not his and therefore is a *mamzer*, the father's claim is accepted, as ruled by the halakhic authorities. If the wife avers that the child is the result of extramarital intercourse, she is not believed.[29]

If an unmarried woman gives birth and claims that the father was a Jew of pure lineage, even though she refuses to disclose his identity her claim is accepted, provided she lives in a Jewish community where most of the men are of pure lineage, and consequently the child's status as a Jew of pure lineage is confirmed.[30] If she discloses his identity and he admits that he is the father and is of pure lineage, the child's status as being of pure lineage is confirmed even if the mother was under suspicion of having lived a loose life. If, however, the man denies that he is the father, and she has had intercourse with other men as well as with him, we accept his denial.[31]

These halakhic rulings were formulated in talmudic times when questions of pure lineage were paramount, as I have pointed out in Chapter 2. Today, questions of putative paternity revolve around questions of support for the problematic child, and the courts—even rabbinic courts—are inclined to rule in favor of the mother if there is some circumstantial evidence to support her claim. Today many civil courts rely on results of sophisticated blood and genetic tests, though rabbinic courts may hesitate to rule upon such evidence.

IT'S A BOY

Among Jews, as among other ethnic groups, a son is preferred over a daughter (in Judaism, of course, not to the extreme of infanticide). In fact, it was customary for a man to pray that his wife bear him a son. However, the Mishnah rules that if a man's wife is already pregnant, it is useless to pray then for a son, since the sex of a child is determined at the moment of conception. But the Talmud tells us that there was an exception in the case of Leah, the wife of Patriarch Jacob. After she had given birth to six sons and conceived another child, she reasoned as follows: "Twelve tribes are destined to be sired by Jacob. I have already given birth to six of them, and the two handmaidens Bilhah and Zilpah have each given birth to two sons. If the child of this pregnancy is a son, my sister Rachel [who until then had given birth to only one son] will not have produced as many sons as even one of the handmaidens." So Leah prayed that the sex of the child she was bearing be changed from that of a male to that of a female, and her prayer was granted. This was a miracle, explains the Talmud, not to be granted to an ordinary individual. There is another explanation: Possibly Leah prayed for the change within forty days after conception, and at that early stage the sex of the embryo was not yet determined, and a prayer then might be helpful.

The Talmud continues the discussion by telling us what really determines the sex of a child: "If the man emits his seed first, the child will be female; if the woman emits her seed first, the child will be male. Only if both emit their seed simultaneously will the sex be determined forty days after conception."[32] This theory about the sex of the embryo was derived by the Sages from the verse that begins, "If a woman conceives and gives birth to a male" (Leviticus 12:2). The word employed by the Torah for "conceives" is *tazria*, literally, "will emit seed," hence the assumption that if a woman emits seed first the child will be male. This phrase introduces a distinction the Torah makes between the birth of a male and that of a female. After the birth of a male, the period of the mother's impurity is seven days; after the birth of a female it is fourteen days. Why this distinction? asked the disciples of Rabbi Shimon bar Yochai. He explained, "When a male is born everyone is happy; when a female is born everyone is sad."[33] Whether or not this explanation is true, if upon birth the midwife or attending nurse announces, "It's a boy," the joy is great in a Jewish household.

Jewish law recognizes this joy in making the following ruling: "If a man's wife gives birth to a boy, he pronounces the benediction 'Blessed is He Who is good and bestows goodness,' for even the wife is pleased with the birth of a son." Consequently, the *Shulchan Arukh* rules that even the wife must recite the benediction, though the Rema comments that it is no longer customary to recite the blessing.[34] A later halakhist, Rabbi Israel Meir Hacohen, in his commentary to the *Shulchan Arukh*, asserts that at the birth of a daughter the father may recite the benediction "Blessed . . . Who has kept us alive . . . [the *She-hecheyanu* blessing]."[35]

The joy at the birth of a son becomes more manifest shortly after the birth of a boy in the custom called *Shalom Zakhar* (Welcome to a Male), which some maintain was already prevalent in talmudic times.[36] The first Friday evening after the son is born, friends are invited to the parents' home to partake of refreshments and sing liturgical songs.[37]

BRIT MILAH: CIRCUMCISION

The celebration of the birth of a son reaches its climax on the eighth day after his birth, when the *brit milah* or circumcision ceremony takes place. *Brit* is a covenant, and *brit milah* is the covenant between God and the People of Israel, first sealed when God said to Abraham, "This is My covenant which you shall keep, between Me and you and your offspring after you; circumcise every male among you . . . and it shall be a sign of the covenant between Me and you. Every male eight days old shall be circumcised throughout your generations" (Genesis 17:10–12). It was reaffirmed as one of the 613 *mitzvot* of the Torah in the Book of Leviticus (12:3). It is so fundamental a mark of belonging to the Jewish people that the penalty for not observing it is *karet*, being cut off from the people.[38] And any male non-Jew who wishes to become a member of the Jewish people by conversion must first undergo the rite of circumcision. Indeed, Scripture refers to non-Jews as *areilim*, uncircumcised, even though they may be circumcised.[39] The Mishnah, uncharacteristically, lists a series of statements by various *Tanna'im* extolling the greatness of circumcision, concluding with the panegyric "Great is *milah*, for if not for it God would not have created the world, as is said, 'Thus says the Lord, "If not for My covenant with day and night [an allusion to *brit milah* that remains with the person day and night] I would not have established the laws of heaven and earth" ' " (Jeremiah 33:25–27).[40]

Though some modern heretics have branded the rite of

circumcision as primitive and even barbaric, causing unnecessary pain to the infant, it is to this day observed by practically all Jews regardless of the extent of their religious commitment; and the attempt by early proponents of Reform Judaism to eliminate its practice has failed.[41] However, it must be understood that in addition to being a surgical practice with hygienic advantages to boot (hence many non-Jews undergo the procedure[42]), it is a religious rite and therefore must be conducted according to the *Halakhah*. Thus, it may not be done by a non-Jewish physician even if a rabbi conducts the ceremony and recites the blessings.

METZITZAH

One part of the procedure became controversial among halakhists in modern times. The Mishnah states that an integral part of circumcision, after cutting off the foreskin and pulling down the membrane beneath it, is *metzitzah*, sucking off by mouth the blood from the organ. To this an *Amora* commented, "A surgeon [i.e., the circumcisor] who does not suck the blood endangers the child and should be removed."[43] Over a century ago, at the suggestion of physicians, it was argued that oral *metzitzah*, rather than preventing harm to the child, actually increases it because of some infection that might be transmitted by the circumcisor's germs, and that removing excessive blood can best be done by manual compression with a sponge. Traditionalists, who regard every talmudic statement as divinely inspired and therefore may not be discarded despite scientific judgment to the contrary, to this day insist upon oral *metzitzah*. More liberal halakhists agreed that *metzitzah* may be dispensed with. Many *mohalim* (plural of *mohel*, the performer of the rite) have compromised:

they use a glass tube, one end of which is placed upon the organ, and remove the blood by suction from the other end, a method approved by most latter-day *poskim*. Today, with the spread of the HIV virus and AIDS, this method is a must. Recently, refinements of the procedure, such as the use of a shield or clamp and sterile bandages, are employed in order to make the circumcision safer.

THE *BRIT MILAH* CEREMONY[44]

As in the performance of many other *mitzvot*, so in that of *brit milah* ancillary customs have been adopted. One of the earliest, though not mentioned in the Talmud, is the appointment of an honored individual to hold the infant on his knees during the circumcision. He is called the *sandak*, a word of Greek origin meaning "representative," perhaps representing Elijah. Tradition has it that the *sandak* is rewarded with riches for his participation in the *mitzvah*, and therefore the same person should not be honored as *sandak* at another *brit milah* in the same family, to allow another person to receive the reward. In some communities it was customary to honor the local rabbi to act as *sandak* at all circumcisions. In addition to the *sandak*, a couple is appointed, the woman to receive the infant from the mother and the man to receive him from his wife.[45] They are called *k'vatter* (godfather) and *k'vatterin* (godmother). When the infant is brought into the room where the circumcision is to be performed, the assembled guests rise and welcome him with the traditional greeting "*Barukh Ha-Ba*" (Blessed is he who arrives). In chasidic circles, the infant—who is borne on an embroidered cushion—is handed over to the guests' *seriatim* to be held for a moment.

It was customary in most communities—and still is with

many celebrants—to conduct the ceremony in the synagogue, where recognition is given to the presence of the celebrants (father, *sandak, mohel*) by eliminating from the prayer service certain penitential prayers (*tachanun*), which are not said on festive days. In many medieval synagogues there was a special chair known as "the chair of Eliyahu" for a *brit milah*. According to legend, Elijah the Prophet is the "angel of the covenant" and is said to attend every circumcision. The *sandak* takes his seat on this chair, the infant is placed on his knees, and he grasps the feet of the infant in his hands so that they do not interfere with the procedure.

According to the basic *Halakhah*, the *mitzvah* to perform this rite devolves upon the father.[46] However, most fathers are not competent to perform it personally, and therefore a specially trained person, a *mohel*, is called on to be the circumciser. It is the latter who, just before cutting the foreskin, recites the benediction "Blessed are You . . . Who has commanded us concerning *milah*." Immediately thereafter the father recites the benediction "Who has commanded us to bring him into the covenant of Abraham our father." The assembled guests then respond, "As he [the infant] entered into the covenant, so may he enter into Torah, *chuppah*, and *Maasim Tovim* [Good Deeds]."[47] In Israel, the father adds the *She-hecheyanu* blessing, "Who has kept us alive . . .," but it is not recited in the Diaspora "because of the pain inflicted upon the child."

After the circumcision has been completed, a celebrant chants a special benediction over a cup of wine. It reads:

> Blessed are You . . . Who has sanctified a beloved [Isaac] [see Genesis 22:2] from the womb, impressing a statute in his flesh, and has sealed his descendants with the sign of the covenant. Therefore, O Living God, as a reward for this, command to deliver our beloved kin from destruction; blessed are You, O Lord, Maker of the covenant.[48]

Then a name is bestowed on the infant, accompanied by an informal blessing for the health of the child and the joy the parents will hopefully derive from him. A drop of wine is placed in the infant's mouth, and he is then returned to his mother. A festive meal follows, with special blessings for the various participants added to the Grace after Meals.

The Talmud mentions that at the time the Roman government decreed against Jews' observing their religious rituals, a clandestine signal was used to summon people to a *brit milah*. In one place, the signal was the grinding of the mill, in another the kindling of many candles.[49] Because Jews defied the evil decree at a risk to their lives, this *mitzvah* was never abandoned.

The Sages were sensitive to the health risks involved in circumcision and therefore regulated that if the infant is not completely healthy (e.g., is underweight) or displays symptoms of an infection (particularly jaundice), the *brit milah* must be postponed until a week after health has been restored. If there is a history of hemophilia in the family, the child should not be circumcised at all. It is related that Rabbi Natan, a *Tanna*, once visited a Mediterranean city and was approached by a woman whose first and second sons died after being circumcised. She brought her third son and asked the rabbi if he should be circumcised. The rabbi said, "I saw that the child was jaundiced, so I said to the woman, 'Wait until his blood is absorbed in his body.' She waited and then had him circumcised, and he lived; so they called him 'Rabbi Natan the Babylonian' after my name."[50]

THE FEMINIST REACTION

Traditionally, the only ceremony attendant on the birth of a daughter is naming the infant when the father is called up to the reading of the Torah, and the sexton recites a blessing for the health of the mother and her newborn child.[51] Even this ceremony is of posttalmudic origin and perhaps explains why most feminine names are in the vernacular, in contradistinction to the names given boys, which are in Hebrew.[52]

Modern feminists, who demand equality between the sexes in religious ritual, are not happy with the traditional pomp and ceremony given to a son and not to a daughter and therefore are seeking some corresponding ceremony to celebrate the birth of a girl. One, called *Shalom Bat* (see p. 111), is becoming quite popular, though not among the ultra-Orthodox. Other tentative proposals have not yet caught the fancy of the modern Orthodox; innovation does not come easily in traditional Judaism.[53]

PIDYON HA-BEN: REDEMPTION OF THE FIRSTBORN

The Talmud rules, "A father is obligated to do the following for his son: to circumcise him; to redeem him; to marry him off; and to teach him a craft."[54] "To redeem him" is to fulfill the *mitzvah* of redeeming a firstborn son, as is written, "Every firstborn human among your sons you shall redeem" (Exodus 13:13), and is explained in the verse, "For unto Me belongs every firstborn; from the day I smote every [Egyptian] firstborn in the land of Egypt I have sanctified unto Myself every firstborn in Israel, from human to animal shall be to Me" (Numbers 3:13). This redemption is executed by giving five shekels to a *kohen* when the child is thirty days old, as is said, "You shall redeem a month-old firstborn with silver, five shekels in the sacred shekel" (Numbers 18:16).

No particular ceremony, other than reciting a benediction for the fulfillment of the *mitzvah*[55] and handing over the five shekels to the *kohen*, is prescribed by the Torah or the Sages. However, the *Geonim* instituted the following procedure: The father brings the child to a *kohen* and informs him that the infant is a firstborn to his mother.[56] The *kohen* then asks the father, "Which do you prefer, your firstborn son or the five shekels with which you have to redeem him?"[57] The father replies, "I prefer my firstborn son, and here are the five shekels for his redemption,"[58] then recites the benediction "Blessed are You . . . for the *mitzvah* of *pidyon ha-ben* and *She-hecheyanu*" ("Who has kept us alive . . . "). Then the *kohen* is given a cup of wine, recites a long prayer corresponding somewhat to the prayer recited at a *brit milah*,[59] blesses the infant with the priestly blessing (Numbers 6:24–27), and hands over the child to its father. A festive meal concludes the ceremony.

The Torah refers to the firstborn as *peter rechem*, opener of the womb (Exodus 13:2). Hence, an oldest son born after his mother has had a miscarriage does not have to be redeemed since the aborted fetus opened her womb. By the same token, a firstborn delivered by cesarian section is exempt from the *mitzvah*, as is the son born after him; the former did not open the womb, and the latter, even though he did open the womb, is not a firstborn to his parents. Furthermore, if the mother is the wife or a daughter of a *kohen* or a Levite, the child is excluded from the *mitzvah* of *pidyon ha-ben*.

UPSHEREN

A custom of rather recent origin, observed primarily by *chasidim*, adds another festive occasion in the life of a young son. It is called *upsheren*, a Yiddish term for cutting the hair. Until a boy reaches the age of three his hair is not cut; it grows long like a girl's. A supposed intimation of such a custom is found in the verse, "When you shall come into the land and plant any food-bearing tree, you shall abstain from its fruit; three years it shall be forbidden to you, it shall not be eaten" (Leviticus 19:23). (By transposition, a child is the fruit of the womb; what grows on him shall not be touched for three years.) Upon reaching the age of three (in Israel the custom is to wait until Lag B'Omer, when pilgrimage to the tomb of Rabbi Shimon bar Yohai in Merom takes place, and conduct the ceremony there) the hair is cut and thrown to the flames, after which a festive meal, to which relatives and friends are invited, is served. It is possible that this custom developed after it became customary to bring children to school at the age of three.[60]

THE *MITZVAH* OF *CHINUKH* (TRAINING)[61]

Until a boy reaches the age of thirteen he is considered a *katan*, a minor, and he is under no personal obligation to perform any of the *mitzvot* of the Torah. However, his father is obligated to train him beforehand how to perform them properly in accordance with the *Halakhah*. This obligation is called *chinukh* ("training"). In several instances Scripture commands us to involve young children in the performance of a *mitzvah*. King Solomon summed it up in the verse, "Train a lad in the way he ought to go; he will not swerve from it even in old age" (Proverbs 22:6). The age to begin training a child depends on his maturity. I have already mentioned what the child has to be taught as soon as he is able to speak. In addition, say the Sages, "As soon as he knows how to wave the 'four species' [on the Festival of Sukkot] the child is obligated to do so; how to wrap himself in a [four-cornered] garment, he is

obligated to attach *tzitzit* [fringes; see Numbers 15:37–41];
how to guard *tefillin* [phylacteries] from uncleanness [that is,
not to enter the lavatory before removing them], his father
buys them for him."[62]

We are told that Shammai the Elder (colleague of Hillel the
Elder, end of first century B.C.E.) was very strict in this regard.
When his daughter-in-law gave birth to a son during the
Festival of Sukkot, he removed the plaster from between the
rafters in the roof of the bedroom and put *sukkah* covering in
the open spaces so that the infant could suckle in a *sukkah*.[63]
Once he refused to feed his young son on Yom Kippur until
the Sages compelled him to do so.[64] His disciples, the school
of Shammai, continued his stringency and ruled that a child
who is not yet able to walk but can be carried on the shoulders
of his father should be taken to the *Bet Ha-Mikdash* in Jerusalem on a Pilgrimage Festival.[65]

TRAINING FOR A LIVELIHOOD

Fulfilling the obligation to marry off a son (marrying off a
daughter is the father's privilege) has been discussed in
Chapter 2. The obligation to teach a son a craft is not specified
in Scripture, but the Sages understood it from a pragmatic
point of view; if not taught a craft, which would enable him to
earn a livelihood for his family, the son might turn out to be a
bandit.

The Sages gave wise advice concerning this paternal obligation. First of all, a son should not be taught a business that
deals exclusively with women, so that he may be kept from
temptation. Furthermore, he should be taught a craft that is
"clean and easy." They argued, "Even though the world

needs both perfumers and tanners, happy is the man whose children are perfumers." One should always pray for success in business: "It is not the craft which brings wealth or poverty; it is God's blessing."[66]

Today Jewish parents strive to fulfill some of this advice. They want to spare their children the struggles and hardships they endured in order to provide for their families. They scrimped and saved so that their children could enter a lucrative profession, particularly in medicine or law. Many a Jewish mother expressed her pride in saying, "My son the doctor" or "My son the lawyer." A more recent trend in Jewish families is for children to pay less attention to their parents' wishes and choose for themselves a career more in accordance with their own inclinations.

One sage added that a father is obliged to teach his son how to swim. A growing child must be taught to become self-sufficient, able to take care of himself and not continue to be dependent on his parents. This transition from dependence to independence must be done in stages; far too often adolescents wish to assert their independence by ignoring the patient guidance of their elders, which they still require. On the other hand, parents must respect and understand this desire for independence on the part of their growing children. Thus, the Sages have warned against a father's whipping his grown-up son, lest this cause the son to rebel against him.[67] Similar advice was given to a father reacting to his young child's misbehavior: "One should not pull his ear before a child [to indicate that he is going to punish him by pulling his ear]; he should either punish him immediately or keep quiet." This advice was given after two examples were cited in which a child whose father had threatened him committed suicide.[68]

Bar Mitzvah

When a boy reaches the age of thirteen he passes from the status of *katan* (minor) to that of *gadol* (adult). The *Halakhah* recognizes him now as a mature person in practically every aspect of Jewish life. Prior to age thirteen he may not serve as a witness in court, but on turning thirteen his testimony is valid. The same applies to the signing of documents, his signature valid only upon his having reached age thirteen.[69] By the same token, the Mishnah rules, "Thirteen years old is the age for performing the *mitzvot*."[70]

Technically speaking, a child reaches his legal majority upon showing signs of puberty, but the assumption is that these signs appear at age thirteen, and no examination of his body—except in questions relating to marriage and divorce—is required before admitting the young man to ceremonies requiring a Jewish adult. He is now counted in a *minyan*, the quorum of ten adults required for the public recitation of certain prayers.[71] And now he may be called up to the congregational reading of the Torah. Indeed, his becoming *Bar Mitzvah* is marked by this honor.

The Sages aver that, coincident with physical maturity, thirteen is also the age when a boy reaches psychological or moral maturity. Commenting upon the passage in Ecclesiastes (4:13), "Better a poor but wise child than an old foolish king," the *Midrash* expounds, " 'the poor wise child' symbolizes the *yetzer tov*, the inclination to do good. Why is it called 'child'? Because it does not attach itself to a person until he reaches age thirteen. Why is it called 'wise'? Because it teaches mankind to follow the proper path. Why is it called 'poor'? Because not many heed its teachings."[72]

We have seen above that before a boy reaches the age of

thirteen, it is the father's responsibility that he perform *mitzvot*; but upon turning thirteen it is the personal responsibility of the child. To mark this transfer the *Midrash* states, "One has to supervise his son up to the age of thirteen; afterward he has to say, 'Blessed [is He] that He has relieved me from punishment because of this child [when he misbehaved].' "[73] It is said by the father when the *Bar Mitzvah* completes his reading of the Torah portion.

THE *BAR MITZVAH* CELEBRATION

We do not find in the Talmud or in the posttalmudic writings any mention of a special ceremony or celebration on the occasion of a boy's becoming *Bar Mitzvah*. However, by the sixteenth century we find discussions among the halakhists as to whether the festive meal in honor of a *Bar Mitzvah* is in the category of a *se'udah shel mitzvah*, a religiously sanctioned meal.[74] As time went on, the celebration of a *Bar Mitzvah* took a more fixed routine. If called up to the Torah on *Shabbat*, he is usually called up to the concluding section, the *Maftir*, so that he can chant the *Haftarah*, the reading from the Prophets. If he is competent, he reads the entire weekly portion from the Torah scroll, which requires much preparation since it does not have phonetic or cantillation signs. Frequently, a youngster begins training for his *Bar Mitzvah* duties many months before the crucial day arrives.[75]

Just as a groom is pelted with sweets from the women's gallery, so is the *Bar Mitzvah* after he finishes reading from the Torah, and the young children scramble to pick them up. Invariably, the rabbi of the congregation delivers from the pulpit a special message to the *Bar Mitzvah*, admonishing him to live up to his newly acquired obligation to observe the *mitzvot* of the Torah. After the services, the congregation is usually invited by the boy's parents to an elaborate *Kiddush*. A dinner in celebration of the occasion is held for family and friends, either on *Shabbat* or some weekday evening. There is a modern tendency to have very lavish and costly *Bar Mitzvah* celebrations, even providing entertainment not in keeping with the spirit of the occasion, a tendency decried by many spiritual leaders. To make the festivities appropriate for a *se'udah shel mitzvah*, "words of Torah"—a message based on Scripture and/or Talmud—must be delivered. Hence, the custom is for the *Bar Mitzvah* boy himself to deliver a speech, at which time he also expresses his gratitude to his parents for his benevolent upbringing.

Ever since the Six-Day War in 1967, when the Israeli defense forces captured the Old City of Jerusalem and gave Jews access to the Western Wall, it has become customary for *Bar Mitzvah* boys to be called up to the Torah at the Wall on a Monday or Thursday or on *Rosh Chodesh*, days when the Torah is read. Parents may prefer to have their son called up on a weekday since traveling to the celebration is not prohibited as it is on *Shabbat*.

Now that I have discussed the obligations that Jewish law has imposed on a father toward his son, I must discuss the obligations of the son to his father. In this area, practically all distinctions based on gender do not apply; both father and mother, as well as son and daughter, are treated equally.

The Severity of Offending Parents

In no other code, ancient or modern, do we find such harsh punishment for offenses against parents on the part of children as that legislated by the Torah: "Who strikes his father or his mother shall be put to death" (Exodus 21:15); "Who curses his father or his mother shall be put to death" (Exodus 21:17, Leviticus 20:9). The Sages qualify "striking" only if the child inflicts a wound; for a mere slap he would not incur the penalty of death. The Talmud raises an interesting question: Does the injunction against inflicting a wound apply even to a son who is a surgeon; is he allowed to operate on his father or mother? The answer is "Yes," though some Sages would not allow their son to remove from them a thorn stuck in the flesh, or lance a blister, lest inadvertently they might inflict a wound.[76]

HONOR YOUR FATHER AND YOUR MOTHER

Being admonished against offending one's parents is not enough; the Torah commanded that we pay homage to them. In the Decalogue we are commanded to *honor* father and mother (Exodus 20:12); in Leviticus, chap. 19, the so-called Holiness Code, we are commanded to *revere* father and mother.[77] The Sages explain how we are to fulfill these commandments. To "revere" obliges us not to stand in father's place[78] not to sit in his place (i.e., the seat usually occupied by him in the home), nor to contradict him.[79] To "honor" obliges us to feed him and give him drink, to clothe him and assist him in going and coming.[80]

A discussion arose about honoring parents when expenditures are involved; who provides the money, the parent or the child? The ruling is: If the parent has his own means, he must bear the expense; if he lacks the means, the child has to provide the necessities out of his own pocket.[81] Important is the manner in which the assistance is given, as illustrated in the following examples given in the Jerusalem Talmud.

There was a man who would feed his father fattened fowl. Once his father asked him, "Son, where do you get all this?" He replied, "Old man, eat and keep quiet, like dogs that eat and keep quiet." There was another man, a miller, whose elderly father was being conscripted for the king's service. The son said to his father, "Father, you tend to the mill; I will serve the king in your place. If they abuse me, better me than you; if they whip me, better me than you." The first son—avers the Talmud—though he fed his father fattened fowl, will inherit *Gehenna*; the second son, though he tied his father to the mill, will inherit *Gan Eden*.[82]

The importance of this *mitzvah* of honoring parents is underscored in that it is included in the Decalogue, which adds the reward "That your days be lengthened" (Exodus 20:12). Indeed, the Sages equate the honoring of parents with honoring Heaven and recount many instances illustrating the extent to which a child must go in order to fulfill the *mitzvah*. It is related of a jeweler, a non-Jew in the city of Ashkelon by the name of Dama ben Netina, that the Sages wanted to purchase from him very costly precious gems for the High Priest's vestment. It so happened that the key to the gems was under the pillow of his sleeping father, and he would not disturb his father's sleep. (Apparently, the Sages then went to another jeweler and Dama lost the sale.) However, the following year he received his reward. A red heifer was born in his herd (see Numbers, chap. 13), and the Sages went to Dama to purchase it (its rarity makes it very costly). Dama said to them, "I know you, that if I were to demand of you any amount of money for the heifer you would pay it. However, I will demand of you only the amount I lost because of honoring my father." Furthermore, Dama would not act disrespectfully to his parents even if they embarrassed him in public. Once, while sitting in silk robes among the elite of Rome, his mother came and tore his robe, hit him on the head, and spit in his face, yet he did not shame her. Another example of diligence in honoring parents is that of Rabbi Tarfon. Once his mother went for a stroll on *Shabbat* and her shoe fell off, so he put his two hands under her feet and she walked on them till she reached her bed. Also, every time that his mother wanted to go to bed and she found it difficult to mount, he would crouch down by the bed so that she could use his back as a step.[83]

The Sages did set certain limits to the obligation to honor parents, which includes obedience to their demands. If a parent asks a child to commit a transgression—for example, he is asked to perform a service that entails desecration of the Sabbath—he may not do so; obeying God's command is superior to obeying a father's command.[84] Many halakhists rule that a son need not obey a father when the latter objects to his marrying a certain woman or conversely insists that he marry a certain woman. The same applies to an unmarried son's desire to leave home in order to study Torah under a certain master; he may do so despite his father's objection.[85]

The Sages also ruled that one must honor one's parents even after their demise. During the parents' lifetime a child does not call his or her parents by their first names, a familiarity that leads to disrespect. Rather, a father should be called *"Abba"* ("Father" or "Daddy") and a mother *"Imma"* ("Mother" or "Mommy"). After their demise, one should add, "May his (her) memory be a blessing."[86] Invariably, when a child quotes his or her father or mother, he or she refers to them as *avi mori*, "my father, my teacher," or *imi morati*, "my mother, my teacher."[87]

KADDISH

Jewish children honor the memory of their deceased parents primarily by observing the laws of mourning.[88] Though technically speaking, the period of mourning for a deceased relative is thirty days from the day of death,[89] for parents it has been increased by the Sages to twelve months. During this period the garment torn at the time of death (keriah) is not to be repaired, and the children refrain from participating in festive affairs. It is during this period that the sons recite the Kaddish, the prayer for mourners, beginning at the burial service and continuing at all congregational services. Since the period of purgatory during which sinners are punished in Gehenna is twelve months,[90] and it is not seemly for a son to assume that his parent is among the full-time sinners, the period of saying Kaddish has been reduced to eleven months. Kaddish is also recited every year on the anniversary of the day of death, known as Yahrzeit. (The calculation of the day of death is made according to the Jewish, and not the secular, calendar.) In talmudic times and later, the custom was for a son to fast on the day of the Yahrzeit.[91] Though the mourner's custom of reciting Kaddish is of posttalmudic origin, legend has it that it was instituted by Rabbi Akiva, who once suggested to an orphan that he lift up his father's soul from purgatory by leading the congregation in prayer. Thus, the greater honor is for the son to lead the congregation in the prayer service, which includes the saying of Kaddish several times. Hence, it is customary for a mourner to conduct the prayer service, especially during the first thirty days after death and on the day of the Yahrzeit. Also, a mourner is called up to the Torah reading on the Sabbath preceding the Yahrzeit.[92]

Several centuries ago halakhists were asked whether

daughters are allowed to recite the *Kaddish* if the parent left no sons. (Daughters, of course, were excluded from leading the prayer services.) Opinions were divided, some rabbis vehemently opposed, while others, more sensitive to feminine emotion, did not object, with the understanding that the daughter is restricted to the women's section in the synagogue. With the recent increase in women's participation in religious ritual, many daughters recite the *Kaddish* even if their brothers are also doing so. Though the *Kaddish* has no direct reference to the departed, it is nevertheless widely observed as a token of respect to parents even by those who are lax in their observance of other rituals.

The memory of departed parents is also honored at festival services with the reciting of the *Yizkor* prayer ("May He remember . . . "). Originally this prayer was recited only on Yom Kippur, the Day of Atonement, when according to the *Midrash* we seek atonement not only for ourselves but also for the departed. This is the custom in many oriental communities today.[93]

In all past Jewish generations, the relationship between parents and children was a happy combination of respect and affection. A token of this respect among oriental Jews, observed to this day, is for the children to stand while their father is called up to the reading of the Torah in the synagogue. However, among modern Westernized Jews, concurrent with the more permissive attitude of parents toward children, the tendency is for parents to act more like "pals" to their children. Consequently, the commandment to revere parents in the traditional way has been weakened. Abandoning the advice to "spare the rod and spoil the child" (Proverbs 13:24), we have succumbed to the Freudian theory that many pathological emotional problems are due to an overbearing parent.

A better understanding of the filial–parental relationship, garnered from Jewish tradition, places the blame for juvenile
delinquency more on the parent's relinquishing his or her
proper role as teacher and moral mentor.

The Sages extended the obligation to honor parents to
include honoring one's stepfather and stepmother, as well as
one's older brother[94] Furthermore, one is obliged to observe
mourning rites for his or her parents-in-law out of respect for
the spouse.[95]

THEOLOGICAL IMPLICATIONS OF THE *MITZVAH* TO HONOR PARENTS

One of the basic principles of Judaism, affirmed repeatedly in
Scripture, is the belief in divine reward for observing the
commandments of the Torah. However, in only two instances does the Torah attach a promise of a reward of good
and lengthy days to the commandment itself: for honoring
father and mother (Exodus 20:12) and for "sending away the
mother bird" before taking her young (Deuteronomy
22:6–7). A tragic incident involving the performance of these
two *mitzvot* led to a fundamental theological principle of
Judaism concerning reward and punishment. Once a father
asked his son to go to the roof and fetch him some fledglings.
The son went up, sent away the mother bird as required by the
Torah, and took the fledglings to bring to his father. Unfortunately, while descending from the roof he fell and died.
"Where," asked the Sages, "is the goodness and length of days
promised the doer of these *mitzvot?*" They therefore came to
the conclusion that reward for fulfilling *mitzvot* is not given in
this world but in the world-to-come, where life is of infinite
goodness and length.[96] The promises of the Torah that obser-

vance of its *mitzvot* will be rewarded with material prosperity are spoken for society in general, not for the individual. As far as the individual is concerned, the advice is, "Do not serve your Master [i.e., God] for the sake of receiving a reward."[97]

Jews who have adhered to the teachings of traditional Judaism have found ample reward, despite persecution and prejudice, in the happiness and contentment they enjoyed within the bosom of the family. It would, however, be self-deluding to assert that all Jewish marriages were a bed of roses. Incompatibility, sharp differences in temperament and outlook, lack of mutual respect and understanding, have made marriage for some an unrealized hope, a bad dream, a chamber of strife and resentment. Contrary to Catholic doctrine, which condemns such unfortunate partners to lifetime misery, the Torah has provided a release from an unsuccessful marriage through the institution of divorce. When and how divorce is implemented is the subject of the second section of this volume.

PART II

DIVORCE IN JEWISH LAW
AND CUSTOM

CHAPTER 9

THE BREAKDOWN OF MARRIAGE: GROUNDS FOR DIVORCE

You cover the altar with tears, weeping and moaning.
But you ask, "Because of what?"
Because the Lord is a witness between you and the
   wife of your youth
With whom you have broken faith
Though she is your partner and your covenanted
   spouse. (Malachi 2:13–14)

THE TRAGEDY OF DIVORCE

The Talmud records an ancient Palestinian custom.[1] When a man got married, people would say to him, "Either *matza*, he found, or *motzei*, I find." They were referring to two biblical verses, reflecting diametrically opposed types of married life, a happy one and an unhappy one. The first verse, "who has found [*matza*] a wife has found goodness" (Proverbs 18:22), speaks of a happy marriage; the second verse, "I find [*motzei*] the wife more bitter than death" (Ecclesiastes 7:26), speaks of the unhappy marriage. "How fortunate," exclaimed one sage, "is the man who found a good wife; how miserable is the man who found a wicked wife."[2]

The unfortunate, indeed tragic, fact of life is that wedded bliss can turn into a chamber of horrors, transforming love into hate and respect into contempt. No better testimony of this can be found than in the divorce courts, with claims and counterclaims, demonstrating that that which heaven designed to be beautiful can become something sordid and ugly. Both Scripture and Sage bemoan this undeniable fact, rebuking thoughtless individuals for taking a precious gift and eroding the happiness it can bring. Thus the Sages comment, "Anyone who divorces his first wife, even the altar sheds tears over him, as it is said, 'You cover the altar with tears . . . the Lord is a witness between you and the wife of your youth with whom you have broken faith' " (Malachi 2:13–14).[3]

I have described earlier the efforts made by individuals in order to restore harmony between husband and wife. Furthermore, certain measures were instituted and certain rules were waived by the religious authorities in order to maintain domestic bliss. We are told that Ezra the Scribe instituted that peddlers make the rounds in the towns to provide cosmetics for the women "so that they do not appear ugly to their husbands."[4] For the same reason the Sages permitted a bride in mourning to pretty herself with cosmetics and jewelry and to wash her face on Yom Kippur.[5] The main idea of granting a woman substantial financial rights as stipulated in her *ketubah* was "that it should not be easy for him to divorce her."[6] Despite all these measures and admonitions, husbands did divorce their wives and Jewish law perforce had to deal with it in all its aspects.

That Scripture looked with disfavor upon divorce, and nevertheless made provision for it, is seen from the following biblical scenario:

> If a man marries a woman and becomes her husband, and it will come to pass that she will not find favor in his eyes because he found in her something indecent, and he wrote for her a bill of divorcement and gave it into her hand and sent her out of his house; and she then left his house and went and became married to another man; and the latter man hated her and wrote for her a bill of divorcement and gave it into her hand and sent her out of his house; or if the latter man who married her should die; then her first husband who sent her away cannot once again marry her after she was defiled, for this is an abomination before the Lord. [Deuteronomy 24:1–4]

Apparently, the Torah is legislating against the temporary exchange of wives, indeed an abomination; thus was it understood by Jeremiah, who railed against such a practice by saying, "Indeed, if a man divorces his wife and she leaves him and became married to another man, can he ever go back to her? Would not such a land be polluted?" (Jeremiah 3:1). Again we see Judaism's affirmation of marriage as being a sacred covenant and at the same time its allowance for its dissolution if the circumstances warrant it. Judaism never did draw the conclusion, as did the New Testament and Catholic doctrine, that "divorce is a sin and inconsistent with the divine institution of marriage"[7] and therefore cannot be effected. It should be pointed out that a second marriage is considered a defilement only with respect to the first husband; there is no biblical restriction against a wife's marrying a third party after the dissolution of the second marriage.

GROUNDS FOR DIVORCE: HATRED

From the above scenario we see that hatred is one of the things that impels a man to divorce his wife.[8] A classic story of love turned into hate is recorded in the Bible (2 Samuel, chap. 13). Amnon, son of King David, fell in love with his half-sister, Tamar, but after she spurned his advances we are told, "Then Amnon felt a very great hatred for her; indeed, his hatred for her was greater than the love he had felt for her." Such instantaneous reversal may be rare, but from Aramaic papyri of the fifth century B.C.E. from the Jewish community in Elephantine in Egypt we learn that a more gradual turning of love into hate was probably not so rare, and it constituted grounds for divorce. Stipulations in several marriage contracts provided for the dissolution of the marriage if one party expressed a hatred for the other. One such contract (*ketubah*) reads:

> Tomorrow or some other day, Anani [the groom] will get up in the Congregation and declare, "I hate my wife Tamat"; he has to pay the price of hating. . . . Tomorrow or some other day, Tamat will get up in the Congregation and declare, "I hate my husband Anani"; upon her falls the financial penalty, and she may go wherever she wishes without further litigation.

Another document of the same period reads, "Tomorrow or some other day Mephatahiah [the wife] will get up in the Congregation and declare, 'I hate my husband As'hur'; upon her falls the financial penalty for hating" and correspondingly for the husband if he initiates the separation.[9]

A lingering practice in later talmudic times of such marriage contracts is recorded in the Jerusalem Talmud[10] as follows: "Those who write [in their *ketubot*] 'If he hates; if she hates,' it is a financial condition [i.e., the penalty imposed on the plaintiff] and therefore is valid." The expression "those who write" indicates that this was an exceptional practice; indeed, not in a single Mishnah in tractate *Ketubot*, nor in any talmudic discussion of the circumstances that lead to the breakdown of a marriage, is there any reference to such a stipulation in a marriage contract. However, a medieval commentator, Rabbi Menachem Ha-Meiri (late thirteenth century), mentions that the teachers of his teachers record that in the period of the *Geonim* (sixth to eleventh centuries) it was customary to include such stipulations in marriage contracts, and furthermore, since the custom became widespread, such a stipulation was implicit even if not written out in the *ketubah*.[11]

A confirmation of this was found in an examination of Palestinian *ketubot* from the Cairo *Genizah*, which revealed that two of fifty *ketubot* contained such a stipulation.[12] Apparently this custom was confined to Palestine, and even there it could not have been as widespread as was claimed by Meiri's teachers. Therefore, it found no place in the discussions in the Babylonian Talmud and its chief commentators. Furthermore, where the papyri indicate that upon such declarations of hating the couple would automatically be divorced without the giving of a divorce document (a *get*), in the talmudic and geonic records it is taken for granted that a properly conducted divorce procedure is required. As we continue our examination of grounds for divorce, we shall see if a petition for divorce on similar grounds was granted in Jewish courts in times past and present.

THE HUSBAND'S PREROGATIVE IN JEWISH DIVORCE

Talmudic law, based on Scripture, affirmed that a husband might divorce his wife of his own volition, without regard to her wishes in the matter. It did, however, affix certain qualifications to this masculine prerogative. The last Mishnah in tractate *Gittin* (Divorces) reads: Bet Shammai declares, "A man should not divorce his wife unless he found in her something indecent,[13] for it is said, 'Because he found in her something indecent' [Deuteronomy 24:1]." Bet Hillel declares, "Even if she burned his food" (i.e., he found something objectionable in her, not necessarily of a sexual nature). Rabbi Akiba says, "Even if he found another woman prettier than his wife, for it is said, 'It will come to pass that she will not find favor in his eyes' [Deuteronomy 24:1]."[14]

The *Halakhah*, following the general principle that in disputes between Bet Shammai and Bet Hillel we rule according to Bet Hillel, rules that a man may divorce his wife if there are some reasonable grounds for his desire.[15] In some instances the court will coerce a man to divorce his wife, for example, if she committed adultery willingly. Discussed both in the Talmud and by posttalmudic authorities is the question of whether a husband whose wife was seen to engage in conduct arousing a suspicion of adultery is obliged to divorce her. Furthermore, if a man divorced his wife because of a rumor that she had an affair with a certain individual, then that individual is forbidden to marry her, and if he did marry her he has to divorce her.[16]

There are other instances in which the court will urge a

husband to divorce his wife, for example, if she dresses immodestly, keeps bad company, or prepares for him nonkosher food while telling him that it is kosher. In fact, the Sages state that it is a *mitzvah* to divorce a wicked woman, namely, one who deliberately does things to cause her husband distress. Nevertheless, eminent sages refused to divorce their irritating wives. Thus, it is related of Rav and his uncle Rabbi Chiyya that they had wives who caused them pain by their contrariness, but would not divorce them. The latter explained, "It is good enough for us to keep them, for they raise our children and save us from sinning [with other women]."[17] In all instances in which the divorce was granted because of the woman's misbehavior, she loses her *ketubah* rights.

Restrictions against arbitrary divorce were in force only when a husband could divorce his wife without her consent. Today, after the *cherem* (ban) of Rabbenu Gershom (who instituted that the wife's consent is a prerequisite to the granting of a divorce), if both husband and wife agree to the divorce there is no such restriction, but it remains for the court to decide as to the extent of the financial benefits due her after the divorce.[18]

WHO IS TO BLAME: HE OR SHE?

As one reviews classic Jewish literature, one perceives a tendency to place the blame for a husband's domestic misery on the nature of the woman. Thus King Solomon, in both Proverbs and Ecclesiastes, does not spare his biting criticism of the promiscuous and the quarrelsome woman, though he does lavish praise on the pious and intelligent woman.[19] Nor did the rabbis of the *Midrash* fail to remark on the disconcerting characteristics of the female, such as her haughtiness, curios-

ity, prattling, jealousy and her being a busybody, an eaves-
dropper, and a gossiper.[20] Disconcerting characteristics,
however, especially quarrelsomeness, are not confined to
women; they are found among men as well[21] and likewise
lead to domestic strife and ultimately to divorce. In fact,
according to one rabbinic record, it seems that as far as being
a good influence on one's spouse, the female surpasses the
male. Thus, it is recorded that a pious man married a pious
woman but they produced no offspring. So they said, "We are
not helping the Almighty at all," and he divorced her. He
married a wicked woman who turned him into a wicked man,
while the first wife married a wicked man and made him
pious. The homily concludes, "You see, everything is from
the woman."[22] A brief survey of grounds for divorce recognized by the *Halakhah* reveals the many causes that bring
about the breakdown of a marriage.

THE JEALOUS HUSBAND, THE STRAYING WIFE

In the Pentateuch, the Torah speaks of a jealous husband who
suspects his wife of infidelity and violating the covenant of
marriage. This is told in the chapter of the *Sotah*, the wife over
whose husband came a fit of jealousy (Numbers 5:12–29), he
suspecting her of having willingly committed adultery. However, there are no witnesses to confirm his suspicion, and
therefore he must bring her to the priest ministering in the
Sanctuary, together with a "meal-offering of jealousy . . .
which recalls sin." The priest prepares "bitter waters that
bring a curse" by putting some earth from the floor of the
Sanctuary in sacred water, writing the curse on parchment
and rubbing it off into the water. He then makes her drink the
water and pronounces the curse, which warns her that if she

indeed did commit adultery the water will cause "her thigh to sag and her belly to distend." If, however, she did not commit adultery, she shall be cleared and will produce children.

The Sages filled in the biblically prescribed procedure with various particulars. Initially, the husband must warn his wife in the presence of witnesses not to be secreted with the suspected paramour, but if she does not heed his warning he will take her to the local court to lodge a complaint, and they will send her to the Great Court in Jerusalem, which will try to persuade her to confess and thus eliminate the need to administer the oath with the bitter waters. They will say to her, "Much sin is done because of wine and frivolity, childishness and evil companions." If she maintains her innocence, she is made a spectacle of derision by publicly letting down her hair and exposing parts of her body, a warning to all women against marital infidelity. If even one witness comes forward and testifies that he saw her commit adultery, she does not go through the ordeal but is divorced without receiving her *ketubah* rights. The Mishnah concludes by recording that Rabban Yohanan ben Zakkai did away with the procedure because there were so many adulterers.[23]

Though the biblical *sotah* is a thing of the past, jealous husbands and wives continued to be subject to rabbinic scrutiny and judgment. One sage considers it a *mitzvah* for a husband to be jealous and remonstrate with his wife if he sees her consorting with another.[24] We are cautioned, however, that there are degrees of jealousy, and an overjealous husband can easily cause a rift between himself and his wife. The Talmud gives three examples of a jealous husband, from one extreme to another: one who locks up his wife in the house before he goes out lest she talk to a stranger;[25] another—the average person—who allows her to speak with her relatives;

the third—a wicked man—who sees his wife dress immodestly in public and mingling with other men but does not divorce her.[26] Standards of dress and associating with other men in public places may have changed, but a jealous husband—and for that matter, a jealous wife—can lead to a breakdown of a happy marriage.

Not only excessive jealousy jeopardizes a marriage; a lack of trust also is a source of domestic dissension that leads to divorce. Thus, the Talmud says that the wife whose husband demands of her an exact accounting of the monies she spends for the usual household expenditures can say to him, "Since you are so exacting with me I cannot live with you."[27] Her complaint is justified on the grounds that "a person cannot live together with a serpent in the one cage," which no doubt also applies to an irascible, constantly faultfinding and nagging spouse.

THE WOMAN'S COMPLAINT[28]

The last Mishnah in tractate *Nedarim* (Vows) reads as follows:

At first they [the Sages] would say, "Three women are divorced" [i.e., the Court compels their husbands to divorce them], taking with them their *ketubah* [i.e., the financial benefits accruing to them from the marriage contract]: She who says, "I am defiled for you" [i.e., I was raped];[29] or "The heavens are between you and me" [i.e., only the heavens can testify that you are impotent];[30] or "I removed myself of Jewish men" [i.e., I vowed not to engage in sexual intercourse]. The Sages then decided that perhaps the woman cast her eyes on another man and wants to get rid of her husband, and therefore in the case of the woman who says, "I am defiled for you" she has to bring proof [that she was raped]; for the woman who says, "The heavens are between you and me" they should effect [a reconciliation] by means of a request;[31] for the woman who says, "I removed myself from Jewish men," he should annul that part of the vow affecting him—thus permitting her to engage in intercourse with him—and she remains removed from all other Jewish men.

Two things are apparent from this Mishnah. First, the basis of marriage is the ability to engage in conjugal relations; if for one reason or another these cannot be satisfied, divorce is justified, even recommended. (In the next chapter we shall see in the case of a spouse's impotence being disclosed after marriage whether the marriage is annulled *ab initio* or a divorce procedure is required.) Second, rabbinic opinion veered from accepting a woman's demand for a divorce as being sincere, to rejecting it on the basis of suspecting her of infatuation with another man. (In today's jaded society, one might say that she simply found her husband boring and therefore is suing for divorce.) The reluctance to accept a woman's complaint and grant a divorce is no doubt based on Judaism's evaluation of the importance of family stability, the family being the major instrument for the transmission of its religious tradition to future generations. That is why a husband is not encouraged to seek out grounds for divorcing his wife. Thus, some latter-day *poskim* are of the opinion that it is not required of the *Bet Din* to seek witnesses to establish the fact of a woman's adultery, and consequently in the absence of the necessary evidence the husband may continue to live with his wife.[32] As we shall see, this ambivalence toward a woman's demand for a divorce has characterized the *Halakhah* from the days of the Talmud to the present day.

In Part I, I mentioned the talmudic statement that the Sages were concerned with the welfare of the daughters of Israel, namely, Jewish women. This can readily be seen in a review of the seventh chapter of tractate *Ketubot*, in which the Mishnah defines the cases in which the court will compel a husband who imposes unreasonable restrictions on his wife to divorce her and pay her the monies due her in accordance with the terms of her *ketubah*. Thus, the husband who denies his wife her conjugal rights, or forbids her to eat certain foods, to use cosmetics and jewelry, to visit her family, to attend a wedding, or visit the house of a mourner, is ordered by the court to divorce his wife and pay her the *ketubah*.[33] Furthermore, if the husband contracts a debilitating disease, the wife is entitled to a divorce.

THE CASE OF THE LOATHSOME HUSBAND

There is one case mentioned in the Talmud[34] that has always been the subject of halakhic controversy. It is the case of the woman who claims that she cannot continue to live with her husband because he is repulsive to her. The exact wording of her complaint is *ma'is alai*, "he is loathsome to me," and she demands a divorce, even willing to forego the financial benefits of her *ketubah*. Generally speaking, the Sephardi authorities were inclined to grant her request, some even granting her some financial benefits. The Ashkenazi authorities were skeptical of her complaint and refused to compel the husband to divorce her. We see this difference in approach in two representative opinions. Maimonides, the outstanding Sephardi halakhist, rules:

A woman who refuses to engage in sexual relations with her husband is called a rebellious wife.[35] They [the court] ask her why she rebelled. If she says, "I loathe him and cannot engage in sexual relations with him," they compel him to divorce her right

away, because she is not like a captive woman who is forced to
submit to one who is hateful to her,[36] and she leaves him without
her *ketubah*.[37]

On the other hand, Rabbi Asher ben Yechiel (the Rosh,
1250–1327), a preeminent Ashkenazi halakhist, writes in a
responsum as follows:

> Jewish women in this generation are impudent. If a woman can
> free herself from her husband by saying "I don't want him," no
> Jewish daughter will continue to live with her husband, for they
> will cast their eyes upon another and rebel against their husbands.
> Therefore it is best to keep away from compelling [the husband
> to divorce her].[38]

Until very recently, rabbis followed this hard-line opinion
and refused to rule that the husband is obliged, let alone
compelled, to divorce his wife, unless there is an objective
evaluation that her claim is justified. However, in view of the
changes that have taken place in contemporary society, some
poskim have ruled that *ma'is alai* is sufficient grounds to order a
divorce.[39] No longer can it be asserted, as did a talmudic sage
centuries ago, "A woman prefers an unhappy married life
than to dwell as a widow [i.e., single]."[40]

THE HUSBAND WHO DISAPPEARED: THE *AGUNAH*

The Mishnah, at the very beginning of tractate *Kiddushin*
(Betrothals), reminds us that a marriage is terminated not only
by divorce; the demise of one of the partners also dissolves the
marital union. However, there is the anomalous case of the
"living widow," whose husband has left home and failed to
return when expected, and efforts to contact him were fruit-

less. In other words, he disappeared. In Jewish law there is no presumption of death even after a person's many years of absence. Until the religious authority or the *Bet Din* receives concrete evidence that the husband has indeed died, it will not issue a permit to the wife to remarry. She remains bound by the ties of marriage, anchored to him even though he is missing, and therefore she is known as an *agunah*, whose root meaning is "anchor."

Volumes have been written by the halakhists over the centuries in order to solve the problem of these hapless *agunot*. The Talmud has laid down very strict rules of evidence in such cases, essentially requiring positive identification of the corpse if found. Thus, in the case of a husband who was shipwrecked on the high seas and his body was not found, the presumption is that he may finally have made his way to some distant shore and is unable or unwilling to return to his wife.

Several stories are related in the Talmud to confirm such a presumption. Thus Rabbi Akiba relates:

> Once I was traveling in a ship and I saw another ship nearby being shipwrecked, and I was distressed at the loss of a great scholar, Rabbi Meir [who was aboard that ship]. When I arrived in Cappodoceia, he came and sat before me and engaged with me in an halakhic discussion. I asked him, "My son, who raised you [from the sea]?" He answered, "One wave pushed me on to another, and the other to another, until they threw me up on shore." At that time, I said, "How great are the words of the Sages when they said, If a man drowned in a limited body of water [i.e., its limits are within eyesight, then even if his body was not found] his wife is permitted to remarry;[41] in an unlimited body of water [and his body was not found] his wife is forbidden to remarry [perhaps he resurfaced and is still alive].[42]

Nevertheless, the Sages took cognizance of the desperate situation of the woman whose husband has disappeared and

relaxed the biblical rules of testimony that require two qualified witnesses in all major cases. Thus, they ruled that even if
only one otherwise unqualified person (e.g., a woman)—
indeed, even if the wife herself—testifies that the husband
died, the wife is permitted to remarry, but she will suffer a
severe penalty if such testimony is proved to be false by the
husband's return.[43]

Especially in times of war, when there are losses on the
battlefield and bodies may lose signs of identification, the
problem of the *agunah* becomes acute. Shortly after World
War II, during which millions of Jews were incinerated in the
Nazi crematoria, rabbis were faced with thousands of men
and women whose spouses were lost and whose bodies could
not be identified. Following certain precedents, rabbis began
to argue in favor of presumptive evidence. Thus, if witnesses
testified that they saw a particular individual being taken into
one of the wagons that led to a crematorium and he did not
show up for at least one year after the end of the war, he was
presumed dead and his wife was given permission to remarry.
An analogous case is that of the wives of the crew of the
Israeli submarine *Dakar*, lost without a trace in the Mediterranean. Rabbi Goren, then chief rabbi, argued that in view of
today's modern methods of search, if all efforts to find the
missing men fail we can halakhically assume that they have
drowned, and their wives may remarry. Even more recently,
the chief rabbis in Israel ruled in a case of victims in a plane
crash, in which there were no survivors and the bodies could
not be identified, that the passengers are presumed dead
and their wives may remarry. Here we see how the *Halakhah*
as "a law of life" adapts its rulings to unprecedented
circumstances.

In the next chapter I discuss the case of a different *agunah*,
whose husband is alive and present but refuses to release his

wife from the ties of marriage by his refusal to give her the Jewish bill of divorcement, the *get*.

Now that we have reached the point where the court (*Bet Din*) authorizes the granting of a divorce, we turn to the actual mechanics of writing and delivering the divorce document, which is the subject of the next chapter.

CHAPTER 10

THE RITE OF JEWISH DIVORCEMENT: THE GET

IN BIBLICAL TIMES

From the verses about divorce quoted in the previous chapter we learn how a husband in biblical times would proceed in order to divorce his wife. He would first write a special document of divorcement called *sefer keritut* (literally, "a bill of sundering"), then hand it over to her and send her out of his house. He would do so if he found that she acted indecently (it is not clear if she actually committed adultery)[1] or if he simply hated her. There is no indication that in order to divorce his wife a man would have to appear before any judicial body or the elders of the community.

To date, no divorce document from the First Temple period has been discovered, and so we do not know the wording of the *sefer keritut*. We do know that it was written by the husband and handed over to the wife with some expression

185

that he is sending her out of his house. It should be noted, however, that when Sarah demanded that her husband Abraham send Hagar out of his house, she used the term *garesh*, "drive out," much stronger than *shalach*, "send out," as in the previously quoted passages. In subsequent halakhic literature, the harsher term became the common usage, and divorce was henceforth called *geirushin*.

TALMUDIC EXPOSITION

In the course of the centuries, each generation of halakhic teachers expounded the laws of Jewish divorcement, so that in addition to the basic rules found in tractate *Gittin* (Divorces) of the Talmud, we now have numerous rules and regulations governing every jot and tittle of the procedure. In fact, in the nineteenth century the detractors of rabbinic law by the so-called *maskilim*, "intellectuals," wrote diatribes mocking the rabbis for insisting on all the halakhic minutiae, the absence of any one of them possibly rendering the *get* invalid. Many of the regulations were controversial, some authorities insisting upon them, others considering them inessential. Maimonides, in his Laws Concerning Divorce,[2] distinguishes between two categories of defects in the writing and delivering of a *get*: (1), in which the *get* is totally invalid according to biblical law, and if delivered is of no consequence and the woman remains married to her husband; and (2), in which the invalidity is only according to rabbinic law. With such a *get*, the woman should not marry another until she receives a proper *get*, but if she does remarry she may remain with her second husband. The difference between the two is also crucial as far as the children of the second marriage are concerned; if that marriage was entered into after the first kind of invalid *get*, the children are *mamzerim*, for the woman is considered still married to her first husband; if it was entered into with the second kind of *get*, the children are not considered *mamzerim*.

Then there also are supererogatory directives to which the writer of a *get* should adhere as a matter of custom, but they do not affect its validity if inadvertently ignored. To facilitate the procedure of divorcement, including both the writing and the delivery of the *get*, latter-day authorities have composed a *seder ha-get*, outlining in detail the procedure step-by-step.[3] Later we shall see how the various biblical terms for divorce were incorporated in the bill of divorcement instituted by the Sages of the Talmud.

THE SERIOUSNESS OF THE PROCEDURE

Since the entire procedure is crucial in changing the status of the woman from an *eshet ish*, a married woman, to a "free" or available woman, the ceremony must be conducted with scrupulous attention to all the rules established by the *Halakhah*. To highlight the seriousness with which the rabbis regarded the Jewish divorce procedure, I present the famous case known as "The *Get* of Cleves," which involved a dozen of the leading halakhic authorities in sharp and bitter controversy. In 1776, a young Jew of Mannheim, Germany, married a young woman from Bonn. A few days after the wedding, the groom, who acted rather strangely, told his bride's family that he could not remain in Germany, and that he was ready to give his wife a *get*. The *get* was duly given in the town of Cleves on the German-Dutch border. A short time later, the father of the groom claimed that the *get* was given in order to extort the dowry, and he turned to the rabbi of Mannheim, who decided that the *get* was invalid on the grounds that the groom was not of sound mind at the time of giving the *get*. As was not unusual, the rabbi of Mannheim turned to the *Bet Din* of Frankfurt for confirmation of his decision, which it gave. The rabbi of Cleves, on the other hand, turned to other halakhic luminaries—a veritable "Who's Who" of halakhic scholars from Western Germany and Holland—who sided with him. The controversy raged for almost a year, with scores of *responsa* written on the question. The issue died down after the groom "remarried" his bride, but the case was recorded for posterity in several volumes.

Because of this possibility of questioning the validity of a *get* after its delivery, centuries earlier Rabbenu Tam (twelfth century) had already issued a decree against questioning the validity of a *get* after its delivery, provided the arranger was recognized as a reliable scholar. If some of the documents that are ancillary to the *get* were found upon inspection to be improperly drawn, the assumption was that the arranger was not competent, and in such case the validity of the *get* had to be ascertained by a qualified authority.

I have already mentioned the talmudic statement that "he who is not familiar with the nature of divorce and betrothal should not involve himself in them,"[4] and in the Talmud we find that a particular rabbi was designated by the religious leader of the community to be in charge of conducting divorce procedures.[5] To make sure that it is not conducted in haste, it should not be planned for a Friday, the eve of the Sabbath. And it should be started in the earlier part of the day, for if the writing is completed just before sundown, but before the husband can hand over the *get* it was already nighttime, the *get* is invalid.[6]

DIVORCE: A RELIGIOUS COURT PROCEDURE

In Chapter 9 I cited certain stipulations in marriage contracts of the fifth century B.C.E., in which the plaintiff for a divorce gets up in the Congregation and declares his or her intention to divorce. In talmudic times a couple who decided to divorce had to appear before a rabbinic authority or *Bet Din*, who would decide whether a petition for divorce is justified, and if so, instruct the husband to give his wife a bill of divorcement.[7] It should be clear that the decision of the religious authority that the couple be divorced did not—and does not to this day—constitute the act of divorcement, as it does in civil non-Jewish courts. In Judaism, it is only the actual transfer of the bill of divorcement from the husband, or his duly appointed agent, to the wife, or her duly appointed agent, that constitutes the act of divorcement. The religious authority does rule, however, as to the financial and property rights of the parties, which to a large extent depend upon the motivation for the divorce.

The Sages built their rulings in divorce procedures upon the language and the exposition of the verses in Deuteronomy cited earlier. Thus when they ruled that the woman should be divorced they used the term *yotzeit*, "she goes out," from the word *ve-yatzah* in Scripture (Deuteronomy 24:2). The bill of divorcement they called *get*, the Aramaic term for documents in general,[8] but in the *get* itself it is denominated by the Aramaic form of the biblical *sefer keritut*. In fact, the Sages gave three different Hebrew-Aramaic names to the divorce document: a book of driving out (Genesis 21:10), an epistle of leaving (Isaiah 54:6), and a document of sending away (Jeremiah 3:1). In the course of this discussion we shall see how their interpretations led to a host of rulings, which in effect have made the writing of a *get* a rather complicated procedure.

CONSENT UNDER COMPULSION

A basic rule in the giving of a divorce is the consent of the husband. (A later regulation of Rabbenu Gershom provided for the consent of the wife as well.) Nevertheless, in the many cases cited in Chapter 9 the *Halakhah* has ruled that the husband is compelled to divorce his wife. This has raised a basic question: Is consent given under compulsion valid consent? In connection with the bringing of an obligatory offering to the Temple—which requires the consent of the offerer[9]—the Talmud rules, "We force him [to bring the offering] until he says 'I am willing.' "[10] The same resolution of the contradiction between compulsion and consent was applied to the giving of a *get* under compulsion; we compel the husband until he says "I am willing."[11]

Maimonides offers a rational explanation of this resolution as follows:

> We do not say that a person acted under duress [and consequently the act is void] unless he was pressed and forced to do something that he is not obligated by the Torah to do—for example, he was beaten until he sold or gave something away. But a person whose evil inclination took hold of him, forcing him not to perform a certain *mitzvah* or commit a transgression and was whipped [by the religious authorities] until he did what he was obliged [by the Torah] to do . . . he was not acting under duress because of us; rather, he had forced himself [to be compelled] because of his corrupt opinion. Therefore, one who doesn't want to divorce his wife yet wants to be considered a Jew and wants to perform all the *mitzvot* and keep away from transgressions but his evil incli-

nation takes hold of him, since he is whipped until his evil inclination is weakened and he says, "I am willing," he is already giving the divorce willingly.[12]

This rationalization has led to serious reservations against using compulsion if the husband is an apostate Jew or one who does not observe any *mitzvot* of the Torah; for we cannot say of him, "Yet he wants to be considered a Jew and wants to perform all the commandments." Unfortunately, this is the situation in many cases today and is the reason for the reluctance of the rabbinic courts to employ physical compulsion.[13]

METHODS OF COMPULSION

King Solomon avers, "With words alone a slave cannot be disciplined" (Proverbs 29:19), and therefore the Sages ruled that words are not sufficient to compel a recalcitrant husband to give his wife a *get*, and he must be whipped until he says, "I agree."[14] In general, by the late Middle Ages most Jewish communities abandoned the practice sanctioned by the Talmud of administering lashes to enforce compliance with Jewish law[15] and substituted the *cherem* or excommunication. In the case of compelling to give a *get*, even that was considered too harsh a method, and instead they substituted some form of social ostracism, and that is the normal practice today. In the State of Israel, the rabbinic courts are empowered to imprison a recalcitrant husband, though this power has rarely been exercised.[16] Instead, the court prefers to levy a heavy fine by raising the amount of alimony the husband is obliged to pay. Nevertheless, the problem remains universal, wherever vindictive or blackmailing husbands are obdurate in their refusal to free their wives from the bonds of a marriage that has become intolerable and has led to the physical separation of the couple. To alleviate this problem, rabbis are suggesting that it become standard practice to include in the writing of the *ketubah* a stipulation that will impose a heavy fine upon a husband who refuses to give a *get* when ordered to do so by a rabbinic court.[17] As yet, the established Orthodox rabbinic bodies have failed to implement these suggestions and to respond to the plight of these women, the *agunot*, anchored to their husbands though no longer sharing their lives with them.

COMPULSION THROUGH A NON-JEWISH AUTHORITY

For much of Jewish history, Jews living under non-Jewish regimes enjoyed a large measure of autonomy as far as their internal religious life was concerned. Their religious leaders, rabbis learned in Jewish law, wielded much authority over the members of their community, even to the extent of punishing those who deviated from the normative practices of Judaism. However, there were occasions when the rabbis were unable to enforce their decisions over rebelling members, and they had to resort to the more potent powers of the non-Jewish authorities. One such occasion arose when a recalcitrant husband refused to obey the order of the Jewish tribunal to divorce his wife. Thus, the Talmud found it necessary to lay down the following rule: a *get* compelled by Jewish authorities is valid; by non-Jewish authorities it is invalid. When resorting to non-Jews, they beat him and say to him, "Do what the Jews tell you to do."[18]

An interesting question arose among halakhists concerning the stipulations in marriage contracts that impose a heavy fine on a recalcitrant husband. Suppose the husband refuses to pay the fine, can the injured wife present her claim in a secular court that has the means to enforce payment? For the legalists in the United States, where the constitution provides for the separation of state and religion, the question revolves around the jurisdiction of the secular court in a matter that might be regarded as purely religious. For the halakhists, the question revolves around the employment of a non-Jewish authority to enforce payment that in consequence compels the husband to abandon his refusal and to grant the *get*. Is this a *get* enforced by non-Jewish authorities and consequently of dubious validity?[19] The question, to date, is still debatable in both jurisdictions.[20]

PRELIMINARY PREPARATIONS FOR THE WRITING OF A GET

Since the Torah calls the divorce document *Sefer Keritot,* a book of sundering, the Sages ruled that in certain respects the writing of the divorce document must be similar to the writing of a *sefer Torah*. Thus, it has to be written and not stamped as with a seal.[21] Shortly after the invention of printing, the question was raised as to whether a *get* could be printed (is it considered stamping?), and it was decided that printing is not a valid method. By the same analogy, it was ruled that the *get* has to be written by a qualified scribe with a quill on durable material, preferably parchment, with durable ink. It is customary for the *get* to be written in twelve lines, which are marked with a stylus prior to the writing.[22] Since the scribe is acting as the agent of the husband, the paper, the ink and the quill must be the property of the husband, and therefore it is customary for the scribe to hand over these items to the husband, who takes possession of them, and he then hands them back to the scribe.[23] Incidentally, it is the husband who has to pay the fee for the supervising rabbi, the scribe, and the witnesses. However, the Sages instituted that if the husband refuses to pay, the wife may do so in order to expedite the writing.

In addition to arranging for a scribe, the officiant must arrange for the presence of two qualified witnesses who are able to read the document and sign their names in proper Hebrew.[24] The rabbi must explain to the parties and to the witnesses the nature of the ceremony. All the persons involved should be sober and aware of the seriousness of the occasion. I have already mentioned that a *get* must be given by the husband of his own free will. To make sure that this is so, the husband must make a declaration that he is not giving the *get* under any constraint whatsoever, and that he did not make any prior statement to the effect that his giving the *get* is under duress. As far as the woman is concerned, ever since the *cherem* of Rabbenu Gershom (eleventh century) her consent is also required, and she must declare that she is accepting the *get* of her own free will.

LISHMAH, FOR THE SPECIFIC PURPOSE

From the phrase "and he shall write for her," the Sages derived a basic rule, namely, that the divorce document must be written *lishmah*, that is, for this particular wife, and so must the scribe say expressly when he begins writing. In addition, the scribe adds that he is writing for this particular husband and for the express purpose of divorce. Similar statements are made by the witnesses, that they are signing for this particular husband and wife for the purpose of divorce. Thus, a scribe cannot write up a number of *gittin* (plural of *get*) to keep in stock for some future divorce, nor can a supply of *gittin* be printed.[25] The scribe actually acts as the agent of the husband, who must order the scribe to write for him a *get* for the specific purpose of divorcing his wife. Ever since the invention of the telephone, rabbis have debated whether a husband, who happens to be in a place where there is no scribe, can give the order over the phone.[26]

The Names of the Parties

"For this particular woman and for this particular husband" implies that they must be identified as such. This is done by ascertaining their names, which must be spelled correctly in the divorce document, leaving absolutely no ambiguity. This requirement has led to an almost infinite number of problems, which in turn led to the writing of numerous *responsa* and the composition of special tracts listing the various names adopted by Jews. Invariably, Jews living in different countries with different languages adopted names in the vernacular, and these must be transliterated into Hebrew. Furthermore, most people have both personal names given shortly after their birth—for males at the circumcision ceremony (*brit milah*), and for females when the father is called up to the Torah reading—and different derivatives of those names given by family and friends, by which they are better known and more readily identified. Also in many cases, at a time of serious illness anxious relatives would add names to those given at birth, to ward off the angel of death.[27] The rabbi conducting the procedure must decide which names to include and their proper spelling, and in the case of two names (e.g., one Hebrew and the other non-Hebrew) which to write first. It is Sephardi practice to add to the names the phrase "and every name and nickname that he (she) has." Proper identification and spelling must also be ascertained for the name of the city in which the document is being written. In many instances, Jews called the city in which they resided one way, and the Gentiles another way (e.g., Cracow in Poland was called by Jews by its earlier name, Cazmiri). A city was also identified by its river, and it became customary not to write a *get* in a city that had no river.

Up until several hundred years ago—the exact time depending on the particular regime—Jews did not use family names.[28] A Jew was known by his personal name and the name of his father (occasionally of his mother), and to this day this is the way a Jew is called up to the Torah reading. If a Jew moved from his native town, he was often referred to in his new place of residence by adding to his name the name of the town from which he came. (Eventually, the name of the town became the family name.) Family names for Jews came into vogue initially at the insistence of the local government, but by now they have become accepted practically for all purposes. Nevertheless, the laws of writing bills of divorcement did not change with the times, and the ruling of the *Shulchan Arukh*, that we do not write in a *get* the family name, remains.[29]

The exact date of the writing, including the day of the week and the Jewish month, is an absolute requisite. After the death of Alexander the Great in 323 B.C.E., Jews generally adopted for all their documents, including the *get*, that date as the year 1. This dating is known as *minyan sh'tarot*, dating of documents. However, in talmudic times most communities dated their documents according to the years of the reigning monarch.[30] It seems that Ashkenazic Jewry had in the early middle ages adopted the *minyan yetzirah*, dating from the Creation, though Sephardic Jewry used the *minyan sh'tarot* well into the Middle Ages. By now, the universal practice is for all Jewry to use the *minyan yetzirah* for all *ketubot* and *gittin.*[31]

THE DOCUMENT

As is the case with the *ketubah*, the *get* is written in Aramaic, the common language in the days of the Talmud and the *Geonim*. Today, despite suggestions that these documents be written in Hebrew, rabbis have opposed any departure from traditional practice even though it has become archaic. What is strange is the argument advanced by the opponents of change, namely, that we cannot translate accurately from Aramaic to Hebrew. The contrived nature of this argument is seen in the fact that crucial terms in the *get* are in themselves translations into Aramaic from the original biblical Hebrew.[32] Following is an English rendition of the document:

On the . . . day of the week, the . . . day of the month[33] . . ., in the year . . . *anno mundi* according to the number [of years] that we count here in (name of place of writing), I Yaakov called Jacob called Jack, son of Yitzchak called Isaac, standing today in [name of place], desire of my own free will, without any duress, to leave and release and divorce you my wife Sarah called Surka, daughter of Moshe called Moses called Morris, standing today [if applicable] in . . ., who has previously been my wife, and now I release and send away and divorce you so that you will be free and govern yourself to go and be married to any man you desire, and let no person oppose you, from this day and forever, and behold you are permitted [to be married] to every person. And this shall be for you from me a bill of divorcement and an epistle of sending away and a bill of releasing according to the law of Moses and Israel.[34]

_____ Witness

_____ Witness

TRANSFER OF THE *GET*

After the scribe has completed the writing of the *get* and the ink has dried, the two witnesses read it and then affix in turn their signatures, comprised of their proper name and that of their father (i.e., the name by which they are called up to the reading of the Torah). Again the document is read word for word by the supervising rabbi and the witnesses, the scribe certifying that he wrote it specifically for the parties named therein. The woman is then asked if she is ready to accept the *get* of her own free will. The *get* is then folded and handed over to the husband. The witnesses are then charged to witness its transfer from the husband to the wife. The husband raises his hand above his wife's hand and says to her, "Behold this is your *get*. Accept it for with it you will be divorced from me from this moment and be permitted [to be married] to all men," and drops it into her hand. (The declaration is made in Hebrew and, if necessary, translated into a language understood by the parties.) After the woman grasps the *get* firmly in both hands, it is taken by the rabbi to be read once again by him and the witnesses. He then makes a cut in the document, to indicate that it has been used to execute the divorce, and issues a certificate attesting to the fact that she has been divorced. The rabbi then admonishes the woman not to remarry before the lapse of ninety days to make sure of the paternity of a child that may be born after she remarries. (A child born in less than three months after the divorce may be either a prematurely born child of the second husband or a full-term child of the first husband.) The rabbi also admonishes her not to marry a *kohen*, who is enjoined by the Torah against marrying a divorcée, and not to live in close proximity to her former husband lest they be tempted by virtue of their erstwhile familiarity to resume their intimate relationship.

DELIVERY BY MESSENGER OR POST

If the wife happens to be in another city at the time of the writing of the *get*, or even if she is in the same city but refuses to accept the *get* directly from her husband, he appoints a specific person to act as a messenger on his behalf and deliver the *get* to her personally; for a general rule in Jewish law states, "A person's agent is as the person himself." In addition to the *get*, the agent is given a power of attorney (*harshaah*) to testify that he was appointed to act on the husband's behalf. It includes certain signs (usually holes punched in the document in specified places) to identify the document as the one written specifically for the parties named therein. Of course, arrangements had to be made for a rabbi residing in the locale where the *get* is to be delivered to supervise its delivery and to execute its transfer in the halakhically proper manner.

Several hundred years ago the question was raised whether a *get* can be sent by the postal service, some *poskim* objecting on the basis of certain rulings in the Talmud.[35] However, other *poskim* were able to argue the halakhic propriety of such procedure, and now it is a means of delivery accepted by all. In such a case, the husband personally appoints an agent present at the writing of the *get*, who then appoints another agent residing in the wife's locality, and the document together with the *harshaah* is mailed to the supervising rabbi in the wife's locality.

CONDITIONAL DIVORCES

A *get* may be handed over to a woman with the husband specifying that it should become effective only if a certain condition is met. (A condition is not written in the document itself; it is only expressed verbally at the time of transfer.) This was a frequent procedure in talmudic times on two occasions. The first was when the husband was about to embark on a long journey. Travel in those days was quite hazardous, and means of communication between distant places were sparse, so the husband would say, "This is your *get* on condition that I do not return home within twelve months."[36] Thus, if he did not return within the specified time, and presumably he may never return, she need not remain an *agunah*; she is divorced and may be married to another. The second occasion was when a man was seriously ill and the couple had no children—in which case if he dies, his wife would be subject to the law of *Yibbum*, the levirate marriage, which in most cases they sought to avoid. The husband would give his wife a *get* on condition that it be effective only if he dies from this sickness. If he recovers, no harm was done and they could resume their normal relationship. If he died, she was exempt from the law of *Yibbum* since she was considered divorced from the day of the giving of the *get*.[37]

The Talmud says that every soldier in King David's army gave a conditional *get* to his wife before leaving for the battlefield, so that in the event he was killed or captured she would be free to remarry.[38] In both world wars in this century, the suggestion was made by several rabbis that Jewish soldiers write such a *get* before going off to battle. However, a doubt as to the effectiveness of such a *get* was raised inasmuch as soldiers would from time to time return home on leave and have conjugal relations with their wives and thus render the *get* invalid, necessitating the writing of a new *get* each time a soldier returns to the battlefield, a rather cumbersome procedure.[39] Furthermore, couples were reluctant to go through the ceremony of a divorce based on the possibility of the husband's being missing in action, and the suggestion was not implemented.

THE ANNULMENT OF MARRIAGE

The first Mishnah in tractate *Kiddushin* (Betrothal) states that a woman gains her freedom from her husband—enabling her, if she wishes, to marry another—in one of two ways: either by means of a *get* or by the demise of her husband. There is, however, a third way in which the bond of marriage is sundered: if the marriage is declared by the religious authority to have been invalid *ab initio*. Even though the couple may have lived together as husband and wife and may have produced offspring, they can separate and marry another without benefit of a *get*.

A marriage can be declared null and void in one of several instances:

1. There was no religious ceremony of the marriage, for example, a common-law marriage, or one registered only by a civil authority. Many halakhic authorities in such cases ask the husband to give his wife a *get* in order to remove any doubt as to the permissibility of remarriage. However, if the husband absolutely refuses, or if he is unavailable, the permission to remarry without a *get* would be granted.[40]

2. There was a defect in the marriage ceremony, for example, there were no proper witnesses to the ceremony.[41] It is on this basis that the late Rabbi Moshe Feinstein ruled that a marriage performed by a Conservative or Reform rabbi is null and void, the assumption being that such officiants did not observe the halakhic requirements for the *Kiddushin*.[42]

3. The marriage was entered into under false pretenses, for example, one of the parties was represented as enjoying a certain status or possessing certain conveniences, and it was later ascertained that the representations were false.[43]

4. If a stipulation was made at the time of the marriage that it is being entered into under certain conditions and it was

later ascertained that these conditions were not maintained, for example, the groom said, "I marry you on condition that you [the bride] have no physical blemish," but it was later established that she did have a blemish.[44] There are instances in which a condition of marriage need not be stated explicitly, such a condition being understood to apply to all marriages, for example, impotence of one of the parties, since a fundamental purpose of marriage is the producing of offspring.

5. Special instances in which the Sages decided to declare a marriage null and void for some technical reasons,[45] or because the groom acted improperly.[46]

6. Consanguineous or incestuous marriages,[47] or if one of the parties is non-Jewish.

In talmudic times, rabbis exercised their authority and declared such marriages null and void, but in posttalmudic times a halakhist did so only in very rare instances, for example, when the marriage was absolutely fraudulent. Otherwise, a *get* was required before remarriage.

THE RITE OF *CHALITZAH*:
RELEASE OF A CHILDLESS WIDOW

In Chapter 1 I referred to the biblical law of the levirate marriage, which provides that if a man dies without issue, the widow may not marry outside the husband's family. Her husband's brother must marry her so that a child born to them will perpetuate the name of the deceased. (If there is no surviving brother, the widow may remarry without further ceremony.) If, however, the brother refuses to marry her, he has to submit to the humiliating ceremony of *Chalitzah*, after which she is free to marry outside the family. We have already mentioned that levirate marriage is no longer practiced today, and every widow of a childless marriage (i.e., childless as far as the husband is concerned; if he has a child from a previous marriage the rite is not required) must go through the rite of *Chalitzah.*

The procedure is as follows: A court of at least three, preferably five, must convene at a predesignated place. The widow declares to the court, "My husband's brother refuses to establish a name for his brother. He will not perform the duty of a brother-in-law." He then affirms this by declaring, "I do not want to marry her." Whereupon, she approaches him, pulls his shoe from his foot, spits in his presence,[48] and declares, "Thus shall be done to the man who will not build his brother's house."

As in the case of the *get*, the Sages have elaborated on the biblical procedure with various incidental regulations as to which procedures are vital—without which the rite is invalid—and which are not essential. In talmudic times, the *Bet Din* provided a special shoe that the brother-in-law put on for the rite. The Sages also instituted that just as a woman who received a *get* is forbidden to a *kohen*, so also is the woman who went through the rite of *Chalitzah*.

THE AFTERMATH OF DIVORCE

Though the *get* is a *sefer keritot*, a sundering of the relationship between two persons who formerly were husband and wife, the relationship is by no means completely severed. First of all, the woman has to sue for payment of her *ketubah*, the amount promised her upon the dissolution of the marriage. Very often this involved litigation before the courts to ascertain that the woman has not already seized certain assets prior to the divorce, and also to assess and identify the property held by the husband that is liable for the payment of the *ketubah*. It should be borne in mind that until the twentieth century, Jews enjoyed legal autonomy, and fiscal matters related to the *ketubah* were adjudicated by the rabbinic authorities. Through the centuries numerous *responsa* were written by them describing claims and counterclaims of the parties and/or their heirs.

Furthermore, if minor children are in the custody of the mother, the father remains responsible for their upkeep, an arrangement that invariably involves contact between the divorced parents. In the days of the Talmud the later courts extended the period during which the father was obliged to support his children, and it has been extended further in modern Israel, where such support is imposed by the rabbinic courts even for children in their late teens. Today, rather than awarding a woman a lump sum and thus acquitting the husband from further alimentary support of his divorced wife, the court orders him to continue such support (alimony) until she remarries. The amount of alimony is fixed by the court, depending on the capacity of the husband to pay and the cost of living. Needless to say, the courts are filled with litigation concerning such matters.

In connection with postdivorce support, an interesting story is related in the Jerusalem Talmud.[49] We are told that the wife of Rabbi Jose the Galilean sorely oppressed him. Once his colleague Rabbi Eleazar ben Azariah visited him, became aware of the latter's predicament, and advised him to divorce his wife. Rabbi Jose countered that the amount of her *ketubah* was considerable and he did not have the means to pay her. Rabbi Eleazar then offered to give Rabbi Jose the necessary funds, which Rabbi Jose reluctantly accepted and divorced his wife. Subsequently she married the town sentry, but he lost all his possessions and became blind. She then led him around the town to beg for charity. One day she made the rounds with him but she did not receive any charity, so he asked her, "Isn't there another neighborhood where we can go to beg?" She replied, "I left out one neighborhood, and I have no more strength to go there." (Actually it was Rabbi Jose's neighborhood, and she was embarrassed to go there.) Whereupon he began to beat her and she started to wail out loud. Rabbi Jose heard her cries and became aware of her predicament, so he gave them one of his houses for them to live in, and he supported them for the rest of their lives. He did this, explains the Talmud, in order to comply with the rabbinic exposition of the verse in Isaiah (58:7), "Do not ignore your own kin," which he interpreted as including his divorced wife.

Money matters are not the only source of postdivorce arguments. Matters such as child custody, visitation rights, and the child's education can engage divorced parents in personal and legal conflict if not settled before the divorce. Even the country of residence may be a bone of contention. Though divorce was designed to keep the parties separated from each other, regrettably they are forced to meet on many an occasion during the divorce proceedings.[50] In general, the welfare of the children of divorced parents remains a joint concern of both parties. And when their children celebrate happy occasions, again divorced parents are involved together, though unfortunately these occasions may reawaken feelings of resentment and bitterness.

It also should be noted that according to Jewish law, the woman prohibited to a man by virtue of his marriage to one of her relatives—for example, his wife's daughter from another marriage—remains prohibited to him even after he has divorced his wife, and even after she is deceased. The exception is a wife's sister; she remains prohibited after his divorce only as long as his wife is alive; after her death he may marry her sister. Thus, the ties created between a man and woman by marriage are never completely sundered, and therefore the need for mutual respect and consideration so essential for domestic harmony persists after divorce.

REMARRIAGE AFTER DIVORCE

Jewish tradition distinguishes between a first marriage and a second one. A first marriage, described in the Bible as "the wife of one's youth,"[51] though mingled with feelings of trepidation as to its future, is a very happy occasion, attended by elaborate celebration. A second marriage, however, is invariably celebrated in subdued fashion. After a first marriage—even if it is the first for only one of the parties—there are "the seven days of feasting;[52] for a second marriage one day suffices.[53]

According to the Sages of the Talmud, there is a more basic difference between a first and second marriage. A first marriage is predestined, whereas the second marriage depends on one's deeds.[54] This expresses the idea that a first marriage is usually due to a falling in love, a natural phenomenon that oftimes can be understood only on the basis of predestination (*bashert* in Yiddish), whereas a second marriage is usually entered into after more serious deliberation. There is a difference, however, between a second marriage entered into after the demise of the first spouse and one entered into after the previous marriage was terminated in divorce. The Sages did not look kindly upon the man who marries a divorcée. In accordance with the verses from Deuteronomy, chap. 24, cited earlier (p. 171), they declared, "The first husband dismissed an evil woman from his house,[55] and the second husband took an evil woman into his house. The end will be, either he will hate her or she will bury him."[56]

We may not agree that all divorces are due to the evil character of one of the parties. The contemporary prevalence of divorce is such that it is no longer a stigma, and marriages are terminated for less serious reasons than those advanced by Scripture and Talmud. Whatever the reason, the Jewish tradition maintains that failure in one marriage should not deter a person from entering into a second one despite the inevitable complications involved.[57] The biblical assertion that it is not good for man to dwell alone applies to the widowed and the divorced as well. Judaism seeks for second marriages the same stability it seeks for a first, even though they are based on different motivations. The wedded bliss in a second marriage may not be as romantic as in a first marriage; nevertheless, our tradition calls for the recital of the same benediction as invoked on the former: "May the Almighty make abundantly happy the beloved companions as He made happy the first couple in the Garden of Eden."

Epilogue

I hope that this cursory survey of Jewish marriage and divorce through the ages will serve to demonstrate how Judaism, on the one hand, has conceived of the union of man and woman in the basic social unit, the family, as inherent in their very biological nature, and, on the other hand, has understood that at times the pairing of this particular man with this particular woman was a mistake that can be rectified by dissolving the union. Furthermore, Judaism has understood that marriage was designed to contribute to the happiness of the parties involved and to their psychological and spiritual development, which can be achieved through their conscious efforts, based on the ingredients of both love and mutual respect, which are essentially the two sides of the one coin.

Beyond the universal human aspect of married life, Judaism—with the development of the unique character of Jewish peoplehood—also looks upon marriage as a force for the continuity of its traditional values. The Jewish community as such has an interest in the stability of the families of its members and therefore has instituted the Jewish ceremony of marriage—known by its halakhic terms as *chuppah* (wedding canopy, symbolizing the home) and *kiddushin* (consecration and devotion)—in order to impress upon the newlyweds the importance of their union and its significance for Jewish life in general. In the course of time certain customs surrounding the wedding ceremony arose in order to enhance this perception of marriage and to invoke upon the young couple the blessings of happiness and fertility.

It is because of this sacramental view of marriage that Judaism proceeds with extreme caution when there is a question of its dissolution and has therefore surrounded the act of divorcement with numerous rules and regulations. These halakhic scruples may at times redound to the disadvantage and prolonged unhappiness of individuals caught in the web of circumstance, and therefore the masters of Jewish law have relaxed certain stringent requirements in order to alleviate individual suffering. But it must be acknowledged that such suffering is often due not to the requirements of the law but to the obduracy of those who refuse to abide by the law for selfish reasons, such as husbands who refuse to give their wives a *get* because of hatred and spite.

CHALLENGES TO THE TRADITION

Modern life, with its complexity and radical departure from traditional life-styles, along with the rejection of and indifference to religious values engendered by the fascinating achievements of scientific research, has led to a worrisome devaluation of the importance of marriage. The sense of its sanctity, or of a lifelong commitment to one's marital partner, has diminished, and consequently the desire to terminate a marital relationship by divorce is easily aroused and implemented. The feeling of one's responsibility to the Jewish community at large as opposed to one's individual happiness is no longer dominant, and therefore there is less hesitation to marry outside the faith. The statistics of both divorce and intermarriage bear this out, and they are appalling.

Other manifestations of this contemporary devaluation of marriage are the increase in premarital and extramarital liaisons and common-law marriages. The consequences thereof are a host of social problems; children growing up without parental guidance and love are easily led to crime and drug addiction. Add to these frustrating problems the AIDS epidemic. Strangely enough, instead of leading to a more cautionary approach to extramarital liaisons, it has led to a more public discussion of sex—frowned upon in the Jewish tradition[1]—and the distribution of contraceptives to teenagers by many schools. According to the Talmud,[2] Jews were not suspected of the sin of sodomy even though it was prevalent among non-Jewish idolators. Today, however, homosexuality among Jews is being paraded publicly, and so-called gay synagogues have been established, challenging the community to recognize aberrations that have been condemned by the Torah as an abomination. (Though not condoned by the Sages, lesbianism is not as serious an offense as homosexuality committed by males.)[3]

This book was written to call for a response to these challenges. Perhaps reading it will help some young couples recapture the sense of the sanctity of marriage as manifested in the Jewish tradition. Though married life among Jews in the past may not always have been as idyllic as portrayed by some romanticists, it certainly was a source of happiness and self-fulfillment and characterized by devotion and fidelity. A model that can serve those who are joined by the Jewish ceremony of marriage is the covenant between God and the Children of Israel as portrayed by the prophet Hosea (2:21): "And I will espouse you forever; I will espouse you with righteousness and justice, with kindness and mercy; and I will espouse you with faithfulness; then you shall be devoted to the Lord."

NOTES

PREFACE

1. For a guide to a happy marriage, I recommend Reuven P. Bulka, *Jewish Marriage: A Halakhic Ethic* (Hoboken, NJ: Ktav, Yeshiva University Press, 1986), and for a "happy" divorce his *Jewish Divorce Ethics: The Right Way to Say Good-Bye* (Ogdensburg, NY: Ivy League Press, 1992).

2. For the connection between the Books of the Prophets and the *Halakhah*, see M. Lewittes, *Principles and Development of Jewish Law* (New York: Bloch Publishing Co., 1987), pp. 31–33.

3. For a description of these works, see ibid., chap. 3.

4. For those interested in scholarly treatments of this subject, I recommend the following works: M. A. Friedman, *Jewish Marriage in Palestine* (Tel Aviv and New York: Tel Aviv University and Jewish Theological Seminary, 1980); Z. W. Falk, *Dinei Yisrael* (Jerusalem: Mesharim Publications, 1983); Z. W. Falk, *Tevi'at Gerushin Mi-tzad Ha-Ishah* (Jerusalem: Institute for Legislative Research, Hebrew University, 1973); L. Epstein, *The Jewish Mar-*

213

riage Contract (New York, 1927; reprint, Salem, NH: Ayer, n.d.); Philip and Hannah Goodman, *The Jewish Marriage Anthology* (Philadelphia: Jewish Publication Society, 1965); *Studies in Marriage Customs* (Jerusalem: Magnes Press, 1974).

CHAPTER 1

1. Cf. *Sotah* 2a, which states that the pairing of couples is as difficult as the splitting of the Red Sea.

2. *Vayikra Rabbah* 8:1.

3. *Mo'ed Katan* 18a.

4. *Sotah* 2a. Maimonides explains the statement in the same way as Resh Lakish, namely, a happy marriage is a reward for a good deed, while a quarrelsome marriage is a punishment for a misdeed; see J. Blau, ed., *Teshuvot Ha-Rambam,* Vol. II (Jerusalem: Rubin Mass, 5749 [1989]), p. 715, no. 436.

5. *Sotah* 2a.

6. *Mo'ed Katan* 18a.

7. According to the Sages, Bilaam was impressed by the entrances to the Israelite homes, designed to ensure privacy; cf. Rashi to Numbers 24:5.

8. *Berakhot* 8a; see commentaries ad loc. in Yaakov ben Shlomo Habib, *Ein Yaakov* (Jerusalem: Foundation for the Publication of Books of Babylonian Rabbis, n.d.).

9. *Kiddushin* 2b.

10. *Pesachim* 49b. An ignoramus, asserted one sage, assaults his wife sexually without any shame.

11. *Kiddushin* 70a.

12. *Kiddushin* 41a.

13. *Bava Batra* 168a.

14. *Sanhedrin* 76a–b.

15. *Yevamot* 64b.

16. *Avot* 5:21. Some see an allusion to this in that the word *adam* (man) in Genesis appears eighteen times from the creation of man to the creation of woman; see *Tosafot Yom Tov* ad loc.

17. *Sotah* 44a.

18. *Kiddushin* 29b–30a.

19. *Pesachim* 113a. See, however, p. 42, advice not to marry off a minor daughter.

20. *Yevamot* 62b.

21. Rabbi J. B. Soloveitchik, "The Lonely Man of Faith," *Tradition* 7:2 (Summer 1965).

22. Philadelphia: Jewish Publication Society, 1964.

23. *Niddah* 45b. That is, in practical and domestic matters; in intellectual and spiritual issues the husband is deemed superior.

24. *Bava Metzia* 59a.

25. *Yevamot* 63a.

26. Cf. *Niddah* 31a: "There are three partners in the creation of a human: God, his father and his mother. From his father's white semen develop bones, sinews, nails, brain matter, white of the eye; from his mother's red blood develop skin, flesh, hair, and black of the eye; and God gives him spirit and soul, countenance, eyesight, hearing, speech, ability to walk, intelligence."

27. Cf. *Midrash Ha-Ne'elam*, p. 15, comment on the word *laasot* (to do) (Genesis 3:2), "When God completed the works of Creation He commanded them to produce in their likeness."

28. *Yevamot* 61b; Rambam, *Hilkhot Ishut* 15:1. See also *Sefer Ha-Mitzvot*, ed. Chaim Heller (Jerusalem: Mosad Harav Kook, 1946), no. 212, n. 6. Cf. discussion in Maharsha to *Sanhedrin* 59b.

29. *Yevamot* 61b.

30. *Yevamot* 62b.

31. *Yevamot* 62b.

32. Cf. Genesis 38:9.

33. Leviticus 22:24. However, it may be permitted in cases of prostatitis cured only by surgery. Similarly, the spilling of seed for purposes of diagnosis in cases of infertility may be permitted.

34. Cf. *Ketubot* 39a. For more details, see M. Lewittes, *Principles and Development of Jewish Law* (New York: Bloch Publishing Co., 1987), pp. 216–217. For a comprehensive treatment of contraception in Jewish Law, see David M. Feldman, *Marital Relations, Birth Control and Abortion in Jewish Law* (New York: New York University Press, 1975).

35. *Yevamot* 64a. The assumption was that the wife is the cause of

the infertility. However, another man may marry her, since possibly it was the first husband who was infertile. Cf. *Nedarim* 90b, where it is said that the woman is better able to judge that the husband is impotent.

36. *Yalkut Shimoni, Bereishit*, sec. 17.

37. See *Encyclopedia of Religion and Ethics*, Vol. III, ed. James Hastings (Edinborough: T. and T. Clark, 1964), s.v. "celibacy." The only exemption in Judaism was in the case of Moses, who separated himself from his wife after having fathered two sons because of his need to be ever ready in communication with God; see *Shabbat* 87a.

38. *Yevamot* 65b.

39. Ibid. According to Maimonides (*Hilkhot Issurei Biah* 16:11), female sterilization by removal of her reproductive organs is forbidden; see, however, *Shabbat* 111a and *Tosafot* ad loc.

40. *Yevamot* 65b.

41. *Eruvin* 100b.

42. Cf. the statement of Ben Azzai (*Yevamot* 63b); see also *Kiddushin* 29b about which has priority, the study of Torah or marriage.

43. *Shulchan Arukh, Eben Ha-Ezer* 1:3, Rema ad loc. For further references, see Jeremy Cohen, *Be Fertile and Increase* (Ithaca, NY: Cornell University Press, 1992).

44. *Bereishit Rabbah* 23:3.

45. *Sanhedrin* 22a.

46. *Sanhedrin* 22a.

47. *Yevamot* 65a.

48. *Yevamot* 118a.

49. *Yevamot* 65a.

50. Subsequent authorities argued as to the force of the ban in exceptional circumstances, for example, in the case of the mental derangement of the wife, making normal relations impossible, or the refusal of the wife to maintain conjugal relations yet refusing to accept a divorce. There is also great deal of discussion as to the original scope, both in time and area, of the ban, though that discussion is now theoretical, as all Ashkenazi communities abide by the ban. The ban is called *Cherem d'Rabbenu Gershom, Cherem*

meaning excommunication, the means by which Jewish communities enforced their regulations; see *Encyclopedia Talmudit*, Vol. XVII (Jerusalem: Yad Harav Herzog, 1973–1993), for details.

51. The standard practice in medieval Egypt was to add a clause in the *ketubah* whereby the groom undertakes not to marry an additional wife; cf. Blau, *Teshuvot Ha-Rambam,* Vol. I, p. 73, Vol. II, p. 650.

52. See ibid., pp. 650–652, even if he had undertaken not to marry an additional wife.

53. *Sanhedrin* 58a. Thus, adultery is prohibited to non-Jews as well.

54. *Bava Batra* 109b.

55. *Yevamot* 42a.

56. *Sotah* 28a. Also, the husband must divorce his adulterous wife.

57. *Yevamot* 95a.

58. *Sotah* 47b.

59. Some explain the term as *p'lag ishah,* a half-wife.

60. *Sanhedrin* 21a.

61. Cf. *Shulchan Arukh, Eben Ha-Ezer* 26:1 and Rema ad loc. Curiously, an eighteenth-century rabbi, Yaakov Emden, wrote a lengthy *responsum* refuting all those who maintained that a concubine was prohibited, though at the end he hesitated to give carte blanche to anyone desiring such a liaison (*She'eilot Yavetz,* pt. II, no. 15).

62. The Talmud (*Yevamot* 24a) explains that establishing a name does not mean the child born of the new union should be given the same name as the deceased, rather that the brother-in-law who marries the widow will inherit the property of the deceased. Rashi to Genesis 38:8 explains it as giving the same name, though in the passage in Deuteronomy he explains it as the Talmud does. Nachmanides to Genesis 38:8 sees some mystical significance in the levirate marriage, but he does not elaborate. The *Sefer Ha-Chinukh, mitzvah* no. 598, explains that the child to be born will take the place of the deceased in serving God and thus confer merit upon the soul of the deceased. A more pragmatic understanding of the law of *Yibbum* lies in the fact that according to the Torah's laws of inher-

itance, if a man dies without child his brother, and not his wife, inherits his property, and therefore it behooves him to marry the widow and support her; otherwise she would remain penniless. See also the Book of Ruth 4:5, 10.

63. Moses Maimonides, *Guide to the Perplexed*, trans. M. Friedlander, pt. III, sec. 49. New York: Hebrew Publishing Co., n.d. Cf. Ruth 4:5.

64. *Yevamot* 30b, 39b, 101b.

65. For the status of the betrothed woman, see p. 75.

66. J.T. *Ketubot* 3:6(27d).

67. The payments every assaulter must pay; see *Bava Kamma* 83b.

68. *Ketubot* 39a–b.

69. J.T. *Sotah* 4:4(19d).

70. Ibid.

71. *Yevamot* 107a.

72. *Yevamot* 112b. For details, see *Encyclopedia Talmudit*, Vol. XVII , s.v. *"heresh."*

73. Cf. *Mo'ed Katan* 23a.

74. *Yevamot* 49a.

75. *Yevamot* 62b.

76. Cf. Maimonides, *Guide to the Perplexed,* pt. III, chap. 49.

77. *Yevamot* 21a.

78. Cf. *Tosafot* to *Yevamot* 21a, s.v. *"U-mutar."*

79. Cf. *Kohelet Rabbah* to Ecclesiastes 4:1, "I have seen all the oppressed under the sun": "These are the *mamzerim*; after all, what sin did they commit! Nevertheless, they will enter the world-to-come [heavenly bliss] as is said, 'Behold the tears of the oppressed who have no comforter.' " It should be remembered that a *mamzer* is a Jew, obliged to observe the *mitzvot* of the Torah, and is heir to his father's property. Also, calling a person a *mamzer* in a pejorative manner is a punishable offense. However, it is not construed to be offensive to the parent, as is also the case in English when one insults another by calling him a son-of-a-bitch.

80. Rambam, *Hilkhot Issurei Biah* 15:7.

81. *Kiddushin* 71a. See, however, detailed discussion in Rabbi Y.

I. Herzog, *Responsa Hechal Yitzchak*, Vol. I (Jerusalem: Herzog Publication Society, 1972), no. 10.

82. *Yevamot* 24a. See Deuteronomy 23:7–10.

83. *Sifre* to Deuteronomy 23:8. See Rashi ad loc., who adds that members of other nations may marry an Israelite immediately after conversion. A similar distinction between physical and spiritual harm was made between the holidays of Purim and Hanukkah. The former saved Israel from a threat to its physical existence and therefore is celebrated with feasting and drinking; the latter posed a threat to its spiritual identity and therefore is celebrated with the kindling of candles, the light being the symbol of Torah.

84. *Berakhot* 28a.

85. *Yevamot* 75b.

86. Cf. discussion in *Sanhedrin* 21b.

87. See Herzog, *Responsa Hechal Yitzchak*, Vol. I, no. 18, for an opinion that the prohibition is only against a convert who is not virgin. It should be noted that Reform and many Conservative rabbis maintain that the special restrictions imposed upon *kohanim* no longer obtain since *kohanim* no longer minister in the Temple. However, *kohanim* continue to serve today both in the ceremony of *pidyon ha-ben* (redemption of the firstborn) and in the blessing of the congregation (*birkat kohanim*), even though their direct lineage may be in doubt.

88. *Yevamot* 24a.

89. *Kiddushin* 68b.

90. *Yevamot* 41a.

91. *Yevamot* 42a. See *Encyclopedia Talmudit*, Vol. VI, pp. 29–30, for details.

92. *Yevamot* 42b. Many modern authorities agree that this restriction no longer applies, since in our modern society the supposed harm to the infant is most improbable.

93. *Yevamot* 64b. Maimonides already disregarded the ban against marrying a *katlanit*; see Blau, *Teshuvot Ha-Rambam*, pp. 387 ff. (no. 218).

94. Cf. Rema to *Shulchan Arukh*, *Eben Ha-Ezer* 9:1.

95. *Yevamot* 64b.

CHAPTER 2

1. *Hilkhot Ishut* 1:1. Maimonides is assuming here that the rabbinic interpretation of "take" (*yikach*) refers to betrothal; see p. 66.

2. See p. 19 that this is a parental obligation. Cf. *Ketubot* 52b, where it is assumed that it is more appropriate for a father to seek a bride for his son, rather than to seek a groom for his daughter; see p. 6, that it is the role of the man to seek a woman.

3. Cf. *Sanhedrin* 28b, that *mechutanim* are not among the relatives disqualified as witnesses for each other because of kinship.

4. Rabbenu Nissim's commentary to the *Rif*, *Shabbat* 12a. The *Arukh* explains it as the tranquility of the parents, who are now at ease having arranged a match for their children.

5. For details, see S. W. Baron, *The Jewish Community*, Vol. III (Philadelphia: Jewish Publication Society, 1942), p. 208; Rema to *Shulchan Arukh*, *Choshen Mishpat* 185:10, 264:7.

6. *Chaftez Chayyim*, sec. 9.

7. E. Waldenberg, "Is One Obliged to Inform a Prospective Groom of the Girl's Infertility," in *Studies in Memory of Yitzchak Nisim* (Hebrew) (Jerusalem: Yad Harav Nisim, 5745 [1985]), pp. 99–103. Cf. Leviticus 19:16, "Do not stand idly by the blood of your neighbor."

8. *Ketubot* 102b. See p. 45 for a discussion concerning these commitments.

9. See M. Lewittes, *Tzemichat Ge'ulateinu* (Jerusalem, 5744 [1984]), p. 221.

10. *Ketubot* 52b.

11. *Kiddushin* 50b.

12. *Bava Batra* 146a. Cf. Lewittes, *Tzemichat Ge'ulateinu*, p. 224.

13. Called *tekiat kaf*, a gesture also used to confirm commercial agreements not committed to writing.

14. *Bava Metzia* 49a.

15. *Taanit* 8a. In *Arukh*, s.v. "*chalad-chuldah*."

16. Cf. *Shabbat* 130a, "There is no *ketubah* over which there is no quarreling."

17. Cf. Nehemiah 7:5, *sefer ha-yachas*. See also *Pesachim* 62b, where the Book of Chronicles is referred to as *Sefer Yuchasin*.

18. The beginning of the grape harvest.

19. *Taanit* 26b.

20. *Kiddushin* 69a–b.

21. *Kiddushin* 70b.

22. *Kiddushin* 45b.

23. *Eduyot* 8:2.

24. No doubt the girl was held as a domestic; cf. 2 Kings 4:1 that children were taken as slaves for nonpayment of a debt.

25. *Ketubot* 28b. The Jerusalem Talmud adds that if he divorced that woman, they would again conduct the ceremony, announcing that he had returned to the good graces of the family.

26. *Kiddushin* 76a.

27. *Ketubot* 62b. Occasionally, *yichus* had a disparaging effect; see *Kiddushin* 49a, that if a groom's *yichus* is superior to the bride's, she may object to the *shiddukh* on the grounds that "she cannot walk in a shoe too big." On the other hand, a man is advised to marry a woman beneath his social standing, lest she lord it over him; see *Yevamot* 63a.

28. *Ketubot* 59b. Cf. p. 129, one wife for children and one wife for beauty.

29. *Nedarim* 9:10.

30. *Horayot* 13a.

31. *Kiddushin* 1b.

32. This was so, some explain, because of the confusion that might occur if the identical name is used for two members in the same family.

33. See, for example, Yechezkel Landau, *Responsa Nodah Bi-Yehudah*, Vol. II (Vilna, 1899), *Eben Ha-Ezer*, no. 9.

34. J.T. *Megillah* 3:1(74a).

35. *Ketubot* 62b. Cf. *Kiddushin* 29b, commentaries to "*ha lun, ha lehu.*"

36. *Ketubot* 62b–63a.

37. *Ketubot* 62b–63a.

38. From the German *kost*, "food."

39. At first Rebecca's father, Bethuel, negotiated for his daughter, with brother Laban intruding (see Rashi to verse 50), but because he wanted to object to the match he was smitten by an angel; see Rashi to verse 55.

40. *Bereishit Rabbah* ad loc. quoted by Rashi.

41. *Kiddushin* 41a. According to one *midrash*, this was not followed in the case of Rebecca, who was purported to be three years old at the time; see *Tosafot, Yevamot* 61b. A more bizarre instance of premature betrothal discussed in the Talmud is that of a man who says to his friend whose wife is pregnant, "If your wife gives birth to a female, I hereby betroth her" (*Kiddushin* 62b).

42. See *Tosafot* ad loc.

43. Rema to *Shulchan Arukh, Eben Ha-Ezer* 37:8.

44. Yosef Chayyim of Baghdad, *Chukot Ha-Nashim* (Jerusalem, 5739 [1979]), p. 36.

45. Baron, *The Jewish Community*, Vol. III, p. 204.

46. Rema, *Shulchan Arukh, Yoreh De'ah*, end of sec. 240.

47. Rabbi Yitzchak Ohlboim, author of *Sefer Eizer Le-Yitzchak* (Czechoslovakia, n.d.), on marriage customs and documents.

48. See Yechiel Weinberg, *Responsa Seridei Eish*, Vol. II (Jerusalem: Mosad Harav Kook, 1962), nos. 101, 105; Y. I. Herzog, *Responsa Hechal Yitzchak*, Vol. II (Jerusalem: Herzog Publication Society, 1972), nos. 19, 20, 21. The rabbinate in Israel has adopted the same lenient stand with respect to the many immigrants who have come from Russia with non-Jewish spouses.

49. *Kiddushin* 12b; see also *Shulchan Arukh, Eben Ha-Ezer*, end of sec. 20, that such punishment is no longer administered by Jewish authorities.

50. *Shabbat* 150a.

51. *Ketubot* 102b. Commentators disagree if there was a *kinyan* in front of witnesses to make the agreement binding; see Rashi (no *kinyan*) and *Tosafot* (yes *kinyan*) ad loc.

52. *Tosafot, Kiddushin* 9b, s.v. *"hein hein,"* and Rambam, *Hilkhot Ishut* 23:17.

53. *Hilkhot Mekhirah* 11:18.

54. For further developments and distinctions, see *Shulchan Arukh, Eben Ha-Ezer*, sec. 50 and 51, and Rema ad loc.

55. *Responsa* no. 1180, quoted in A. H. Frieman, *Seder Kiddushin Ve-Nissuin* (Jerusalem: Mosad Harav Kook, 1964), p. 25.

56. Yaahov Moellin, *Minhagei Maharil* (Brooklyn, NY: Ungar Publications, n.d.), p. 64.

57. Rema to *Shulchan Arukh*, *Eben Ha-Ezer*, sec. 51. See also *Otzar Ha-Poskim*, Vol. XVI, p. 50, for an explanation, though second *tena'im* are no longer customary.

58. Joseph Teomim, *Pri Megadim* to *Shulchan Arukh*, *Orach Chayyim*, sec. 560, also quoted by Rabbi Chayyim of Volozhin in the name of his mentor, the Gaon of Vilna. I do not understand how a pottery vessel is less amenable to repair than a glass goblet; see Jeremiah 18:4 for a statement to the contrary. For other reasons for the breaking of a dish, see Ohlboim, *Sefer Eizer Le-Yitzchak*.

59. *Pesachim* 49a.

60. *Mo'ed Katan* 18b.

61. This is a typical version; other versions with somewhat different phraseology are legitimate. Of course, if the parties agree, they may include additional stipulations.

62. Cf. Isaiah 58:11.

63. That is, an undertaking made casually with the assumption that it will not have to be honored.

64. Similar to the cancellation of a betrothal if such defects become known after the wedding; see p. 202.

65. *Shulchan Arukh*, *Eben Ha-Ezer* 50:5.

66. Ibid.

CHAPTER 3

1. Usually referred to as the "Jewish Marriage Contract." For a detailed exposition of the terms of the *ketubah*, see M. A. Friedman, *Jewish Marriage in Palestine* (Tel Aviv and New York: Tel Aviv University and Jewish Theological Seminary, 1980).

2. *Ketubot* 10a; J.T. end of *Ketubot*. Cf. *Tosafot* to *Ketubot* 10a, s.v. "*Amar*."

3. All agree that the *ketubah* of a nonvirgin (widow or divorcée) is *d'rabbanan*. See, for example, S. W. Baron, *A Social and Religious*

History of the Jews, Vol. VI (Philadelphia: Jewish Publication Society, 1958), p. 24, that the dispute in geonic times was between the academies of Sura and Pumbeditha, the former following the Babylonian practice and the latter the Palestinian practice.

4. *Mekhilta* to Exodus 22:15, Rashi ad loc.; see M. Lewittes, *Tzemichat Ge'ulateinu* (Jerusalem, 5744 [1984]), p. 222, for other opinions.

5. Fifth century B.C.E. Elephantine; see Baron, *Social and Religious History*, Vol. I, p. 113; A. Cowley, *Aramaic Papyri of the 5th Century* B.C.E. (Oxford: Clarendon Press, 1923). A few fragments of marriage contracts from the Dead Sea area from the early second century C.E. have also been found; see Friedman, *Jewish Marriage in Palestine*, pp. 7–8.

6. Also known as a dinar (dinarius), estimated to be worth approximately four grams of pure silver; for details, see *Encyclopedia Talmudit*, Vol. VII (Jerusalem: Yad Harav Herzog, 1973–1993), s.v. "dinar." See also A. Reifenberg, *Ancient Hebrew Arts* (New York: Schocken Books, 1950) for Hebrew coins of different periods.

7. *Ketubot* 82b.

8. Actually, the father would pay; cf. *Kiddushin* 29a: "A father is obligated to marry off his son." Also, "A father should pledge for his daughter as much as for his son" (*Ketubot* 52b). See, however, the statement of Ra'avad (Rabbi Abraham ben David of Posquieres, eleventh century), quoted by Baron, *Social and Religious History*, Vol. VI, p. 74, "It is customary for a person not to give much money for his daughter. . . . He who is quarrelsome about his wife's possessions . . . his marriage is bound to fail."

9. The father is reimbursed for the loss in his daughter's value caused by the loss of her virginity.

10. *Ketubot* 38a.

11. Cf. n. 6. The Mishnah records that the Court of Priests doubled the minimum sum as a mark of priestly families distinction, and the Sages did not protest. The Gemara adds that nonpriestly families of distinguished lineage did likewise.

12. *Ketubot* 81a.

13. This perhaps confirms Rambam's statement (*Hilkhot Ishut*

1:2) that betrothal by this transfer of coin is *midivrei soferim*, a regulation of the Sages derived by inference from a hermeneutic principle, a statement that aroused a great deal of amazement; see commentaries ad loc. For Rambam's explanation, see J. Blau, ed., *Teshuvot Ha-Rambam*, Vol. II (Jerusalem: Rubin Mass, 5749 [1989]), p. 632 (no. 355).

14. See *Tosafot* ad loc.

15. *Ketubot* 39b.

16. Mishnah *Ketubot* 39b.

17. This is a biblical mandate; cf. Exodus 21:10: "He must not withhold her food, her clothing, or her conjugal rights."

18. *Ketubot* 46b, 51a.

19. *Ketubot* 52b. In Judea, however, the heirs had the right to say to the widow, "Take your *ketubah* (i.e., the sum of money) and leave."

20. *Ketubot* 2a.

21. *Ketubot* 52b.

22. *Ketubot* 66a.

23. *Hilkhot Ishut* 23:12.

24. Cf. *Encyclopedia Talmudit,* Vol. IX, s.v. *"hakhnasat kallah"* for sources and ramifications.

25. *Ketubot* 67a–b.

26. It is not explicit in the Torah but is inferred by the Sages from their exposition of the verse, "You shall give his property to his nearest relative" (Numbers 27:11; *Bava Batra* 111b). Hence, Maimonides categorizes this ruling as *divrei Soferim*, a ruling of the Scribes.

27. M. Elon, *Ha-Mishpat Ha-Ivri*, Vol. II (Jerusalem: Institute for Research in Jewish Law, Hebrew University, 5733 [1973]), pp. 635, 661. A precedent is found in the Talmud; cf. J.T. *Ketubot* 9:1 (33a), "Some would write that if she dies without leaving children, her possessions should be returned to her father's house, and this is a valid stipulation." Such a condition was customary in medieval oriental communities; see Blau *Teshuvot Ha-Rambam*, p. 656 (no. 34). For the text of one of these regulations, see *Responsa* of Asher b. Yechiel (Rosh, fourteenth century, no. 5).

28. *Ketubot* 95a.

29. *Bava Metzia* 104a.

30. J.T. *Ketubot* 5:10(30b); cf. Mishnah ad loc.

31. *Tosefta, Ketubot* 4:9; *Bava Metzia* 104a.

32. Apparently the Alexandrians did not regard betrothal as already endowing a woman with married status.

33. *Yevamot* 38a.

34. *Ketubot* 9:1.

35. "Iron-sheep" were a flock transferred to an entrepreneur for breeding, with a distribution of the profits.

36. *Yevamot* 7:1.

37. To this very day, when many of these stipulations have lost their significance, the rabbinate in Israel does not budge from tradition and includes them in the standard form of the *ketubah*. They have also resisted all suggestions that the *ketubah* be written in Hebrew and not in the anachronistic Aramaic. Some concession has lately been made in some Israeli communities by giving the couple, in addition to the standard traditional *ketubah*, a separate folder with a précis of the *ketubah* in Hebrew. In other countries, such a précis is usually appended to the *ketubah* in the local language.

38. Cf. *Shabbat* 133b, "A pretty *sefer* Torah . . . with pretty ink, with a pretty quill, by a skilled scribe."

39. If not a virgin, that is, a widow or divorcée or convertee, the proper status is indicated and the basic sum is one hundred zuz instead of two hundred.

40. Cf. *Ketubot* 64b.

41. In the case of an orphan, substitute "her family" (*nesha*); in some *ketubot* this phrase is omitted.

42. See p. 49.

43. Usually a kerchief; cf. Ruth 4:7.

44. In some communities, in addition to the two kosher witnesses, they would honor relatives or close friends by inviting them to add their signatures; cf. *Gittin* 18b and *Shulchan Arukh, Eben Ha-Ezer* 66:13; cf. *Responsa* of Rahsba, no. 1092, and *Nachlat Shivah*, n. 73.

45. *Ketubot* 69a. See Y. I. Ta-Shema, *Mishag Ashkenaz Kadmon* (Jerusalem: Magnes Press, Hebrew University, 5752 [1992]), pp. 43–44, custom in some medieval communities to have youngsters

sign the *ketubah*. See also there, p. 29, the custom to write the *ketubah* on Friday and have it signed Saturday night.

46. *Gittin* 18a.

47. *Sanhedrin* 27b. See n. 44.

48. Cf. the betrothal formula, "the law of Moses and of Israel," the former referring to biblical law, the latter to rabbinic law.

49. *Ketubot* 72a. This is the case provided her husband had warned her and she has ignored his warning (*Sotah* 25a). Here we find the rabbinic ruling (some authorities say that it is biblical) that a married woman may not go out in public with the hair on her head uncovered, which led to the custom among certain religious groups for wives to wear a wig, thus evading the letter of the law. See M. Lewittes, *Principles and Development of Jewish Law* (New York: Bloch Publishing, 1987), p. 9 n. 25.

50. *Ketubot* 63a.

51. *Ketubot*, chaps. 1–2. Cf. J. T. *Ketubot* 1:2, if the zuzzim were of local currency or of the coin of Tyre, which was much more valuable. See also Mishnah, *Ketubot* 13:11, that if either the wedding or the divorce took place in *Eretz Yisrael*, payment is made in the coin of *Eretz Yisrael*, but if both the wedding and the divorce took place outside *Eretz Yisrael*, payment is made in local currency.

52. *Ketubot*, chap. 9.

53. The Sephardi chief rabbi of Tel Aviv, Chayyim David Halevy, has encouraged couples in Israel to make such premarital contracts; see *Shanah Be-Shanah* (Jerusalem: Hechal Shlomo, 5751 [1991]), pp. 226ff.

CHAPTER 4

1. The JPS translation reads, ". . . who has spoken for a woman in marriage [with a note, "i.e., has paid the bridal-price"] but has not yet married her." As we see from our discussion, this translation helps clarify the term *aras* but not the phrase *lo lakach*, "not yet married her," which is somewhat ambiguous since betrothal already confers upon the woman a married status in many respects. A more apt translation is "taken her as his wife."

2. See *Mandelkern's Concordance*, 4th ed. (Jerusalem and Tel Aviv: Schocken Press, 5712 [1952]), s.v. *"aras"* for its etymological origin. In the Bible the word is spelled with a left-pointed *"sin"*; in later Hebrew it is spelled with a *"samekh."*

3. Cf. Numbers 30:17, "These are the statutes which the Lord has commanded to Moses between a man and his wife, between a father and his daughter in her youth in her father's house."

4. Cf. Ezra 9:12; Nehemiah 13:25; 2 Chronicles 11:21, 24:3.

5. See, for example, Numbers 16:15, "I have not taken" [*lo nasati*] and the expression *masa u-mattan*, "taking and giving."

6. It is difficult to accept Ramban's commentary to Deuteronomy 22:13 on *yikach*: "That is, when a man takes a woman by the taking of the Torah, which is the *kiddushin* with money, and she is the betrothed mentioned elsewhere."

7. Leviticus 25:14. Cf. Ruth 4:10. It should be noted that the term for taking, *kichah*, in talmudic parlance means "purchasing." For taking, they used the Aramaic *natal*.

8. Actually, the "taking" is the taking of the purchase-price (money) by the vendor.

9. *Kiddushin* 2b.

10. *Yevamot* 66b; *Ketubot* 57b.

11. Cf. *Nedarim* 66b.

12. *Kiddushin* 6a.

13. See, for example, J. Blau, ed., *Teshuvot Ha-Rambam* (Jerusalem: Rubin Mass, 5749 [1989]), p. 624 (no. 348), regarding the appointment of special officiants at betrothals and divorces for many villages.

14. See p. 71 for explanation of perutah.

15. *Kiddushin* 7a.

16. Ibid. The *Shulchan Arukh* adds that a scholar has to determine whether the recipient in such case is truly important.

17. Cf. *Makkot* 6a and *Tosafot* ad loc. For persons disqualified to serve as witnesses, see p. 63.

18. *Bava Batra* 48b. *Poskim* are divided if the same rule applies to a groom proposing under duress; see Rambam, *Hilkhot Ishut* 4:1; *Tur, Eben Ha-Ezer*, sec. 42.

19. See M. Elon, *Ha-Mishpat Ha-Ivri*, Index s.v. *"Hafka'at Kiddushin,"* especially pp. 687ff.

20. The prohibition is by rabbinic regulation, confirming biblical custom.

21. For the value of a dinar, see above p. 224 n.6.

22. Cf. *Shabbat*, chap. 6.

23. *Kiddushin* 46–48b, "any article that has a fixed value." See Saul Lieberman, *Tosefta Ki-Pshuta* (New York: Jewish Theological Seminary, 1955–1973), *Kiddushin*, p. 931.

24. Cf. A. H. Freiman, *Seder Kiddushin Ve-Nissuin* (Jerusalem: Mosad Harav Kook, 1964), p. 85.

25. Joseph Kapah, *Halikhot Teiman* (Jerusalem: Ben Zvi Institute, 5728 [1948]), p. 142.

26. Cf. *Berakhot* 31a and *Tosafot* ad loc.

27. Cf. Freiman, *Seder Kiddushin Ve-Nissuin*.

28. This might have been because of the influence of the Christian neighbors, who used a double-ring ceremony; cf. Hastings, ed., *Encyclopedia of Religion and Ethics*, Vol. VIII (Edinborough: T. and T. Clark, 1908), p. 436, where it is characterized as "a harmless heathen custom." Maimonides, and even Karo in *Shulchan Arukh*, does not mention the ring.

29. *Sefer Ha-Chinukh, mitzvah* 552.

30. *Tikkunei Zohar*, sec. 10.10.

31. *Kiddushin* 5b.

32. *Eben Ha-Ezer* 28:19.

33. *Ketubot* 57a.

34. *Tosefta, Ketubot* 5:1.

35. *Kiddushin* 41a.

36. *Kiddushin* 58b–59a.

37. *Ketubot* 83a.

38. *Kiddushin* 63a–b.

39. *Kiddushin* 49b. Maimonides (*Hilkhot Ishut* 8:5) rules that the betrothal is only of doubtful validity, since we do not know for sure that he repented. Cf. *Hilkhot Teshuvah* 7:6, "Great is Repentance, for it brings near those who were distant. Yesterday this fellow was hated, distant, abominable; today he is beloved, close, a friend."

40. *Kiddushin* 49b. See *Tosafot* ad loc. for different degrees of assumption or implied conditions that may qualify a transaction.

41. *Ketubot* 73a. See p. 201 for a list of marriages that can be declared null and void.

42. *Ketubot* 41b, 43b.

43. Mishnah, *Nedarim* 10:1.

44. *Yevamot* 29b, 60a. The corollary of this law is whether he is a statutory mourner upon her demise.

45. *Ketubot* 78a.

46. *Masekhet Kallah* 1:1.

47. Rema to *Shulchan Arukh, Eben Ha-Ezer* 55:1.

48. *Kiddushin* 12b.

49. See p. 69.

CHAPTER 5

1. *Gittin* 57a.

2. *Betzah* 36b; *Mo'ed Katan* 8b.

3. See A. Ziv, *Rabbenu Mosheh Isserles* (New York: Yeshiva University Press, 5732 [1972]), pp. 215–216.

4. The night following Tisha B'Av is also proscribed. However, if Tisha B'Av is postponed (*nidheh*) until Sunday because of *Shabbat*, weddings may be conducted after the end of the fasting.

5. So called because of the "counting" of the *Omer*; see Leviticus 23:15–16. The Talmud (*Yevamot* 62b) relates that during this period the disciples of Rabbi Akiba died because they did not act respectfully amongst themselves, so in the early Middle Ages it was accepted to be a period of partial mourning.

6. *Shulchan Arukh, Yoreh De'ah* 179:2.

7. Cf. Deuteronomy 22:13–21 and p. 76.

8. *Ketubot* 5a. Cf. J.T. *Yoma* 1:1(38d), "Those marrying a widow [on a Friday] have to consummate the marriage before nightfall, so that they should not be as if making an acquisition on the Sabbath." As explained by the commentators, a virgin is acquired (see p. 67) by the *chuppah* ceremony, whereas a widow is acquired only by intercourse, which takes place at night; see *Tosafot* to *Yoma* 13b, s.v. "*l'chada.*"

9. *Ketubot* 5b. See *Tosafot* ad loc., s.v. *"Dam."*

10. *Ketubot* 2a, 4b–5a.

11. See discussion in *Tur*, sec. 64 and *Bet Yosef* ad loc.

12. For the laws of *niddah*, see Chapter 7.

13. Cf. *Shulchan Arukh, Yoreh De'ah*, sec. 192, the ruling that the moment a date is set for the wedding, the bride is considered a *niddah* even though there was no flow or staining, and she has to count the seven clean days before going to the *mikveh*.

14. Ibid.

15. *Ketubot* 8a. The example given is "as soon as the barley is put in the crock [to make the beer]."

16. *Ketubot* 5a.

17. The wines in ancient Palestine were very strong and had to be diluted with water, usually two parts water to one part wine; see *Niddah* 19a.

18. Called *be'ilat mitzvah*, the prerequisite to the *mitzvah* of *Peru u-revu*; cf. *Berakhot* 11a, that because of the groom's preoccupation with this *mitzvah* he is exempt from the *mitzvah* of *kriat shema*, a ruling no longer applicable; see *Orach Chayyim* 70:3. During the period of the *Geonim* the custom developed for the groom to recite a benediction after deflowering his bride, but the practice has long been abandoned; see *Tur Eben Hazer*, sec. 63, and commentaries ad loc. In Yaakov Emden, *Responsa She'ilot Yaavetz* (New York: Israel Wolf Publications, 1960), no. 180, there is mention of a meal held after the *be'ilat mitzvah* called "meal of the fish" to invoke the blessing of fertility given to the fish (Genesis 1:22).

19. *Ketubot* 3b–4a.

20. Cf. *Tosafot* to *Yevamot* 43b, s.v. *"shani."*

21. *Mo'ed Katan* 23a.

22. Probably a development from the custom in talmudic times (see p. 87); see J. Werdiger, *Eidut Le-Yisrael* (Bnai Brak: Institute for the Research of Prayer and Customs, 5725 [1965]), p. 5.

23. Rema to *Shulchan Arukh, Eben Ha-Ezer*, sec. 61.

24. J.T. *Bikkurim* 3:3.

25. Various reasons have been advanced why this is a minor holiday; see *Taanit* 26b and the commentaries ad loc.

26. See *Ezer l'Yitzchak*, p. 25.

27. *Tosefta, Shabbat*, chap. 7(8).

28. *Gittin* 57a.

29. *Ketubot* 17a.

30. Literally, bringing the bride into the *chuppah*; it is now commonly applied to helping a young couple financially to establish their home.

31. *Hilkhot Eivel* 14:1.

32. *Ketubot* 16b.

33. Yaakov Moellin, *Sefer Maharil* (Brooklyn, NY: Unger Publication, n.d.), p. 64.

34. Cf. Joel 2:16, "Let the bridegroom come out of his chamber and the bride from her canopied couch."

35. Called in Yiddish *bedekens*, "covering." In sixteenth-century Poland this ceremony was performed in the morning, hours before the wedding.

36. *Ketubot* 16b.

37. *Sotah* 49b; cf. Rashi ad loc., s.v. *"tanboura."*

38. *Bava Batra* 60a; *Orach Chayyim*, sec. 560. Cf. Psalm 137:5–6, "Let my right hand wither . . . if I do not keep Jerusalem in memory even at my happiest hour." In Israel today it is customary to sing these verses toward the end of the ceremony.

39. Cf. Isaiah 1:18, "If your sins are as scarlet, they will become white as snow."

40. See *Siddur Bet Yaakov* of Rabbi Yaakov Emden, under *Birkat Nissuin*. Cf. *Berakhot* 31a, that Rav Hamnuna Zuti was asked to sing at a wedding, and he sang, "Woe unto us that we are going to die." When asked how to respond to such a dire refrain, he said, "Where is the [study of] Torah and where is the *mitzvah* that protect us."

41. *Berakhot* 61a. The *Midrash* (*Bereishit Rabbah*) adds that God also bedecked Eve and chanted the wedding benedictions.

42. *Bava Batra* 144b; Rambam, *Hilkhot Zekhiah U-Mattanah*. For further details, see Me'iri ad loc.

43. *Chasidim* have her circle him seven times. Many other reasons for the threefold circuit have been advanced; see Werdiger, *Eidut Le-Yisrael*, p. 70.

44. Cf. Psalm 45:10, "The consort stands at your right hand."

45. For a thorough treatment of the subject, see *Encyclopedia Talmudit*, Vol. XVI (Jerusalem: Yad Harav Herzog, 1973–1993), s.v. "*chuppah*."

46. *Ketubot* 48b.

47. Rosh to *Sukkah* 25b. S. B. Freehof, in *The Harvest of Time* (New York, 1963), contends that covering the bride's head with a *tallit* is an innovation of sixteenth-century Poland.

48. Cf. *Sotah* 4a for the many opinions on the length of a tryst for a woman suspected of adultery.

49. *Sotah* 49b.

50. For the many opinions, see Rema to *Shulchan Arukh, Eben Ha-Ezer* 55:1.

51. Ibid. 61:1; cf. Genesis 15:5.

52. Rabbi Moshe Sofer (Chatam Sofer, nineteenth-century Hungary) objected strenuously to having the *chuppah* in the synagogue on the grounds that it is a custom of the Gentiles, who conduct their weddings in the church.

53. Rema to *Shulchan Arukh, Yoreh De'ah*, 245:22.

54. *Eivel Rabbati*, chap. 8.

55. *Ketubot* 8a.

56. Cf. Isaiah 54:1.

57. Again, complying with the vow to remember Jerusalem at every happy occasion.

58. Cf. Genesis 2:8.

59. Cf. Jeremiah 33:10–11.

60. The conclusion of the sixth benediction is a prayer for the happiness of the married couple for the rest of their lives, whereas the conclusion of the seventh benediction is praise for the Lord for making grooms happy with brides at the wedding, see Rashi to *Ketubot* 8a, s.v. *mesameach*.

61. In commemoration of the destruction of the Temple, see n. 38. See also *Berakhot* 30b–31a, where it is recorded that Sages broke expensive glass cups at their sons' weddings because the guests became too raucous. This, according to *Tosafot* ad loc., is the origin of this custom of breaking the glass.

62. See p. 47. Cf. *Berakhot* 6b, "The reward for attending a wedding feast is for the words" (Rashi, "spoken to make the bride

and groom happy"). Indeed, it is still customary for distinguished guests, primarily the rabbi, to deliver a message (*derashah*). In some circles, even the groom delivers a *derashah*.

63. *Ketubot* 17a. Cf. the discussion between *Bet Shammai* and *Bet Hillel*. Another custom ascribed to the West was that when a man takes a woman they would say to him, "Have you found a woman of whom it is said 'Who has found a woman has found good'" (Proverbs 18:22) or a woman of whom it is said "I find the woman more bitter than death" (Ecclesiastes 7:26); *Berakhot* 8a.

64. *Ketubot* 17a.

65. *Kiddushin* 81a.

66. *Gittin* 7a and commentaries ad loc. See also Rif to *Berakhot*, chap. 5.

67. Cf. *Responsa* of Rema, no. 125. The musicians were called *klezmer*, from the Hebrew *k'lei zemer*, "musical instruments."

68. Cf. *Taanit* 10b, "Do not show yourselves satiated in front of Esau and Yishmael lest they become jealous."

69. S. W. Baron, *The Jewish Community*, Vol. II (Philadelphia: Jewish Publication Society, 1942), pp. 303–305.

70. Cf. *Berakhot* 50a.

71. Some versions insert "the sons of Jeshurun." From the acrostic it appears that the author was the noted grammarian and composer of hymns, Donash ben Labrat (tenth century).

72. *Ketubot* 8a. Cf. *Chagigah* 12b, which states that the angels sing in *ma'on*, one of the seven heavens.

73. *Ketubot* 8a.

74. *Shulchan Arukh, Eben Ha-Ezer* 62:13.

75. *Shulchan Arukh, Eben Ha-Ezer* 64:1. According to Maimonides (*Hilkhot Eivel* 1:1) these days were instituted by Moses. However, the custom prevailed even before Moses, at the wedding of Jacob and Leah (see Genesis 29:27). Others derive the requirement for seven days of rejoicing from the verse "I will turn their mourning into rejoicing" (Jeremiah 31:13), "since mourning is for seven days [*shiva*], so is rejoicing [end of *Bereishit Rabbah*]."

76. *Sukkah* 25b. It is understood that the wedding itself was held before the festival.

Chapter 6

1. A phrase from the wedding benedictions, see p. 93.
2. *Yevamot* 62b.
3. *Bava Metzia* 59a.
4. *Gittin* 6b.
5. *Bava Metzia* 59a.
6. *Yoma* 2a; *Shabbat* 116b.
7. *Ketubot* 64b; *Pesachim* 109a.
8. *Hilkhot Ishut* 15:20. S. W. Baron, *A Social and Religious History of the Jews*, Vol. I (Philadelphia: Jewish Publication Society, 1958), p. 146 explains that the leaders of the community deliberately tried to maintain the supremacy of the husband as a means of strengthening the family bonds.
9. *Kiddushin* 30b, 31a.
10. *Shulchan Arukh, Yoreh De'ah* 240:19.
11. *Pesachim* 87a.
12. For a detailed study, see E. G., Elinson, *Ha-Ishah Ve-Ha-Mitzvot*, Vol. I (Jerusalem: World Zionist Organization, 5742 [1982]); also available in English translation.
13. *Kiddushin* 29a. Exceptions include the reciting of the *Kiddush* on Friday night (women usually discharge this obligation by listening to the male head of the household) and the eating of *matzah* at the Passover *seder*.
14. *Eruvin* 96a; see *Chagigah* 16b.
15. *Chagigah* 16b.
16. Examples are listening to the *shofar* on Rosh Hashanah and taking aloft the four species on Sukkot. The Sages did object to the putting on of *tefillin* by women, on the grounds that *tefillin* require a "clean body," which women cannot maintain during their menstrual period.
17. For example, the men recite the benediction "to *read* the *Megillah*," whereas the women recite "to *listen* to the *Megillah*." See the relevant sections in the *Shulchan Arukh*.
18. *Berakhot* 20b; see *Tosafot* ad loc., s.v. "*nashim*."
19. *Kiddushin* 30a.

20. *Berakhot* 17a. Cf. p. 39 regarding absence from home to study Torah.

21. This is based on the well-known statement of Rabbi Eliezer (*Sotah* 20a) that he who teaches his daughter Torah is as if he is teaching her *tiflut*, which may be understood as nonsense, though some take it to mean sexual promiscuity.

22. *Hilkhot Talmud Torah* 1:13.

23. *Bava Batra* 20a.

24. Cf. Rabbi Eliezer's statement that a woman's wisdom is only for the spindle (*Yoma* 66b). For an elaboration of her household duties, see *Ketubot* 59b.

25. *Sukkah* 38a.

26. *Megillah* 23a.

27. See p. 129 for the story about the wife and Rabbi Meir in J.T. *Sotah* 1:4.

28. E.g., Bruriah, the wife of Rabbi Meir, and Yalta, the wife of Rabbi Nachman. In the Middle Ages, the daughters of Rashi and the daughter of the Gaon Samuel ben Ali of Baghdad were allowed to teach men, giving instruction through a window. Recently, the former chief Sephardi rabbi, Ovadiah Yosef, gave a similar ruling when Nechama Leibovitch, noted Bible teacher, was asked to teach in a *yeshivah*.

29. *Shabbat* 31b–32a.

30. Now consigned to the flames because of the *kohen*'s ritual impurity. The term *Challah* is now the name given to the specially baked loaves for the Sabbath meals.

31. Cf. *Tosafot* to *Gittin* 2b, s.v. *"eid achad,"* reliance on a woman's testimony that the food is kosher.

32. A review of the laws of *Niddah* follows in the next chapter.

33. Maimonides asserts that this *mitzvah* was given to the woman because she is usually at home and is occupied with the household chores (*Hilkhot Shabbat* 5:3), though in the absence of the woman, the man is obliged to kindle the Sabbath candles. This kindling has specific halakhic significance for the women; by their kindling they accept upon themselves the holiness of the Sabbath and begin to refrain from work prohibited on the Sabbath. There is a difference in procedure between Ashkenazi and Sephardi women;

the former first light the candles and then pronounce the blessing, whereas the latter first pronounce the blessing and then light the candles.

34. She was called a *zokerkeh*, Yiddish for "reciter."

35. Written by Yaakov Ashkenazi, end of sixteenth-century Poland. It went through dozens of editions.

36. *Likutei Halakhot* to *Sotah* 20a.

37. So called because the Sages understood *Bet Yaakov* in Exodus 19:3 to refer to the women; see Rashi ad loc.

38. This is not to be confused with the *Ezrat Nashim* of the *Bet Ha-Mikdash*, which was a large community hall for public assembly attended by both men and women. It was so called in order to mark it off as the area beyond which women as a rule were not allowed to enter. Men were permitted to approach farther toward the Temple building (*Hechal*) into *Ezrat Yisrael* or *Azarah* (Temple Court), which had a higher sanctity than the *Ezrat Nashim*; see Mishnah, *Kelim* 1:8. Baron, *Social and Religious History*, Vol. II, pp. 240, 413, maintains that in talmudic times there were separate sections in the synagogue for women. See also D. Urman, "Jewish Inscriptions in Debora of the Golan," in *Likutei Tarbitz* 2 (Jerusalem: Magnes Press, Hebrew University, n.d.), p. 75: "An upper section served as a woman's section in ancient synagogues."

39. *Berakhot* 20b. Some commentators maintain that the obligation extends only to one prayer a day, in any language or content, which is the biblical obligation (*d'oraita*) for men as well. Others maintain that it extends to the three daily standard prayers instituted by the Sages.

40. *Megillah* 23b. A woman was not to be called up to the Torah-reading, explains the Talmud, "because of the honor of the congregation," which could not find a sufficient number of men knowledgeable for Torah reading and had to avail itself of a knowledgeable woman.

41. Some Orthodox feminists who assemble for prayer refrain from reciting these sections in order to comply with the *Halakhah*.

42. *Hagahot Maimuni*, *Hilkhot Tefillah* 4:3.

43. *Trumot Ha-Deshen*, no. 132.

44. Bet Yosef to *Shulchan Arukh*, *Orach Chayyim*, sec. 88.

45. Yosef Chayyim of Baghdad, *Chukot Ha-Nashim* (Jerusalem: 1979), chap. 39.

46. *Mishnah Berurah*, 88:7.

47. Rabbi Yisrael Meir Hakohen in his *Mishnah Berurah* 219:3.

48. An expression of the privilege for having been given more *mitzvot* to perform than women.

49. The age of twelve, a year earlier than that of boys, because of girls' earlier physical maturity.

50. Cf. Rabbi M. Feinstein, *Responsa Iggeret Mosheh*, *Orach Chayyim* (New York, 1959), Vol. I, no. 102; Vol. II, no. 97.45.

51. See *The Second Jewish Catalog*, Vol. II, ed. Michael and Sharon Strassfeld (Philadelphia: Jewish Publication Society, 1976).

52. *Niddah* 45b.

53. *Yevamot* 87b.

54. Cf. *Gittin* 49b and commentators ad loc. M. Chigier, author of *Husband and Wife in Israeli Law* (Jerusalem: Harry Fischel Institute Publications, 1985), doubts whether this assertion about women's eagerness to marry is true today. He argues, "The emancipated woman of the present day, with the ability to earn her living and with a strong sense of independence, is entirely different from the woman in the time of the Talmud. Nowadays, they are more selective and take greater care in choosing their consort than did the women of old."

55. *Ketubot* 84a, 88a; see *Tosafot* ad loc., s.v. "*li-ketubot.*"

56. See Aryeh Morgenstern, *Ha-Rabbanut Ha-Rashit Be-Eretz Yisrael* (Jerusalem and Netanya: Shorashim Publications, n.d.), pp. 115–131.

57. *Bava Kamma* 15a. Rashi explains that the word *lifneihem* ("before them") includes women.

58. Mishnah, *Ketubot* 8:1.

59. *Bava Kamma* 15a.

60. Mishnah, *Ketubot* 9:4.

61. *Gittin* 46a.

62. *Hilkhot Ishut* 13:11.

63. Mishnah, *Ketubot* 7:6.

64. *Berakhot* 24a.

65. J.T. *Yoma* 1:1. In the corresponding version in B.T. (*Yoma*

47a) it is added that the Sages said to her, "Many did the same but it didn't help."

66. *Berakhot* 24a.

67. Feinstein, *Iggeret Mosheh, Yoreh De'ah*, Vol. I, no. 137; Vol. II, no. 104.

68. Rabbis BenZion Uzziel and Yehiel Weinberg in their respective *responsa*.

69. *Shabbat* 119b.

70. *Shabbat* 119a.

CHAPTER 7

1. *Ketubot* 8b.

2. Cf. Numbers 30:17; *Nedarim* 79b.

3. Most probably she was preparing herself to go to the *mikveh*, which ordinarily should be kept secret.

4. *Sanhedrin* 97a.

5. *Niddah* 47a. Incidentally, M. Margaliot, in his recording of this incident (*see Encyclopedia of Talmudic Sages*, 4th ed., Vol. II [Tel Aviv: Chachick Publishing House, n.d.], p. 818), concealed the truth out of a false sense of modesty.

6. Cf. *Niddah* 22b.

7. *Niddah* 17b. It must be acknowledged that the Sages' understanding of the process of ovulation and its role in reproduction was deficient. According to them, the offspring is created from the menstrual blood of the female and the white (semen) of the male; see p. 215 n. 26.

8. Even the medieval halakhist-physician Nachmanides, in his commentary to Leviticus 12:2, writes, "Even though a woman has ova like those of a man, either they produce no seed or their seed is excreted and does nothing for the fetus."

9. Cf. *Berakhot* 62a, where it is related that a disciple of Rav, anxious to know how his mentor behaved when having intercourse with his wife, hid under his bed. When Rav remonstrated that this was not proper, the disciple replied, "I have to learn for myself how to behave."

10. *Shulchan Arukh, Orach Chayyim* 240 and *Eben Ha-Ezer* 25.

11. See p. 9 that it is a *mitzvah*.

12. *Berakhot* 22b. Subsequently this restriction was abolished, it being too severe.

13. *Hilkhot De'ot* 5:19.

14. Commentary to Leviticus 19:2.

15. *Ketubot* 5:6.

16. Though if he does force himself, the *Halakhah* would not regard it as rape. See, however, *Bava Kamma* 32a, that if he injured his wife by his intercourse, he has to pay her damages.

17. *Eruvin* 100b.

18. *Shabbat* 140b.

19. *Yevamot* 62b.

20. *Ketubot* 72b.

21. The Talmud records that a man who had intercourse with his wife under a fig tree (i.e., in a public place) was brought to court and punished with lashes (*Sanhedrin* 46a).

22. Cf. *Niddah* 31b, "Why does a man [during intercourse] face downward and a woman face upward? He faces the place from which he was created [the earth], and she from which she was created [the man's rib]."

23. *Nedarim* 20b.

24. J.T. *Taanit* 1:4(64c); cf. T. B. *Taanit* 23b.

25. *Yevamot* 72b.

26. Literally, "separated." In some societies, a woman was placed in a separate dwelling during her menstrual period.

27. This requirement of immersion is not explicit in the Torah, but the Sages understood it to be implicit; see *Tosafot* to *Yoma* 78, s.v. *"mikhan."*

28. *Sanhedrin* 37a.

29. *Niddah* 31b.

30. See *Ketubot* 64b, that denial of sex is more of a hardship for the man than for the woman.

31. See Rivkah Levi Jung, "Taharah—a Way to Married Happiness," in *The Jewish Library*, 3d ser. (New York: Jewish Library Publishing Co., 1934), pp. 363, 364.

32. Cf. *Shulchan Arukh, Yoreh De'ah* 195.

33. *Shabbat* 13a.

34. *Shabbat* 13a–b.

35. *Shabbat* 64b.

36. *Shabbat* 14a.

37. *Teshuvot Ha-Rambam*, no. 242.

38. *Niddah* 6b; cf. J.T. *Megillah* 2:5.

39. J.T. *Berakhot* 9:2.

40. J.T. *Sotah* 1:7; cf. *Gittin* 90a.

41. Cf. *Avot d'Rabbi Natan* 12:1: "Hillel says, Be of the disciples of Aaron, he loves peace, pursues peace, and brings about peace between a man and his wife."

42. J.T. *Pe'ah* 1:1.

43. J.T. *Sotah* 1:4. See a similar story in *Nedarim* 66b.

44. J.T. *Mo'ed Katan* 2:2.

45. S. W. Baron, *The Jewish Community*, Vol. II (Philadelphia: Jewish Publication Society, 1942), p. 318.

46. *Responsa*, ed. Prague, no. 81.

47. Rema to *Shulchan Arukh, Eben Ha-Ezer* 154:3.

48. Z. Falk, *Laws of Marriage* (Hebrew) (Jerusalem: Mesharim Publications, 5743 [1983]), p. 11.

49. A recent halakhist deals with the halakhic propriety of having the husband present at the birth; see Y. H. Henkin, *Responsa B'nai Banim* (Jerusalem, 5741 [1981], no. 33). He concludes that it is permissible if his presence will relieve his wife's anxiety.

CHAPTER 8

1. From the verse "For Abraham listened to My voice and kept My charge, My commandments, My statutes and My teachings" (Genesis 26:5), it is apparent that Abraham observed much more than the ethical aspects of the tradition; cf. *Yoma* 28b, that Abraham observed the entire Torah.

2. See the preface to this volume, regarding the development of the Jewish halakhic tradition through the ages.

3. As described by the *Haggadah shel Pesach* (usually referred by the name *Haggadah* alone). For its development, see M. Kasher,

Haggadah Shelemah (Jerusalem: Torah Shelemah Institute, 5721 [1961]).

4. Cf. Mishnah, *Pesachim* 116a: "If the son has no knowledge [to ask questions about the Seder] his father must teach him."

5. *Hilkhot Talmud Torah* 1:1–2.

6. J.T. *Kiddushin* 1:7(61a); cf. a different version in B.T. *Kiddushin* 30a.

7. J.T. *Kiddushin* 1:7(61a); B.T. *Kiddushin* 30a.

8. See *Tosafot, Bava Batra* 21a, s.v. *"ki mi-tziyyon"*: "Because in Jerusalem the child would see great holiness, priests [*kohanim*] ministering in the Temple, imbuing him with the fear of Heaven and the study of Torah."

9. *Bava Batra* 21a; cf. *Ketubot* 50a for another statement about the age of admission to school. For further details about the development of Jewish education, see N. Drazin, *History of Jewish Education* (Baltimore: Johns Hopkins Press, 1940).

10. *Leviticus Rabbah* 7:3. Cf. J.T. *Megillah* 3:1(74a) and *Soferim* 5:9, that scrolls comprising the first eight chapters of Leviticus were written for schoolchildren. See Drazin, *History of Jewish Education*, pp. 82–84, for an explanation.

11. *Sukkah* 42a.

12. *Horayot* 13a.

13. *Bava Metzia* 33a. For further details, see *Shulchan Arukh, Yoreh De'ah*, sec. 242.

14. *Avot* (Ethics of the Fathers) 4:12. Cf. *Kiddushin* 30a: "Scripture has equated the reverence for father and mother with reverence for Heaven."

15. See *Ketubot* 49a–b for the development of this obligation, further extended by the State of Israel.

16. Cf. the daily prayer, "As a father has mercy over his children, so may You have mercy over us."

17. Cf. the controversy between Rabbi Meir and Rabbi Yehudah, whether we are regarded as God's children even if we do not behave like children, that is, we do not obey Him; *Kiddushin* 36a.

18. *Kiddushin* 29b.

19. *Berakhot* 17a.

20. *Yevamot* 45b. Cf. *Tosafot, Sanhedrin* 36b, s.v. *"chada,"* that by the same token he may be appointed a judge in civil cases.

21. *Bava Batra* 109b.

22. *Kiddushin* 30b–31a.

23. The god to which such sacrifice was offered was called "Molech"; see Leviticus 20:2–5.

24. Cf. Jeremiah 19:5, "They have built shrines to Baal, to put their children to the fire as burnt offerings to Baal, which I never commanded, never decreed, and which never came to My mind." See also the story of Jephtah (Judges, chap. 11), who vowed to offer up his daughter as a sacrifice to God and is said to have fulfilled his vow. The commentators explain that he fulfilled the vow by isolating her from human company for the rest of her life.

25. *Sanhedrin* 71a, b. Not only must both parents agree to bring the son to court, they must be identical in [the quality of] their voice, their appearance, and their height. Cf. *Sotah* 25a, that even the parents could "forgive" their son and not bring him before the court to be punished.

26. *Kiddushin* 73b.

27. *Kiddushin* 74a.

28. *Sotah* 27a.

29. *Kiddushin* 78b. Cf. Rambam, *Hilkhot Issurei Biah* 15:15; *Shulchan Arukh, Eben Ha-Ezer* 4:29.

30. *Ketubot* 15a.

31. *Yevamot* 69b–70a.

32. *Berakhot* 60a. See also *Niddah* 31a–b, that some men would keep back their emission so that their wives would emit first and thus bear a son.

33. *Niddah* 31b.

34. *Shulchan Arukh, Orach Chayyim* 223:1.

35. For an interesting discussion of this ruling, see Jonathan Sachs in M. Sokol, ed., *Rabbinic Authority and Personal Autonomy* (Northvale, NJ: Jason Aronson, 1992), pp. 149–155.

36. Cf. *Niddah* 31b, "As soon as a male is born peace [*shalom*] comes to the world."

37. For details, see J. Werdiger, *Eidut Le-Yisrael* (Bnai Brak: Institute for the Research of Prayer and Customs, 5725 [1965]), pp. 99–101.

38. Genesis 17:14. The Sages have interpreted *karet* as premature death, that is, before reaching age sixty (*Mo'ed Katan* 28a).

39. *Nedarim* 31b.

40. *Nedarim* 31b.

41. For details of this controversy and the one concerning *metzitzah*, see J. Katz, *Ha-Halakhah Be-Meitzar* (Jerusalem: Magnes Press, Hebrew University, 5752 [1992]), pp. 123–182.

42. There is a discussion in the Talmud as to whether a Jew may circumcise a non-Jew for health reasons; see *Avodah Zarah* 26b. The Talmud also discusses whether a woman may perform the rite (*Avodah Zarah* 27a). *Shulchan Arukh, Yoreh De'ah*, sec. 264, says that it is not customary to have a woman perform the circumcision, though today the Conservative Jewish Theological Seminary will license a woman as a circumcisor (*mohelet*) who is engaged by a feminist mother to perform the rite.

43. *Shabbat* 133b.

44. For a comprehensive description and sources, see *Encyclopedia Talmudit*, Vol. IV (Jerusalem; Yad Harav Herzog, 1973–1993), s.v. "*brit milah*."

45. Preferably a childless couple. Performing the *mitzvah* may reward them with a child of their own.

46. *Kiddushin* 29a.

47. *Shabbat* 137b.

48. *Shabbat* 137b.

49. *Sanhedrin* 32b.

50. *Shabbat* 134a.

51. The blessing included the hope that the parents would raise up the newborn "to *chuppah* [i.e., the wedding day] and to good deeds." With the recent inclusion of women in Torah learning, the word *Torah* has been added. Cf. p. 149 regarding the hope expressed by the guests at a *brit milah* for the boy.

52. Another explanation may be the fact that a boy will be called up to the Torah by name, which is appropriate if he has a Hebrew name; girls—except for Reform and some Conservative Jews—will not. It should be noted that today, because of the influence of Hebrew being spoken in Israel, girls are more and more being given Hebrew names, which are not necessarily in memory of departed relatives.

53. See *The Second Jewish Catalog*, ed. Michael and Sharon Strassfeld (Philadelphia: Jewish Publication Society, 1976).

54. *Kiddushin* 29a.

55. *Pesachim* 121b.

56. If, for example, a man had a firstborn by a previous marriage and fulfilled the *mitzvah* of *pidyon ha-ben* with him, he nevertheless has to fulfill the *mitzvah* again with the firstborn of his second wife.

57. This is a rhetorical question; the father has no choice, he being obligated to redeem his son.

58. Contemporary authorities in every generation assessed the equivalent of the biblical five shekels in local currency. The *kohen*, if he so desires, may return the five shekels to the father, but this is discouraged. The *kohen* may also be paid with an object that is worth to him five shekels; cf. *Kiddushin* 8a.

59. Cf. *Tur, Yoreh De'ah*, sec. 310, for the text.

60. Cf. p. 136. *Bet Yosef, Orach Chayyim*, end of sec. 308, mentions an interesting local custom whereby a child is led to synagogue for the first time with a wax candle, even on the Sabbath, a practice to which the *Bet Yosef* objected since one is not permitted to carry a candle, even if unlit, on the Sabbath.

61. For a comprehensive review and sources, see *Encyclopedia Talmudit*, Vol. XVI, s.v. "*chinukh.*"

62. *Sukkah* 42a. The custom is to wear under one's shirt all day a small four-cornered garment called a *tallit katan*—the ultra-Orthodox have the fringes protrude from under the shirt—and a larger wraparound shawl over one's jacket during prayer services called a *tallit. Chasidim*, paradoxically, have their children begin wearing a *tallit katan* at a very young age, but they do not begin wearing the large *tallit* until after marriage. Later, authorities decided that a boy should not put on *tefillin* before age thirteen.

63. *Sukkah* 28a. For the age when a child should be trained to fast on Yom Kippur, see *Yoma* 82a.

64. *Tosefta, Yoma* 4:2.

65. It is in this obligation that posttalmudic authorities found justification for bringing young children not yet able to pray to the synagogue; see *Tosafot, Chagigah* 3a, s.v. "*kedai.*"

66. *Kiddushin* 82a–b.

67. *Mo'ed Katan* 17a.

68. Tractate *Semahot* 2:6. Cf. *Sukkah* 46b, that one should not say

to a child that he is going to give him something and then not give it, for he will be teaching him to lie.

69. An exception to this rule is in commercial matters; some transactions by a minor are considered valid (*Gittin* 59a), while others are not valid until he reaches eighteen (*Bava Batra* 155a).

70. *Avot* (Ethics of the Fathers) 5:24. This is for a boy; for a girl the age of obligation is twelve years. See p. 147 for the celebration of a *Bat Mitzvah*.

71. *Niddah* 45b.

72. *Kohelet Rabbah* 4:15.

73. *Bereishit Rabbah* 63:14. Since this is not a benediction mentioned in the Talmud, it is not recited with God's name.

74. See Shlomo Luria, *Yam shel Shlomo* (commentary to *Bava Kamma*) (Yasmitz, 1713), 7:37.

75. Originally, each person called up to the reading of the Torah (*aliyah*) read from the scroll himself, a custom still observed in some oriental communities. However, this excluded many persons unable to read from the scroll by themselves, and therefore it was instituted that one specially trained person called *baal koreh* would read the entire weekly portion, while the person called up recites the benediction before and after the reading of his portion.

76. *Sanhedrin* 84b. Maimonides adds that they should refrain from treating a parent only if someone else is available; otherwise they may operate (*Hilkhot Mamrim* 5:7).

77. See p. 140 for an explanation of the difference in phraseology between the two commandments.

78. Rashi explains, "In the special place reserved for his father to stand when in the counsel of the elders."

79. That is, if you think that he has erred, point it out to him indirectly.

80. *Kiddushin* 31b.

81. *Kiddushin* 31b.

82. J.T. *Kiddushin* 1:7(61b); cf. version in B.T. ad loc., as cited by Rashi and *Tosafot*.

83. *Kiddushin* 31a–b.

84. *Yevamot* 5b.

85. *Yoreh De'ah* 240:25.

86. After other departed individuals one usually adds, "Peace be upon him (her)." After a distinguished spiritual leader one adds, "May the memory of a *tzaddik* [pious one] be a blessing"; cf. Proverbs 10:7, "The memory of a *tzaddik* is a blessing."

87. Cf. J.T. *Megillah* 4:10(75c), that teachers quoting their father to the students would say, "My father taught," rather than "Rabbi so-and-so taught."

88. For details, see M. Lamm, *The Jewish Way in Death and Mourning* (New York: Jonathan David Publishers, 1969).

89. Cf. *Mo'ed Katan* 27b, "After thirty days God says, 'You do not have to be more merciful than I am' "

90. *Eduyot* 2:10.

91. *Nedarim* 12a.

92. Up until recently, only one mourner in the congregation recited the *Kaddish*, according to a system of priorities; however, the custom in most congregations today is for all the mourners to recite the *Kaddish* in unison.

93. *Sifre* to Deuteronomy 21:8.

94. *Ketubot* 103a.

95. *Mo'ed Katan* 26b; *Ketubot* 4b.

96. *Kiddushin* 39b.

97. *Avot* 1:3.

CHAPTER 9

1. *Berakhot* 8a.

2. *Yevamot* 63b.

3. *Gittin* 90b.

4. *Bava Kamma* 92b.

5. *Yoma* 8b.

6. *Ketubot* 82b. See also *Ketubot* 65b.

7. Saint Paul in 1 Corinthians and Galatians, chap. 5.

8. According to one opinion in the Talmud (*Gittin* 90b), if a man hates his wife he should divorce her.

9. Quoted by Zev W. Falk, *Petition for Divorce by the Woman in Israeli Law* (Hebrew) (Jerusalem: Institute for Research in Legisla-

tion and Equality of Justice, 1973), pp. 17–18. See also A. Cowley, *Aramaic Papyri of the 5th Century* B.C.E. (Oxford: Clarendon Press, 1923), and S. W. Baron, *A Social and Religious History of the Jews*, Vol. I (Philadelphia: Jewish Publication Society, 1958), p. 113, for further details of Mephtahiah's career.

10. *Ketubot* 5:10(30b); *Ketubot* 7:7(31c), where correct reading is *tisni* (will hate) and not *tisbi* (will take) as printed.

11. *Bet Ha-Bechirah* to *Ketubot* (ed. A. Sofer), p. 270.

12. M. A. Friedman, *Jewish Marriage in Palestine* (Tel Aviv and New York: Tel Aviv University and Jewish Theological Seminary, 1980), pp. 40–41.

13. The Jewish Publication Society translation (*The Torah*) reads, "something obnoxious," which does not convey the true meaning of the text.

14. *Gittin* 90a. Some have explained Rabbi Akiba's position—so uncharacteristic of his romantic attitude toward marriage—on the grounds that if a man is willing to divorce his wife merely because he finds another woman more attractive, then surely the marriage is faulty. It can only lead to constant bickering and better be terminated.

15. Maimonides follows Scripture closely and distinguishes between a first marriage, the breaking up of which constitutes a tragedy, and therefore only a sexual misdemeanor can justify its dissolution, and a second marriage, in which a feeling of hatred is sufficient cause; *Hilkhot Geirushin* 10:12.

16. *Yevamot* 24b and commentaries ad loc.

17. *Ketubot* 72a.

18. Rema to *Shulchan Arukh, Eben Ha-Ezer* 119:3.

19. See Proverbs 12:4, 27:15; Ecclesiastes 7:26.

20. *Bereishit Rabbah* 18:3.

21. Cf. *Yevamot* 116a–b, that either man or woman can be the instigator of domestic disharmony.

22. *Yalkut Shimoni* to Genesis 2:18. Cf., however, the comment of *Bamidbar Rabbah* (18:15) to the verse (Proverbs 14:1), "The wisest of women builds her house," that it refers to the wife of On ben Peles (who saved him from Korach's plot), and that "but a

foolish woman tears it down with her own hands" refers to the wife of Korach (who urged him to rebel against Moses).

23. *Sotah* 9:9. "Hence," advises Rabbi Chaninah of Sura, "nowadays that we do not have the bitter waters to test her, one should not say to his wife, Do not secrete yourself with so-and-so, lest she secrete herself and she becomes prohibited to him forever" (*Sotah* 2b).

24. *Sotah* 2a. Cf. J.T. *Sotah* 1:1(16b): "Express jealousy, not playfully or casually, but threateningly." There are different versions of this statement among the Rishonim; see *Tosafot, Sotah* 2b, s.v. *"mai taama,"* and Me'iri (ed. Machon Ha-Talmud Ha-Yisraeli Ha-Shalem [p. 6 nn. 52, 53]. Rambam summarizes the proper attitude at the end of *Hilkhot Sotah*: It is not proper to hastily express one's jealousy right away in the presence of witnesses. Rather, one should express it in privacy, softly and admonishingly, to direct the wife in the proper path and keep her from misconduct. However, one who is indifferent to his wife's and his children's conduct, and does not reprove them until he sees that they are free from sin, is himself a sinner.

25. I do not know of any rabbinic source that might disclose the use of a chastity belt among Jewish husbands.

26. *Gittin* 90a.

27. *Ketubot* 86b.

28. For a detailed treatment of this subject, see Shlomo Riskin, *Woman and Jewish Divorce* (Hoboken, NJ: Ktav Publishing, 1989).

29. This refers only to the wife of a *kohen*, who becomes defiled for him even though the act of adultery was committed under duress; the raped wife of a non-*kohen* does not become defiled for her husband and he does not have to divorce her. For a detailed discussion of this ruling, see J. Blidstein, "The Status of Captive Women" (Hebrew), *Hebrew Law Annual*, Vols. III–IV (Jerusalem: Institute of Hebrew Law Research, Hebrew University, 1976–1977), pp. 42–46.

30. The Jerusalem Talmud (*Nedarim* 11:13[42d]) explains her statement as follows: "Just as the heavens are distant from the earth, so am I distant from you."

31. Some say they should ask her to stop talking. The Jerusalem Talmud says, "Let them make a feast and they will become reconciled" (*Nedarim* 11:13[42d]).

32. *Responsa Chatam Sofer, Eben Ha-Ezer*, pt, II, no. 14. See, however, *Responsa Nodah Bi-Yehudah, Eben Ha-Ezer*, pt. I, no. 72.

33. *Ketubot* 7:3–5. In the last two instances, if the husband claims that he objects because those gatherings include promiscuous persons, his objection is sustained. See also p. 178 for the husband who does not trust his wife.

34. *Ketubot* 63b.

35. In Hebrew, *Moredet*.

36. Cf. the talmudic statement, "A person does not dwell together with a serpent in one cage," *Ketubot* 77a.

37. *Hilkhot Ishut* 14:8.

38. *Responsa* of the Rosh, no. 43.

39. Cf. Riskin, *Woman and Jewish Divorce*.

40. *Yevamot* 118b. See M. Chigier, *Husband and Wife in Israeli Law* (Jerusalem: Harry Fischel Publications, 1985), pp. 256–278, who argues that women today are not as dependent financially on a husband as they used to be.

41. The presumption is, if he didn't drown and resurfaced we would have seen him.

42. *Yevamot* 121a.

43. Mishnah, *Yevamot* 10:1.

CHAPTER 10

1. The fact that the Torah prohibits a *kohen* to marry a divorcée in the same verse that prohibits him to marry a prostitute (Leviticus 21:7) seems to indicate that a woman was divorced because she had committed adultery.

2. *Hilkhot Geirushin*, chap. 10.

3. See, for example, the appendix to the laws of divorce in *Shulchan Arukh, Eben Ha-Ezer*.

4. See p. 69.

5. *Gittin* 5b.

6. *Gittin* 17a.

7. Cf. *Targum Yonatan b. Uzziel* to Deuteronomy 24:1, which adds the words "before the court."

8. Sometimes they specify *get ishah* (pl. *gitei nashim*) and use the term *shtar* for other documents. Some commentators say that the word *get* derives from an Aramaic root meaning "breaking," that is, the breaking up of a marriage. The Gaon of Vilna pointed out that the two consonants forming the word *get* (*gimel* and *tet*) are never juxtaposed in a Hebrew word, symbolizing a man and woman who cannot live together. Some saw in these letters an acrostic for *gemar tov*, "a good ending," which is rather farfetched.

9. Cf. Leviticus 1:3, "He shall offer it willingly."

10. *Arakhin* 21a.

11. *Yevamot* 106a.

12. *Hilkhot Geirushin* 2:20.

13. Rema to *Shulchan Arukh, Eben Ha-Ezer* 154:21.

14. *Ketubot* 77a.

15. *Ketubot* 86a–b.

16. See Z. Wahrhaftig, "Compulsion in Divorce," (Hebrew) *Hebrew Law Annual*, Vols. III–IV (Jerusalem: Institute of Research in Hebrew Law, 5736 [1976]), pp. 153–216.

17. See Shlomo Riskin, *Woman and Jewish Divorce* (Hoboken, NJ: Ktav Publishing House, 1989), and M. Chigier, *Husband and Wife in Israeli Law* (Jerusalem: Harry Fischel Institute Publications, 1985).

18. *Gittin* 88b.

19. See *Encyclopedia Talmudit*, Vol. V (Jerusalem: Yad Harav Herzog, 1973–1993), p. 704, for a general discussion of whether imposition of a fine for persuading to give a *get* is considered compulsion.

20. See I. H. Haut, *Divorce in Jewish Law and Life* (New York: Sepher-Hermon Press, 1983), chap. 12.

21. By the same token, a photocopy or fax of a *get* is not valid.

22. The twelve lines correspond to the numerical value of the word *get* (*Tosafot Gittin* 2a, s.v. *ha-meivi*). The marking of the lines, required in the writing of a *sefer* Torah, is called *shirtut*; see *Shulchan Arukh, Eben Ha-Ezer*, sec. 125:10.

23. This procedure is not mentioned in the Talmud and apparently was instituted in early medieval Ashkenaz but was dismissed

by those who opposed innovations; see Y. I. Ta-Shema, *Minhag Ashkenaz Kadmon* (Jerusalem: Magnes Press, 5752), p. 94. Nevertheless, it has already been codified in the standard Guides for the *Get*.

24. The Mishnah speaks of witnesses who signed in Greek. However, the custom today is to have the witnesses sign only in Hebrew.

25. Mishnah, *Gittin*, chap. 3.

26. See *Ha-Hashmal Be-Halakhah*, Vol. I, ed. A Weissfish (Jerusalem: Technological Institute for Halakhic Problems, 5738 [1978]), pp. 207ff.

27. Cf. *Rosh Ha-Shanah* 16b, "A change in name can avert the evil decree." Also J.T. *Shabbat* 6:9(8d), "A change in name brings about a change in fortune."

28. In medieval Spain some families adopted family names (e.g., Ibn Ezra), but this was not a widespread practice.

29. *Shulchan Arukh, Eben Ha-Ezer* 129:16.

30. Cf. *Rosh Ha-Shanah* 2a, 3a.

31. See *Tosafot* to *Gittin* 80b, s.v. *"zu divrei."*

32. See discussion in *Noam*, Vol. ix, and *Encyclopedia Talmudit*, Vol. V, s.v. *"get."*

33. The term for "month" in a *get* is *yerach*, instead of the usual *chodesh*, a pun on the phrase *geresh yerachim* in Deuteronomy 33:14.

34. The last line is reserved exclusively for the phrase "according to the law of Moses and Israel, which is spaced out to cover the whole line."

35. For example, a non-Jew cannot serve as a messenger to deliver a *get*.

36. *Gittin* 76b. Cf. the *takkanah* of Maimonides and his court in twelfth-century Egypt, that any newcomer to a community who married a local woman and wanted to visit in his native land would not be allowed to leave until he gave his wife a *get* on condition that it become effective if he did not return within a year or two, or at the most three (*Teshuvot Ha-Rambam*, ed. J. Blau, Vol. III [Jerusalem: Rubin Mass, 5749 (1989)], p. 624).

37. *Gittin* 72a.

38. *Ketubot* 9b.

39. Compare Uriah the Hitite's refusal to visit his wife on his return from the battlefield (2 Samuel 11:9). See Y. I. Herzog, *Responsa Hechal Yitzchak*, Vol. II (Jerusalem: Herzog Publication Society, 1972), nos. 35–41.

40. Ibid., nos. 29–33.

41. See p. 63 regarding the qualification of witnesses.

42. No doubt Rabbi Feinstein was moved to make such a bold decision because of the antihalakhic attitudes of these non-Orthodox movements, as well as finding release for the woman whose husband refuses to give her a *get*.

43. *Kiddushin* 49b.

44. Kiddushin 49b. These conditions were made at the time of the betrothal when the betrothal was separate from the nuptials, and the betrothal is annulled. However, if the marriage was consummated before the misrepresentation was disclosed, the marriage is terminated only by means of a *get*, unless the conditions were repeated at the time of the consummation.

45. See *Gittin* 33a.

46. See p. 70 regarding the groom who acted improperly. See also *Yevamot* 100a.

47. See p. 20.

48. Literally, "in his face," but the Sages interpreted the phrase to mean "in front of him," that is, on the ground in the presence of the members of the court.

49. J.T. *Ketubot* 11:3(34b). A somewhat expanded version of this story is recorded in *Bereishit Rabbah* 17:3. Obligation to support an indigent divorced wife is codified in Rema to *Shulchan Arukh, Eben Ha-Ezer* 119:8.

50. Cf. *Ketubot* 28a that they should not come to court together lest they become intimate (codified in *Shulchan Arukh, Eben Ha-Ezer* 119:8).

51. Cf. Malachi 2:14–15; Proverbs 5:18.

52. See p. 96.

53. *Shulchan Arukh, Eben Ha-Ezer* 62:6.

54. *Sotah* 2a.

55. The assumption is that he divorced her because of her misconduct.

56. *Gittin* 90b.

57. Cf. *Yevamot* 64a.

Epilogue

1. Cf. Mishnah, *Chagigah* 2:1, "We do not expound the laws of prohibited marriages with three (or more) present."

2. *Kiddushin* 82a.

3. *Yevamot* 76a.

GLOSSARY

Aggadah   Homiletic, inspirational rabbinic lore; see Preface.

Agunah   A woman whose husband has disappeared and there is no evidence of his death, or a woman whose husband refuses to give her a bill of divorcement (*get*) even though ordered to do so by the religious court.

Aliyah   Being called up to a portion of the congregational Torah reading; in modern parlance, coming to settle in Israel.

Amora'im   Talmudic commentators to the Mishnah, third to sixth centuries C.E.

Ashkenazi (pl. *Ashkenazim*)   Jews of Northern France and German origin, hence primarily European Jews (Ashkenaz was the Hebrew name given to Germany).

Asmakhta   An undertaking made casually with the assumption that it will not have to be honored.

Bar Mitzvah   A boy who just has reached age thirteen; also the ceremony celebrating the occasion.

Bat Mitzvah   A girl who just has reached age twelve; also the ceremony celebrating the occasion.

Bedekens   Yiddish for covering the bride's face with a veil before the wedding ceremony.

Beshert   Yiddish for predestined.

Bet Din   Rabbinic court of law.

Bet Ha-Midrash   Academy for talmudic studies.

Birkat Ha-Gomel   Benediction of thanksgiving for survival from a dangerous situation.

Birkat Ha-Mazon   The Grace (series of benedictions) after a Meal.

Brit Milah   Circumcision ceremony.

Chalitzah   The ceremony releasing a widow whose husband died without issue from marrying the husband's brother.

Challah   A piece of dough set aside for priestly consumption; also the special loaf for the Sabbath meal.

Chatan   Groom; also son-in-law.

Chatunah   Wedding.

Cherem   Ban; excommunication of nonconformist.

Chinukh   Training of young children for religious practice.

Chol Ha-Mo'ed   Intermediate days between the first and last days of a festival.

Chumash   Pentateuch, the Five Books of the Torah.

Chuppah   The wedding ceremony, particularly the canopy used in the ceremony.

Eben Ha-Ezer   The section in the *Shulchan Arukh* dealing with the laws of marriage and divorce.

Ezrat Nashim   The section in the synagogue reserved for women worshipers.

Gemara   Compendium of rabbinic commentary to the Mishnah, including halakhic and aggadic discussions by the *Amora'im*.

Get   Bill of divorcement.

Haftarah   The portion from the Prophets read after the Sabbath and Festival Torah reading.

Haggadah (shel Pesach)   The treatise of directions for the *Seder* ritual.

Hakhnasat Kallah   Assisting a young couple to marry and establish their home.

Halakhah   Rabbinic law; see Preface.

Hallel   The psalms recited on festivals.

Kallah   Bride; also daughter-in-law.

Keriat Shema   Twice daily recital of Deuteronomy 6:1–8 and 11:13–21.

Kiddushin   Act of betrothal.

Kinyan   Act of acquisition.

Klezmer   Yiddish for musicians.

Kohen (pl. *Kohanim*)   Member of priestly family descended from Aaron, brother of Moses.

Kohen Gadol   High Priest.

Kollel   School of talmudic studies for married students.

Maftir   Final portion of the Sabbath and Festival Torah reading.

Mamzer   Child born of incestuous union.

Megillah (Megillat Esther)   Biblical Book of Esther, read on Purim.

Midrash   Rabbinic exposition of Scripture; rabbinic homilies.

Mikveh   A pool of water made in accordance with halakhic specifications, in which one immerses himself or herself to be cleansed from a ritual impurity, especially a woman after her menstrual period. Called Ritualarium.

Minchah   The statutory afternoon prayer.

Minhag   Customary ritual not legislated originally by rabbinic authority; see Preface.

Minyan   Quorum of at least ten adult males for congregational prayer.

Mishnah   Code of Jewish Law comprising opinions of *Tanna'im*, edited by Rabbi Yehudah Hanasi c. 200 C.E.

Mitzvah   Literally, a commandment; specifically, a statutory religious ritual; in common parlance, a good deed.

Naarah   A girl who has reached age twelve, until age twelve and a half.

Nedunia   Dowry given by bride's father.

Niddah   A woman during her menstrual period.

Pidyon Ha-Ben   Redeeming of firstborn son.

Pilegesh   Concubine.

Posek   (pl. *Poskim*) Rabbinic authority who decides questions of Jewish law.

Rema   Acrostic of Rabbi Moshe Isserles, Ashkenazi annotator to *Shulchan Arukh*.

Rishonim   Halakhic authorities of the Middle Ages (1000–1500 C.E.).

Seder   The ritual conducted on the first (in the Diaspora, also on the second) night of Passover.

Sephardi (pl. *Sephardim*)   Jews originating in the Iberian peninsula (Spain in Hebrew is *Sepharad*) and in oriental countries.

Shadkhan   Matchmaker.

She'eilot U-Teshuvot   Literally, Questions and Answers; rabbinic *Responsa*.

Sheva Berakhot   The seven benedictions chanted at a wedding ceremony.

Shiddukh (pl. *Shiddukhin*)   A proposal to match a couple for marriage.

Shulchan Arukh   Sixteenth-century Code of Jewish Law comprising Sephardic rulings by Joseph Karo and Ashkenazic rulings by Moshe Isserles.

Siddur   Prayer book.

Tachanun   Supplementary prayers for divine pardon.

Taharat Ha-Mishpachah   Literally, purity of the family; the laws regulating conjugal intercourse.

Takkanah   A rabbinic regulation or ordinance.

Talmud   Compendium of rabbinic discourse of *Halakhah* and

Aggadah, comprising the Mishnah and the Gemara, in two versions or editions, the Palestinian (called Jerusalem) and the Babylonian.

Tanna'im   Sages whose opinions are recorded in the Mishnah.

Tefillin   Phylacteries; scrolls of four paragraphs from the *Chumash* (Exodus 13:1–16; Deuteronomy 6:4–8, 11:13–21) set in black boxes and placed on arm and forehead.

Tena'im   Generally, conditions to an agreement; specifically, agreement to marry and the document certifying the agreement.

Torah   Literally, instruction; specifically, the Pentateuch or *Chumash*; generally, all rabbinic teaching.

Torah she-be'al peh   The Oral Law, i.e., all rabbinic teaching.

Torah she-bi-khtav   The Written Law, i.e., the Pentateuch.

Tzarah   The co-wife in a polygamous marriage.

Ufruf   Yiddish term for the "calling up" of a groom to the Torah reading.

Upsheren   Yiddish for cutting the hair of a three-year-old son.

Yetzer Ra   The innate inclination to do evil.

Yetzer Tov   The innate inclination to do good.

Yibbum   Levirate marriage of a widow of one who died without issue to his brother.

Yichud   Closeting of bride and groom in a private chamber immediately after the wedding ceremony.

Yichus   Genealogy; family prestige.

Yom Tov   Festival.

BIBLIOGRAPHY

PRIMARY SOURCES, IN CHRONOLOGICAL ORDER

The Bible: *The Torah*. Philadelphia: Jewish Publication Society, 1962.

The Prophets. Philadelphia: Jewish Publication Society, 1978.

The Writings. Philadelphia: Jewish Publication Society, 1979.

The *Mishnah*. Trans. H. Danby. London: Oxford University Press, 1933.

Avot (Ethics of the Fathers). A tractate of the *Mishnah*.

Tosefta. Ed. Saul Lieberman. New York: Jewish Theological Seminary, 1955–1973.

Mekhilta (tannaitic exposition to Exodus). Trans. and ed. Jacob Z. Lauterbach. Philadelphia: Jewish Publication Society, 1933.

Sifra d'Bei Rav (tannaitic exposition to Leviticus). Ed. Isaac Hirsh Weiss. Vienna: 1862. Reprint. New York: Ohm Publications, 1947.

Sifrei d'Bei Rav (tannaitic exposition to Numbers and Deuteronomy). Ed. Meir Ish Shalom. Vienna: 1865. Reprint. New York: Ohm Publications, 1948.

Talmud Yerushalmi (the Jerusalem–Palestinian Talmud). Bamberg-Venice edition. Reprint. New York: Ma'aseh Roke'ah Publishers, n.d.

Talmud Bavli (the Babylonian Talmud). Vilna: Romm Family Publications, 1908.

Avot d'Rabbi Nathan. Trans. Judah Goldin. New Haven: Yale University Press, 1955.

Massekhet Kallah. Trans. J. Rabinowitz. London: Soncino Press, 1965.

Massekhet Semahot (Aivel Rabbati). Trans. J. Rabinowitz. London: Soncino Press, 1965.

Massekhet Soferim. Trans. Israel W. Slotki. London: Soncino Press, 1965.

Bereishit Rabbah (Midrash). Warsaw, 1851.

Leviticus Rabbah (Midrash). Warsaw, 1851.

Vayikra Rabbah (Midrash). Warsaw, 1851.

Kohelet Rabbati (Midrash). Warsaw, 1851.

Targum Yonatan b. Uzziel. Mikra'ot Gedolot edition. Jerusalem: Pardes Publications, 1956.

Nathan b. Yechiel of Rome. *Arukh*. Alexander Kohut *Arukh Hashalem* edition. Tel Aviv, 1954.

Shlomo b. Isaac Yitzchaki (Rashi, commentary to Pentateuch). Mikra'ot Gedolot edition. Warsaw, 1860.

Tosafot (medieval Ashkenazi commentators to Babylonian Talmud). Vilna: Romm Family Publications, 1908.

Moses b. Maimon (Maimonides). *Sefer Ha-Mitzvot*. Ed. Chaim Heller. Jerusalem: Mosad Harav Kook, 1946.

Moses b. Maimon (Maimonides). *Rambam, Mishneh Torah*. Facsimile of 1480 Rome edition. Jerusalem: Mosad Harav Kook, 5715 (1955).

Moses b. Maimon (Maimonides). *Moreh Nevukhim* (Guide to the Perplexed). Trans. M. Friedlander. New York: Hebrew Publishing Co., n.d.

Moses b. Maimon (Maimonides), *Teshuvot Ha-Rambam*. Ed. J. Blau. Jerusalem: Rubin Mass, 5749 (1989).

Moses b. Nachman (Nachmanides). *Commentary to Pentateuch.* Mikra'ot Gedolot edition. Warsaw, 1860.

Sefer Ha-Chinukh. Author unknown. Ascribed to Aharon Ha-Levi of Barcelona. Exposition of the *Taryaq* (613) *Mitzvot.* Vilna: Rosenkrantz Publisher, 1924.

Menahem b. Shlomo Ha-Me'iri. *Bet Ha-Bechirah* (commentary to Babylonian Talmud). Jerusalem: Institute of the Complete Israeli Talmud Publications, 5720 (1940).

Nissim b. Reuben Gerondi (*RA'N*), commentary to Alfasi (*RI'F*). Vilna: Romm Family Publications, 5684 (1924).

Rabbenu Shimon of Frankfurt-a-Maim. *Yalkut Shimoni* (anthology of *Midrashim*). New York and Berlin: Horev edition, 1926.

Asher b. Yechiel (R'O'SH). *Responsa.* Vilna, 1880.

Jacob b. Asher. *Arbaah Turim* (*Tur*) (code of Jewish law). New York: Otzar Ha-Seforim Publications, 5719 (1959).

Karo, Joseph b. Ephraim. *Bet Yosef* (commentary to *Tur*).

_____. *Shulchan Arukh: Orach Chayyim; Yoreh De'ah; Eben Ha-Ezer; Choshen Mishpat.* Reprint. Jerusalem: Chatam Sofer Institute, 5726 (1966).

Isserles, Mosheh b. Israel (R'M'A). Glosses to *Shulchan Arukh.* Reprint. Jerusalem: Chatam Sofer Institute, 5726 (1966).

SECONDARY SOURCES

Ashkenazi, Yaakov. *Tzenah U-Re'enah.*

Baron, S. W. *The Jewish Community.* Vols. II, III. Philadelphia: Jewish Publication Society, 1942.

_____. *A Social and Religious History of the Jews.* Vols. I, II, VI. Philadelphia: Jewish Publication Society, 1958.

Berkowitz, Eliezer. *T'nai B'Nissuin U-ve-Get.* Jerusalem: Mosad Harav Kook, 1967.

Blidstein, J. "The Status of Captive Women" (Hebrew). *Hebrew Law Annual.* Vols. III, IV, pp. 42–46. Jerusalem: Institute of Hebrew Law Research, Hebrew University, 1976–1977.

Bulka, Reuven P. *Jewish Divorce Ethics: The Right Way to Say Goodbye.* Ogdensburg, NY: Ivy League Press, 1992.

_____. *Jewish Marriage: A Halakhic Ethic*. Hoboken, NJ: Ktav, Yeshiva University Press, 1986.

Chigier, M. *Husband and Wife in Israeli Law*. Jerusalem: Harry Fischel Institute Publications, 1985.

Cohen, Jeremy. *Be Fertile and Increase: Fill the Earth and Master It*. Ithaca: Cornell University Press, 1992.

Cowley, A. *Aramaic Papyri of the 5th Century B.C.E.* Oxford: Clarendon Press, 1923.

Drazin, N. *History of Jewish Education*. Baltimore: Johns Hopkins Press, 1940.

Elinson, E. G. *Ha-Ishah Ve-Ha-Mitzvot*. Vol. I. Jerusalem: World Zionist Organization, 5742 (1982).

Elon, M. *Ha-Mishpat Ha-Ivri*. Jerusalem: Magnes Press, Hebrew University, 1973.

Emden, Yaakov. *Responsa She'ilot Yaavetz*. New York: Israel Wolf Publications, 1960.

_____. *Siddur Bet Yaakov*. Vienna: Schlesinger Publications, 1924.

Encyclopedia of Religion and Ethics. Ed. James Hastings. Edinborough: T. and T. Clark, 1908.

Encyclopedia Talmudit. Jerusalem: Yad Harav Herzog, 1973–1993.

Epstein, Louis M. *Marriage Laws in the Bible and Talmud*. Cambridge: Harvard Semitic Series 12, 1942.

Falk, Zev W. *Petition for Divorce by the Woman in Israeli Law* (Hebrew). Jerusalem: Institute for Research in Legislation and Equality of Justice, 1973.

Feinstein, M. *Responsa Iggeret Mosheh*. Vols. I, II. New York, 1959.

Feldman, David M. *Birth Control in Jewish Law*. New York: New York University Press, 1968.

Foster, Brenda. "The Biblical Omein." *Judaism* 42:3 (Summer 1993): 321–331.

Freiman, A. H. *Seder Kiddushin Ve-Nissuin*. Jerusalem: Mosad Harav Kook, 1964.

Friedman, M. A. *Jewish Marriage in Palestine*. Tel Aviv and New York: Tel Aviv University and Jewish Theological Seminary, 1980.

Goodman, Philip, and Goodman, Hannah. *The Jewish Marriage Anthology*. Philadelphia: Jewish Publication Society, 1965.

Ha-Chashmal Be-Halakhah. Ed. A. Weissfish. Jerusalem: Technological Institute for Halakhic Problems, 1978.

Halevy, Chayyim David. "Responsum re Financial Arrangements
for Married Couples" (Hebrew). In *Shanah Be-Shanah*, pp. 226ff.
Jerusalem: Hechal Shlomo, 5751 (1991).

Haut, I. H. *Divorce in Jewish Law and Life.* New York: Sepher-
Hermon Press, 1983.

Herzog, Y. I. *Responsa Hechal Yitzchak.* Jerusalem: Herzog Publication Society, 1972.

Isserlein, Yisrael. *Terumot Ha-Deshen.* Tel Aviv: N. Steiner, 1924.

Jung, Rivkah Levi. "Taharah: A Way to Married Happiness." In
The Jewish Library, 3d ser., pp. 355–365. New York: Jewish
Library Publishing Co., 1934.

Kagan, Yisrael Meir Ha-Kohen (the *Chafetz Chayyim*). *Chafetz
Chayyim.* Frankfurt a. M.: Chermon, 1925.

———. *Likutei Halakhot* to *Sotah.* Pietrikow, 1943.

———. *Mishnah Berurah.* Glosses to *Shulchan Arukh, Orach Chayyim.*

Kapah, Joseph. *Halikhot Teiman.* Jerusalem: Ben Zvi Institute, Hebrew University, 5728 (1948).

Kasher, M. *Haggadah Shelemah.* Jerusalem: Torah Shelemah Institute, 1961.

Katz, J. *Ha-Halakhah Be-Meitzar.* Jerusalem: Magnes Press, Hebrew
University, 5752 (1992).

Lamm, Maurice. *The Jewish Way in Death and Mourning.* New York:
Jonathan David Publishers, 1969.

Landau, Yechezkel. *Responsa Nodah Bi-Yehudah.* Vilna, 1889.

Lewittes, M. *Principles and Development of Jewish Law.* New York:
Bloch Publishing Co., 1987.

Lewittes, M. *Tzemichat Ge'ulateinu.* Jerusalem, 1984.

Lieberman, Saul. *Tosefta Ki-Pshuta.* New York: Jewish Theological
Seminary, 1955–1973.

Lipman, Yom Tov. *Tosafot Yom Tov* (commentary to the Mishnah).
Vilna: Romm Family Publications, 1937.

Luria, Shlomo. *Yam shel Shlomo* (commentary to *Bava Kamma.*
Yasnitz, 1713.

Mandelkern, Solomon. *Biblical Concordance.* Jerusalem and Tel
Aviv: Schocken Publications, 1959.

Margaliot, M., ed. *Encyclopedia of Talmudic Sages* (Hebrew). 4th ed. Tel Aviv: Joshua Chachik Publishing House, n.d.

Meir ben Barukh of Rothenburg. Berlin, 1865. Reprint. Jerusalem, 1968.

Meir Ha-Kohen of Rothenburg. *Hagahot Maimuniyot*. Glosses to Rambam's *Misneh Torah*.

Moellin, Yaakov. *Sefer Maharil*. Brooklyn, NY: Unger Publications, n.d.

Morgenstern, Aryeh. *Ha-Rabbanut Ha-Rashit Be-Eretz Yisrael.* Jerusalem and Netanyah: Shorashim Publications, n.d.

Noam. Vol. IX. Jerusalem: Torah Shelemah Institute, 1966.

Ohlboim, Yitzchak. *Sefer Eizer Le-Yitzchak*. Czechoslovakia, n.d.

Otzar Ha-Poskim (digest of rabbinic *responsa*). Jerusalem, 1931–1992.

Reifenberg, A. *Ancient Hebrew Arts*. New York: Schocken Books, 1950.

Riskin, Shlomo. *Woman and Jewish Divorce*. Hoboken, NJ: Ktav Publishing House, 1989.

Sacks, Jonathan. "Creativity and Innovation in *Halakhah*." In *Rabbinic Authority and Personal Autonomy*, ed. M. Sokol, pp. 149–155. Northvale, NJ: Jason Aronson, 1992.

Samuel ben David Halevi. *Nachlat Shivah*. Warsaw: Argelbrand Press, 1884.

The Second Jewish Catalog, ed. Michael and Sharon Strassfeld. Philadelphia: Jewish Publication Society, 1976.

Sofer, Mosheh. *Responsa Chatam Sofer*. Pressburg, 1879.

Solomon Adret (*Rashba*). *Responsa*.

Soloveitchik, J. B. "The Lonely Man of Faith." *Tradition* 7:2 (Summer 1965).

Ta-Shema, Y. I. *Minhaq Ashkenaz Kadmon*. Jerusalem: Magnes Press, Hebrew University, 5752 (1992).

Teomim, Joseph. *Pri Megadim*. Glosses to *Shulchan Arukh*.

Tikkunei Zohar. Jerusalem: Eretz Yisrael Press, 1943.

Urman, D. "Jewish Inscriptions in Debora of the Golan" (Hebrew). In *Likutei Tarbitz* 2. Jerusalem: Magnes Press, Hebrew University, n.d.

Uzziel, BenZion. *Responsa Mishpetei Uzziel*. 2d ed. Jerusalem: Mosad Harav Kook, 1962.

Wahrhaftig, Z. "Compulsion in Divorce" (Hebrew). *Hebrew Law Annual.* Vols. III, IV, pp. 153–216. Jerusalem: Institute of Research in Hebrew Law, 1976.

Waldenberg, E. "Is One Obliged to Inform a Prospective Groom of the Girl's Infertility." In *Studies in Memory of Yitzchak Nisim.* Jerusalem: Yad Harav Nisim, 1985.

Weinberg, Yechiel. *Responsa Seridei Eish.* Vol. II. Jerusalem: Mosad Harav Kook, 1962.

Werdiger, J. *Eidut Le-Yisrael.* Bnai Brak: Institute for the Research of Prayer and Customs, 5725 (1965).

Yaakov ben Shlomo Habib. *Ein Yaakov.* Jerusalem: Foundation for the Publication of Books of Babylonian Rabbis, n.d.

Yitzchak ben Yaakov. *Tzenah U-Renah.* Vilna: Romm Family Publications, 1878.

Yosef Chayyim of Baghdad. *Chukot Ha-Nashim.* Jerusalem, 5739 (1979).

Ziv, A. *Rabbenu Mosheh Isserles.* New York: Yeshiva University Press, 5732 (1972).

Index of Biblical References

INDEX OF RABBINIC REFERENCES

General Index

About the Author

Mendell Lewittes was born in New York City. He received a bachelor's degree as a member of the first graduating class of Yeshiva College in 1932. Rabbi Lewittes received rabbinic ordination from Rabbi Yitzchak Elchanan at Yeshiva University, a master's degree in Semitics from Harvard University, and an honorary doctorate of Divinity from Yeshiva University. After serving 35 years in the rabbinate in several prominent congregations in the United States and Canada, he settled in Israel in 1969 to devote his time to writing and lecturing. The author of *Book of Temple Service, The Nature and History of Jewish Law, The Light of Redemption, Beyond the Moon and Other Sermons, A Tale to Remember,* and *Zemichat Ge'ulateinu,* he was also a contributor to numerous journals in Israel and abroad. At the time of his death he was editor of the rabbinic annual *Shanah B'Shanah,* published in Jerusalem. He and his wife, Ethel Drazin, had 4 children, 14 grandchildren, and 17 great-grandchildren. On July 23, 1994, during the preparation of this book, Rabbi Lewittes passed away.